HUMAN RELATIONS
IN A CHANGING WORLD

HUMAN RELATIONS
IN A CHANGING WORLD

Observations on the Use of the
Social Sciences

By

ALEXANDER H. LEIGHTON

E. P. DUTTON & COMPANY, INC.

New York, 1949

To

LT. (J. G.) FREDERICK CUSHING CROSS, USNR

Who Died, August 7, 1943

That Others Might Live

CONTENTS

ACKNOWLEDGMENT

THE FIRST DEBT is to the members of the Foreign Morale Analysis Division, whose work is here reported. Since they were a team in which all made contributions at a high level of endeavor, it would be a mistake to single out individuals for particular mention. Nevertheless, a very deep and personal gratitude is felt toward each one, not only for help, but also for the pleasure of the association.

Appreciation and thanks are due the members of the Sponsoring Committee, John W. Coulter, E. W. Gibson, George E. Taylor and Harold M. Vinacke. In this case it is fitting to say that the origin, growth and continued existence of the Division were due to Mr. Taylor's particular interest and action on its behalf.

The writing of the book was made possible through a fellowship from the John Simon Guggenheim Memorial Foundation. For criticism and suggestion I am grateful to the late Ruth Benedict, William M. Doerflinger, Clyde Kluckhohn, Dorothea Leighton, Felix E. Moore, Jr., Morris Opler, Tom T. Sasaki, Katherine Spencer, and Toshio Yatsushiro, all of whom were members of the Division. The following were also kind enough to read the manuscript and make valued comments: Leonard S. Cottrell, Jr., Charles Dollard, Joseph C. Grew, A. O. Leighton, Edward P. Lilly, and Lauriston Sharp.

For essential help in preparing the book for the printer many thanks are due to Florence Mohri, Freda Phelan and Tom T. Sasaki.

For permission to reprint material previously appearing in articles, acknowledgment is made to *The Atlantic Monthly, The American Journal of Psychoanalysis,* the *Philosophical Review, Science, Mental Hygiene,* and the Eighth Conference on Science, Philosophy and Religion.

9

FOREWORD

THE FOUNDATION of this book is a particular experience in applying some of the principles and methods of social science, especially cultural anthropology, sociology and psychiatry, to the wartime analysis of Japanese morale. The work was done for policy makers in the Government who needed to know about the nature of Japanese morale, its strength, what changes were occurring and what, if anything, could be achieved by psychological warfare. After victory it became possible to re-examine many of the conclusions with the benefit of later information; early diagnoses were compared with how things did, in fact, turn out. Now, due to the lifting of security restrictions, it is possible to report the result.

The value in this exercise is not thought to lie primarily in what is said about the past nor in what may be shown about a technique that had a place in war. The value is believed to consist in implications for the present and future. These implications stem from two principal convictions that color this presentation and the conclusions.

One of these convictions has to do with social science. It is believed that social science has potentialities for development and use in human welfare that are comparable with what has been realized in other fields where the scientific method has been employed for several hundred years.

The other conviction bears on the times in which we live. It is believed that the need for better human relations both within nations and between nations is urgent. This includes family relationships, neighborliness, community life, labor relations, "race" relations, and the cooperation of nations. It involves the twin problems of preventing war and utilizing present-day knowledge and skills more effectively for the benefit of all mankind.

11

Foreword

Although the book touches on these matters — matters that are great both in scope and significance — it is itself limited. The aim is to present one set of experiences and some suggestions arising from them in the hope that they are pertinent to the employment of social science in a world situation where it is badly needed.

In short, there is here an orientation in the light of which a particular account is given and some general conclusions drawn. The presentation is planned in that order: *Part I, The Setting,* concerns the point of view that permeates the book; *Part II, A Case History in Applied Social Science,* tells the story of a wartime analysis of Japanese morale; *Part III, The Use of Applied Social Science,* deals with the implications for the present and future.

As the reader pursues his way, he may feel from time to time that loose ends have been left and that some of the evidence is unsatisfactory. Without denying fault, it is my hope that he will not be distracted by this from the central points. The main items are such as can be established only by further testing and not by historical documentation which, however exhaustive, must always be incomplete and therefore susceptible to question. The need is for active finding out, not for restriction of effort due to the possibility of error.

Doubts are valuable indicators of where more work is required. This, indeed, is a central consideration in the whole of social science at the present time. In looking forward, it is not speculation regarding what may or may not be so that is essential, but rather, in the words used again and again by Francis Bacon:

"Let it be further inquired."

"Let trial be made."

PART I

THE SETTING

INTRODUCTION

The viewpoint of this book is largely the result of a visit to Hiroshima. In December, 1945, I was research leader of the team sent to that city by the United States Strategic Bombing Survey in order to study the feelings and attitudes of the survivors.

CHAPTER I

HIROSHIMA AFTERMATH

I

We approached Hiroshima a little after daybreak on a winter day, driving in a jeep below a leaden sky and in the face of a cold wet wind. On either side of the road black flat fields were turning green under winter wheat. Here and there peasants worked, swinging spades or grubbing in mud and water with blue hands. To the north, looming close over the level land, mountains thrust heavy summits of pine darkly against the overcast. To the south and far away, the bay lay in dull brightness under fitful rain.

"Hiroshima," said the driver, a GI from a Kansas farm who had been through the city many times, "don't look no different from any other bombed town. You soon get used to it. You'll see little old mud walls right in the middle of the town that wasn't knocked down. They been exaggerating about this bomb."

Within a few miles the fields along the road were replaced by houses and shops that looked worn and dull, but intact. On the road itself people straggled to work, some on bicycles, most of them on foot; tattered and bandy-legged old men, girls with red cheeks and bright eyes, ancient women under towering bundles, middle-aged men looking stiff in Western business suits. At a bus stop a crowd stood waiting in a line almost long enough to fill a train. Half a mile farther on we passed the bus, small, battered and gray, standing obliterated by the cloud of smoke that came from the charcoal burner at the back, while the driver stood working at its machinery.

Human Relations in a Changing World

Children of all ages waved, laughed and shouted at us as had children in other parts of Japan.

"Hallo-goodabye! Hallo-goodabye!" "Jeepu! Jeeeepu!"

Like the children of Hamelin to the piper, they came rushing at the sound of our approach from doorways and alleyways and from behind houses to line up by the road and cheer. One fellow of about six threw himself into the air, his little body twisting and feet kicking in a fit of glee.

The adults gazed at us with solemn eyes or looked straight ahead.

Presently a two-story trade school appeared, with boards instead of window glass, and then a factory in the same condition. Soon there were shops and houses all along the way with windows missing. A house came into view with its roof pressed down, tiles scattered and walls bulged outward. A shop with no front, like an open mouth, showed its contents public and private clear to the rear window.

The road turned to the Ota River where the tide was running out and boats lay heaved over on the beach. The air came still cooler from the water and with it a damp, dirty smell of shore. Down stream figures small in the distance dug for shellfish and were reflected in pools. A bridge started out and stopped suddenly like a headless neck.

Now every house and shop was damaged and lay with only one end or a corner standing — a disorderly herd of animals with backs broken struggling to rise.

Then all the buildings ended and we came as if from a forest out on to a plain, as if from tumult into silence.

Imagine a city dump with its smells of wet ashes, mold and things rotting, but one that runs from your feet out almost to the limits of vision. As is often the case with level and desolate places on the earth, the sky seemed close above it. The predominant colors were red and yellow, crumbles of stone, bricks, red earth and rust. Low walls made rectangles that marked where

The Setting

houses had been, like sites of prehistoric villages. Here and there in the middle distance, a few large buildings stood about, buttes in the rubble of the plain.

"You see them?" said the driver, as if it were a triumph for his side. "The bomb didn't knock them down."

Running like ruler lines through the waste were black roads surprisingly dotted with people, some on foot and some in carts of all sizes, drawn by man, woman, horse or cow. Clothing was old and tattered, suitable for the denizens of a dump, and of every combination from full European to full Japanese. People looked as if they had grabbed what they could from a rummage sale to cover their bodies.

We slowed down to go around a piece of cornice that lay partly across the road like a glacial boulder and from somewhere in a band of children came the gift of a tangerine that landed on the floor of the jeep. Wondering at them, I picked it up and put it in my pocket.

When crossing a bridge we could see down through the swiftly running water to the stones and shells on the bottom. This clearness gave an odd contrast to the disorder of the land. We passed a number of trees turned black, but still holding up leafless branches in perpetual winter.

The drive ended at one of the large buildings that was still standing, a former bank, now a police headquarters, where I had an appointment with the chief, to arrange for office space and other necessities.

The driver said, as he got out, "This is it."

II

The bank building which housed the police headquarters was a well-made structure of stone, three stories high. Through an imposing entrance my interpreter and I went past tall and solid metal doors that were bent inward like cardboard and no longer usable. The lobby was large and high, but dark, because it had no window glass and the openings were boarded to keep out the wind. Through poor light there loomed the white face of a clock up on one wall, its hands pointing to 8:10, the time it had stopped on August 6.

Behind the counters were the tables and desks where the police officers and clerks worked. At the time we entered, they were in two groups, each around a charcoal brazier, talking together in low voices, their hands held out to the coals.

The chief ushered us into his office, a small square room with a green baize cover on a table and a window in which the pane had been replaced. On the wall was a notice board that had been cut by fragments of glass, some of which were still sticking in it like small daggers.

The police chief was a small man, lean, with a little mustache and gold on his teeth. His hair was gray and his face long. Tea was served as we talked, but though he spoke pleasantly, it was to the point and he did not seem interested in general conversation.

Our business over, I asked to have a look from the roof and was conducted to a parapet from where we could search Hiroshima from all sides.

From warm tea we came back to silence, cold, and the stretches of destruction. Real silence, as Thomas Hood has said, is not under the ocean nor in the uninhabited deserts, but among the ruins where men have been. From the height more miles of rubble were visible than could be seen lower down, and the people on the roads were stragglers who gave scale to the emptiness. The city seemed to have been stripped naked of everything but its cemeteries which stood out in small granite clumps of orderly stones, gray and narrow like teeth in a comb, the hard remaining bones of the city after the flesh had dissolved.

As I looked, I felt angry at the police chief, his men, and even the people I could see walking down below. I felt an impulse to agree with the jeep driver's words, "They been exaggerating about this bomb." Somebody was making too much of all this. That is the way it must be ——

Then there came, like a huge round fish swimming out of vague green into sharp focus, the image of the white-faced clock in the gloom with its hands at 8:10. In the years when that clock had been going, Hiroshima had been a city, at first unknown to Europe and America, then a friendly source of emigrants to the United States, and finally an enemy port. It lay on a delta between the mouths of the Ota and was traversed by canals and an ancient highway that connected Kyoto in the east with Shimonoseki in the west. Close around the city stood mountains covered with red pine, while before it stretched the bay, indented with headlands and spread with islands, in places narrow and deep like a fjord. In shallows near shore rows of poles stood as if in a bean patch, set in the sea to anchor oysters and to catch edible seaweed passing in the tide. In deeper water fishing boats with hawkish prows and planked with red pine tended nets. A few fishermen used cormorants to make their catch.

Since Hiroshima had been a chief source of emigrants to California and there had been much traveling back and forth of relatives, the influence of the United States was marked. On main streets there were movies and restaurants with façades that would have fitted into shopping districts of Bakersfield or San Diego.

But Hiroshima was also ancient. Its feudal castle raised a five-story keep that could be seen a long distance over the level land of the delta. There were three large temples and many smaller ones and the tombs of the Asano family and of the wife and son of the leader of the Forty-Seven Ronin, Oishi Yoshio. There were also Christian churches whose bells mingled with the temple gongs and the honking of auto horns and the rattling of trolleys.

The people of the city made their living by buying and selling farm produce and fish, by making mountain pines into boats for the fishing fleet of the Inland Sea, by meat packing, rubber processing and oil refining, by making textiles from the cocoons of wild silkworms, by brewing rice and grape wine, by manufacturing paper umbrellas, needles, *tabi* socks, small arms, metal castings, and by utilities and services such as electricity, transportation, schools and hospitals.

During the war there was an increase of industrialization, and plants grew up, chiefly on the outskirts.

There was a famous gay district with little streets along which a person walking in the night could hear laughter and the twang of the *samisen* and geishas singing.

Although not a fortified town Hiroshima was a major military command station, supply depot and staging area because of its protected position and because of Ujina Harbor with access to the Pacific, the Sea of Japan and the China Sea. More than a third of the city's land was taken up with military installations and from the harbor troopships left for Korea, Manchuria, China and the southern regions.

However, toward the end of hostilities, most of the shipping had ceased because of sinkings in the Inland Sea.

The population of Hiroshima was given as over 340,000 before the war, but this was reduced by evacuation prior to the atomic bomb, probably to about 250,000.

A movement on the part of the police officer at the parapet broke the reverie and brought me back to Hiroshima of the present and the view from the roof of the bank.

It is not really certain how many the bomb killed, but it was probably between 70,000 and 80,000.

III

In the two weeks of our stay we made our headquarters on the third floor of the bank. Using random selection, some members of the team gathered in a small sample of the population from the ruins of the city, from the damaged suburbs and from untouched outlying towns and villages in mountain valleys and even from an island down the bay. Other members sat all day long interviewing these men and women — shopkeepers, factory workers, laborers, housewives, cooks, teachers, farmers, fishermen and many more. Some of the respondents were frightened and wordless and others were overtalkative, but for the most part they were quiet and willing.

In addition to the work with the selected sample, there were interviews with the police chief, the officials in the city hall, the mayors of near-by towns and with the governor of the prefecture and his assistants. Members of the team struck up conversations with people on bridges, by wayside stalls where cuttlefish were sold, or in the shacks amid the debris. One member of the team developed a friendship with a newspaperman and I spent many hours talking informally with a doctor.

Bit by bit the things we learned fitted together to make a picture of how the atomic bomb had seemed to the people of Hiroshima. Some of the details did not emerge until the total results were in and the findings of other investigators were analyzed and compared. The result has been reported elsewhere together with figures and technical details.* A general descriptive picture will be given here.

IV

The morning of August 6, 1945, was warm with fleeting clouds — not different from a thousand other summer mornings that had

* (1) *The Effects of Atomic Bombs on Hiroshima and Nagasaki:* The U. S. Strategic Bombing Survey, 30 June 1946, Government Printing Office, Washington, D. C.

(2) *Summary Report (Pacific War):* U. S. Strategic Bombing Survey, 1 July 1946, Government Printing Office, Washington, D. C.

(3) *The Effects of Strategic Bombing on Japanese Morale:* June 1947. Government Printing Office, Washington, D. C.

come and gone without incident, the kind of weather that gives confidence in the even tenor of unfolding time. People stirred themselves to get breakfasts, soldiers moved in the barracks and walked across the drill grounds, children prepared for school, housewives pushed back sliding doors to air their homes.

About seven o'clock there was an air-raid warning and three planes were reported in the vicinity. No one was much disturbed. For a long time B-29s flying over in small numbers had been a common sight.

By eight o'clock, the all clear was sounded and people were thinking again of the day's plans, looking forward to their affairs and engagements of the morning and afternoon. The castle keep stood in the sun. Children bathed in the river. Farmers labored in the fields and fishermen on the water. City stores and factories got under way with their businesses. In a mountain town, before its hall, the mayor and his staff were making their regular morning bows to the Emperor.

In the heart of the city near the buildings of the prefectural government and at the intersection of the busiest streets, almost everybody had stopped and stood in a crowd gazing up at "three parachutes" floating down through the blue air.

The bomb exploded several hundred feet above their heads.

"I heaved a sigh of relief," the weaponeer of the plane is reported to have said, "because I knew the bomb was a success. A few fires were visible around the edges of the smoke, but we could see nothing of the city except the dock area where buildings were falling down."

The people around Hiroshima in the fields, in the mountains and on the bay saw a light, brilliant even in the sun, and felt heat.

A small-town official was crossing a bridge on his bicycle about ten miles from the heart of the city when he felt the right side of his face seared and, thinking that he had sunstroke, he jumped to the ground.

A woman who was washing dishes noticed that she felt "very

warm on the side of my face next the wall. I looked out the window toward the city and saw something like a sun in bright color."

At a slower pace after the flash came the sound of the explosion, which some people have no recollection of hearing, while others described it as an earth-shaking roar, like thunder or a big wind.

A black smoky mass, lit up with color, ascended into the sky and impressed beholders with its beauty. Red, gold, blue, orange and many other shades mingled with the black. One man, who looked on from the mountains, thought it like a globe of the world spinning. Nearer to the city almost everyone thought that an ordinary bomb had landed very close to him, and only realized the extent of the damage later.

A man who was oiling the machinery in a factory saw the lights go out and thought that something must be wrong with the electricity. "But when the roof started crumbling down, I was in a daze, wondering what was happening. Then I noticed my hands and feet were bleeding."

Another who was putting points on needles was knocked unconscious and when he came to, found "all my surroundings burned to the ground and flames raging here and there. I ran home for my family without knowing I was burned around my head. When I arrived home, our house was devastated and destroyed by flames. I ran to the neighbors and inquired about my family and learned that they had all been taken to safety across the river."

An invalid who was drinking tea said, "The tin roof sidings came swirling into my room and everything was black. Rubble and glass and everything you can think of was blasted into my house."

A businessman in his office figuring on his advice slip had the roof come down on his head and a body was blown into the next room.

Human Relations in a Changing World

Said a woman, "I was in the back of the house doing the washing. All of a sudden, the bomb exploded. My clothes were burned off and I received burns on my legs, arms and back. The skin was just hanging loose. The first thing I did was run into the air-raid shelter and lie there exhausted. Then I thought of my baby in the house and ran back to it. The whole house was knocked down and was burning. My mother and father came crawling out of the debris, their faces and arms just black. I heard the baby crying, and crawled in and dug it out from under the burning embers. It was pretty badly burned. My mother carried it back to the shelter."

It was in the heart of the city that death prevailed and few who were there are left to tell us about it. In part the picture has to be reconstructed, as in archeology, from the remains.

The crowd that stood gazing upward at the "parachutes," went down withered and black, like a burned-out patch of weeds. Flames shot out of the castle keep. Trolleys bulging with passengers stopped, and all died at once leaving burned figures still standing, supporting each other, and "fingers fused to the straps." The military at their barracks and offices were wiped out. So, too, were factories full of workers, including students from schools, volunteers from neighboring towns working on the firebreaks, children scavenging for wood, the mayor's staff, the units for air-raid precaution, fire, welfare and relief. The large war industries, since they were on the fringe of the city, were for the most part not seriously damaged. Most of the personnel in the prefectural government offices were killed, though the governor himself happened to be in Tokyo. In hospitals and clinics, patients, doctors and nurses all died together, as did the priests and pastors of the temples and the churches. Of 1,780 nurses, 1,654 were killed, and 90 per cent of the doctors were casualties.

People who were in buildings that sheltered them from the instantaneous effects that accompanied the flash were moments later decapitated or cut to ribbons by flying glass. Others were crushed as walls and floors gave way even in buildings that maintained their outer shells erect.

In the thousands of houses that fell, people were pinned below the wreckage, not killed in many cases, but held there till the fire that swept the city caught up with them and put an end to their screams.

The police chief said that he was in his back yard near a chicken coop when the bomb went off. He was knocked down and a concrete wall fell over him, but he was able to extricate himself and go at once toward the police station in the bank. "Houses were all caved in by the road as I went along. Many people were pinned under them, wounded. The sight was pitiful. Many people were running toward safety. When I arrived at the office, I found ten policemen; some were severely wounded. These were evacuated to a place of safety where they could get aid. We tried to clean up the glass from the windows, but fire was spreading and a hot southerly wind was blowing. We used a hose with water from a hydrant and also formed a bucket brigade.

"About 1 P.M. we began to apply first aid to the people outside, since the fire seemed under control as far as this building was concerned. A doctor came to help. He himself was wounded in one leg. By night this place was covered by a mass of people. One doctor applied all the first aid."

Another doctor who was at a military hospital outside Hiroshima said that about an hour after the bomb went off, "many, many people came rushing to my clinic. They were rushing in all directions of the compass from the city. Many were stretcher cases. Some had their hair burned off, were injured in the back, had broken legs, arms and thighs. The majority of the cases were those injured from glass, many had glass imbedded in the body. Next to the glass injuries, the most frequent were those who had their faces and hands burned, and also the chest and back. Most of the people arrived barefooted, many had their clothes burned off. Women were wearing men's clothes and men were wearing women's. They had put on anything they could pick up along the way.

"On the first day about two hundred and fifty came who were so injured they had to stay in the hospital and we also attended about five hundred others. Of all of these about one hundred died."

A talkative man in a newspaper office said that the most severely burned people looked like red shrimps. Some had skin which still burned sagging from the face and body, with a "reddish-white skin underneath showing."

A reporter who was outside the city at the time of the explosion, but who came in immediately afterward, noticed among the dead a mother with a baby held tightly in her arms. He saw several women running around nude, red from burns, and without hair. Many people climbed into water tanks kept for putting out fires, and died there. "The most pathetic cases were the small children looking for their parents. There was one child of about eleven with a four-year-old on his back, looking, looking for his mother in vain.

"I was unhurt and I felt ashamed to walk around among so many tragic persons."

Shortly after the bomb fell there was a high wind or "fire storm" engendered by the heat that tore up trees, and whirling over the river made waterspouts. In some areas rain fell.

Although the fire burned for days, major destruction did not take very long. A fisherman who had been out on the bay said, "I saw suddenly a flash of light. I thought something burned my face. I hid in the boat face down. When I looked up later, Hiroshima was completely burned."

V

Hiroshima, of course, never had been prepared for a disaster of the magnitude which overtook it, but in addition the organized

sources of aid that did exist were wiped out along with everything else. As a result, rescue had to come from surrounding areas
and soon trucks and trains were picking up the wounded while
hospitals, schools, temples, assembly halls and tents were prepared to receive them. However, the suburbs and surrounding
areas were overwhelmed by the rush of immediate survivors out
of the bombed region, and so for about a day help did not
penetrate far into the city. This, together with the fact that
survivors who were physically able were stunned and bewildered,
resulted in great numbers of the wounded dying from lack
of aid.

The vice-mayor of a neighboring town that began receiving
the wounded about 11:30 in the morning said: "Everybody
looked alike. The eyes appeared to be a mass of melted flesh.
The lips were split up and also looked like a mass of molten flesh.
Only the nose appeared the same as before. The death scene
was awful. The color of the patient would turn to blue and
when we touched the body the skin would stick to our hands."

Those who ventured into Hiroshima were greeted by sights
they were reluctant to describe. A businessman reported that
"the bodies of half-dead people lay on the roadside, on the
bridges, in the water, in the gardens and everywhere. It was
a sight no one wants to see. Practically all of these people were
nude and their color was brownish-blackish and some of their
bodies were dripping. There was a fellow whose head was half
burned so that I thought he was wearing a hat."

In the public parks great numbers of both wounded and dead
were congregated, the former adding constantly to the ranks
of the latter. There were cries for aid and cries for water and
there were places where nameless shapes merely stirred.

In the late afternoon aid began to come farther into the city
from the outer edges. Rice balls and other food were brought.
From their mission up the valley a number of Jesuits came, and
one of them, Father Siemes, gave a vivid and careful description

of what he had seen, when he was later interviewed by members of the Bombing Survey in Tokyo. He said, "Beneath the wreckage of the houses along the way, many have been trapped and they scream to be rescued from the oncoming flames. They must be left to their fate."

On the bridge, he encountered a procession of soldiers, dragging "themselves along with the help of staves or carried by their less severely injured comrades. . . . Abandoned on the bridge there stand, with sunken heads, a number of horses with large burns on their flanks.

"Fukai, the secretary of the mission, is completely out of his mind. He does not want to leave the house as the fires are burning closer, and explains that he does not want to survive the destruction of his fatherland." He had to be carried away by force.

After dark, the priests helped pull from the river two children who suffered chills and then died. There was a sandspit in the river covered with wounded who cried for help and who were afraid that the rising tide would drown them.

After midnight, "only occasionally do we hear calls for help."

Many of the injured were brought to an open field right behind Hiroshima station and tents were set up for them. Doctors came in from the neighboring prefectures and from near-by towns such as Yamaguchi, Okayama and Shimane.

One of the newspapermen reported that when he came into the city ashes were everywhere. "They got into my ears and nose; and for a month it was difficult to clear out the damage because of the hot ashes."

A fisherman who came to Hiroshima to see what had happened said: "I cannot describe the situation in words, it was so pitiful. To see so many people dead was a terrible sight. Their clothes were shredded and their bodies puffed up, some with tongues hanging out. They were dead in all shapes."

As late as the second day the priests noted that among the

cadavers there were many wounded who were still alive. "Frightfully injured forms beckoned to us and then collapsed."

They carried some to the hospitals, but "we cannot move everybody who lies exposed to the sun." It did not make much difference anyway, for in the hospitals there was little that could be done. They just lay in the corridors, row on row, and died.

A businessman came into Hiroshima on the third day. "The guards," he said, "told us that we would have to wait before we could come looking for missing persons. They said that maybe in a week there would be lists from which you could find if your relatives were in a hospital, school, or killed. There were trucks busy with rescue work.

"I went to my brother's house in the suburbs and found that all were wounded but none killed. They were stunned and could hardly speak. The next day, one of the four children died. She got black and blue in the face, just as if you had mashed your finger, and died fifteen minutes after that. In another half hour, her sister did the same thing, and she died also."

People were very nervous when American planes flew over, fearing that more bombs would be dropped. The doctor reported that whenever a plane was seen, people would rush into shelters. "They went in and out so much that they did not have time to eat. They were so nervous that they could not work."

The businessman said: "Before the bomb fell, people were so used to American planes that they would not go to a shelter. Afterward, they were so nervous that any kind of spark would scare them, any kind of spark they saw. That was because of the flash of the atomic bomb."

The destroyed heart of Hiroshima consisted of 4.4 square miles. The police chief told how the dead were collected and burned. "Many could not be identified. In cases where it was possible, the corpses or the ashes were given to the immediate family. Mostly, the cremation was done by the police or the soldiers, and the identified ashes given to the family. The ashes of those not identified were turned over to the City Hall. There still are boxes in the city hall. Occasionally even now one is identified, or is supposed to be identified, and is claimed."

For many days funeral processions moved along the roads and through the towns and villages all around Hiroshima. The winds were pervaded by the smell of death and cremation. At night the skies were lit with the flames of funeral pyres.

VI

Very few if any of the people we interviewed at Hiroshima attempted to make a play for sympathy or to make us feel guilty. The general manner was one which might be interpreted as due either to apathy and absence of feeling consequent on shock, or to reserve that masked hate. It was probably a mixture of both, in varying degrees in different people. However, over-lying this with almost everyone, there appeared to be a deter-mination to cooperate and oblige.

When asked for their views regarding the atomic bomb, many spoke with apparent frankness and gave a variety of opinions. An official of a small town outside of Hiroshima that was un-touched said, "Everyone was resigned to the fact that it was part of the war."

The vice-mayor of another town felt that "if America had such a weapon, there was no use to go on. Many high-school students in Hiroshima who were wounded in the raid spoke incoherently on their deathbed saying, 'Please avenge that raid for us some-how.' However, most of the people felt that since it was war, it was just *shikata ga nai*, could not be helped. But we were united in the idea that we had to win the war."

The newspaper reporter said that after the bomb some felt that this was the end, while others wanted to go on regardless. "Those who had actually experienced the bomb were the ones who wanted to quit, while those who had not wanted to go on."

The Setting

The doctor reported that people said: "If the enemy has this kind of bomb, everyone is going to die, and we wish the war would hurry up and finish. We cannot fight against a bomb like that."

A woman whose soldier husband was killed in the blast said: "When I first saw the destruction I wondered if mankind could make such a bomb. I felt sharply the difference in advancement between the American and Japanese scholars. Personally,though many are resentful against America, I feel no animosity. It was an understood war and the use of weapons was fair. I only wonder why they didn't let the people know of this bomb and give us a chance before bombing us to give up."

The police chief believed that the general reaction among the people was one of surprise and a feeling that "we have taken the worst beating, we have been the goats." He said: "They felt that America had done a terrible thing and were very bitter, but after the surrender they turned on the Japanese military. They felt they had been fooled and wondered if the military knew that the bomb was coming and why they did not take steps.

"The bomb made no difference in the fighting spirit of the people, it drew them together and made them more cooperative.

"My eldest son was killed, but I felt that it was destiny that ruled. When I see people who got away without any injury, I feel a little pang of envy naturally, but I don't feel bitter toward them."

A businessman thought "It was cruel to drop the bomb where ordinary people are living. I don't see why they didn't drop it in some army camp or something."

A housewife wondered, "Is there any use in such a bomb? I saw so many burned people streaming past our home, I saw so many of them."

A woman who escaped with her family, but whose house was burned, said: "After the atomic bomb exploded, I felt that now I must go to work in an ammunition plant. After seeing all the injured people, it seems that only one out of a hundred people escaped with no bad effects. My sons told me that they would not forget the atomic bomb even when they grew up."

Another wife and mother said: "When I reached where my husband worked, I saw the building crumbled. I went almost crazy. I searched for him but could not find him. I found my only son dead, crushed under a stone. I carried my son back home and cremated his body, but my husband's body was not found. There were so many dead who could not be recognized. I felt bitter against the enemy and the war."

There was one woman who said, "If there is such a thing as ghosts, why don't they haunt the Americans?"

Perhaps they do.

For one thing, pity has persistent and haunting qualities, and is the more terrible for being fruitless. There are of course semi-automatic devices of mind for warding off its full poignancy. Preoccupation with work, jokes with teammates, playing with the responsive children, giving away candies and similar actions can overlay perceptions with a temporary padding. Even feelings of anger at the victims for threatening your composure by existing can for a time displace other thoughts. Reasoning can seem to make the present tragedy less by showing that it is not so bad as things that others have done or would have done. Arguments of justification can be conjured up on grounds of necessity, and one can try to prove that lives have been saved and that the future as a result is really brighter for everybody.

But, in spite of all, a consciousness creeps in that all this is irrelevant and does not make the tragedy less. Then moments come when the recollection of a tangerine given by a child, a stopped clock, or an old woman picking about in the rubble of what had been her life, causes the protecting mists to vanish and leaves one alone with an unbearable realization of human suffering.

One afternoon an elderly schoolteacher spent several hours

The Setting

telling me in careful English about life in Hiroshima as it used to be and how the city had become "transformed from Paradise to Hades." He was a gray-haired man with a quiet manner and his tone was not one of bitterness, but rather of wonder. When we parted he was standing on the steps of the shattered city hall within which were the stacks of white boxes full of the ashes of the unidentified dead. His farewell word was, "Godspeed."

VII

The streets of Hiroshima ran through the rubble like perspective lines in a surrealist desert. From them came images of similar streets with names like "Broadway," "Constitution Avenue," "Michigan" and "Kearney," and the Hiroshima scene enacted again and again between the coasts of the United States, on a larger scale, but with no detail of suffering omitted. Looking at the ruins one felt impelled to think:

"This is a preview of things to come where I live. These thousands dead will not be strangers. They will include friends, brother, sister, father, mother, wife and children. Some will die instantly and some will survive a while to realize their slow death and to beckon for help where there will be no one to answer."

It is said sometimes that, after all, Japanese cities are really a collection of "tinderboxes," while those in America are built more substantially. In Hiroshima there were many buildings of types common in the United States and some, prepared against earthquakes, that were stronger. The engineers of the Bombing Survey concluded from their examination that "the overwhelming bulk of buildings in American cities could not stand up against an atomic bomb bursting at a mile or a mile and a half from them." To this must be added the probability that the bomb dropped at Hiroshima is crude by later standards in methods for destruction — the newer bombs, radioactive gas and biological poisons designed to wipe out plants, animals and people.

Human Relations in a Changing World

One of the effects of being in Hiroshima was to move thought after a time not only from the victims to the people of one's own country but eventually to the people of the world.

It is always easy to talk about "the people of the world," but not often is it possible to feel about them in the way one feels about known individuals, or even about those who merely live in a familiar place. In the ruined city, the whole world came into consciousness. The dead streets in the rubble rendered vivid living streets with names in the languages of every continent, streets where people walked, with their aspirations, petty and large, and with the curve of the earth between them and Hiroshima.

Harder to grasp than a realization of the potential building up for world suffering was the possibility of extinction for the human race — a world of ocean, sky and wilderness from which even the ruins of man's works have vanished. This too, however, came at times like a quick look into interstellar space, like a momentary comprehension of spinning spheres and nebulae amid limitless time and distance, marking the brevity of human life.

On the whole, it seemed more probable that some fringe of humanity would survive and gradually spread again like new vegetation over burned land. These people might be simple and primitive and come from those who now live behind mountains, in jungles or on arctic tundra. Or they might come from some maimed fragment of one of the contestants.

At all events, whoever these people might be, it is very likely that they would have learned the lesson. It is possible that they would, like the citizens of Erewhon, ban all machines, but more probable that they would turn their science to the mind and society of man so that machines and other physical powers could be safely handled and put to work solely in the interests of humanity. They might tackle squarely the causes of war instead of dealing opportunistically with the symptoms. They might consider it worth while to maintain an order of existence wherein the relations between nations followed naturally from the relations between men in nations.

They would have to be different in many respects from us, for nothing is more certain than that the power now possible, in the hands of people as they now are, means disaster.

VIII

When scuffing about the stones and pieces of fused glass in Hiroshima, one could not help wondering why, if the human race were capable of learning this lesson at all, it could not do so without first going through the fearful experience that was coming. The requisite would be for people everywhere to know in advance what the survivors would know afterward. Such knowledge means more than an intellectual formulation. It means the kind of knowledge which, rooted in the emotions and the sense of reality, leads to sustained doing.

Looking from Hiroshima at the state of the world, there appeared to be no physical block to such awareness and action, no lack of facilities for communication, yet the outlook was bleak.

Although much has been said and written, most people go about their business as if they did not quite believe in the implications of Hiroshima, or did not believe it would affect them. Sometimes it is said, "Well, there is nothing an individual can do." Yet this can hardly be an adequate reason, for when men and women are alive to something that affects their welfare, they find out what it is that they can do and band together in accomplishing it.

With the war only a short time over, we who fought for ideals and for peace are deep in the historic cycles of postwar self-seeking, disillusionment, apathy, realigned hostilities and witch-hunting. The situation is similar in other nations. There is passionate striving for reform and passionate striving to prevent change; there is demand for the new and for the old — both in the name of fulfilling basic human values. The whole makes up a familiar constellation of activities and attitudes that lead to new catastrophe. It is as if we danced to the music of words about peace and a better world while executing age-old figures that have always led to war.

Yet peace and fruitful living are things people really want. Thus we demonstrate that curious progress in directions opposite to the hope of humanity which impressed the Greeks as the dominance of Fate.

IX

It did not require Hiroshima to bring realization of the slowness of man in rising to meet his needs and his opportunities. Progress in civilization has been a slow business and both need and knowing how have generally run far ahead of adequate practice.

However, always before in thinking of these matters there had appeared to be time. Given a long enough period, humanity seemed generally able to "muddle through" to some solution of most of its problems, even if this took several generations and entailed enormous wastage and suffering. The Spanish Inquisition, child labor, torture as legal means of securing confession, resistance to public-health measures — each lasted, but not forever. Those working to improve human relations could always feel that time is long and that we need not expect great results tomorrow or the next day.

Hiroshima with its clock at 8:10 brought realization that time has almost run out. It is not sure that nothing can now be done to avert the disaster that is imminent, but, the habits of our minds and the set of our society being what they are, such is the probability. It is certain that if there is any time left in which to alter an otherwise downward course, it is very, very short.

This means that one can no longer work in problems of human relations, either in big issues or in small, with the feeling that any progress made, however minute, is something gained. An inch made is not now an inch gained. No progress is of value unless it adds up to crossing soon the threshold between things as they are now and a world order in which there will be no war.

These effects are obviously not limited to work in the field of improving human relations. They embrace every activity. Unless the threshold is crossed there can be little significance beyond the present moment in scholarly work, in creative art and literature, in political careers, in building a business, in developing a labor union, in finding new cures for disease, or in any other item on the list of things people do, including raising a family. No one can be confident any more of achieving in his lifetime anything "enduring."

When the impact of these circumstances is felt, it is natural for one to look for a remedy. It is also natural for each to turn to his own trade and to feel that within it is an important part of the answer if people would only recognize it and apply it. The lawyer is likely to find what is necessary in control by law, the educator in the spreading of knowledge for enlightened understanding; the statesman looks to political strategy, the soldier to the strength of weapons and the placing of them, the philosopher to the insight of a unifying concept, the religious man to faith and the practice of God's laws. Many answers and formulas for solution are put forward. It is difficult to choose between them, especially since it is an evident fact that none of these fields of thought and activity, despite long history and many great contributions to human welfare, has ever produced a workable answer to the problem of war. On the contrary, conflict between peoples has grown extensive and destructive beyond anything that could have been anticipated in the Dark Ages.

Like other workers, the social scientist is inclined to look to his own field and to believe that there is help to be found there. In this he shares the common bias. When he examines his resources, however, he finds that there are some distinctive features. The fact that social science is relatively new means in part lack of knowledge and skill, but it also means lack of trial as compared to other kinds of endeavor. Something effective might be uncovered. The need being what it is, such a possibility deserves close attention.

Another difference is that it has no assured answers ready. Not only does it lack answers of its own, but it increases skepticism of all existing ready-made solutions. It directs attention away from the question, "What to do?" on the ground that it cannot be dealt with until another matter is explored first. This is the question, "How to find out what to do?"

In place of answers, the one substantial thing which social science has to offer is the element that is common to all sciences — the scientific method. In this there is promise, if the history of science in other fields is any guide. It is not a promise of an immediate answer, but it is a reasonable assurance that there exist now the knowledge and skills necessary to make the tools which in turn will yield the desired results.

There is in this no guarantee of success, but it is a substantial hope and where else, in any realistic sense, can that be found?

PART II

A CASE HISTORY IN
APPLIED SOCIAL SCIENCE

INTRODUCTION

DURING THE WAR, there was extensive use of social science. It played a part in the selection of men and women for particular jobs, in the maintenance of morale both in the armed forces and at home, in the prevention and treatment of neuropsychiatric disorders, in propaganda analysis, in selling war bonds, in studies of the social and psychological make-up of the enemy, in training military government personnel for dealing with many kinds of people from Germany to the Pacific islands, and in numerous other operations.*

One set of problems had to do with the Japanese. The morale of their fighting forces was exceedingly high and it seemed probable that the situation was similar for the civilians on the home front. Policy makers required information as to why this morale had such strength, whether it had flaws, what changes could be expected, and what could be done to influence it. These questions were important in military and political strategy as well as in psychological warfare.

The problem was but a particular instance of a general fact. Policy makers are always faced with matters that hinge on human psychology, social behavior and patterns of culture. This is true both on the international scene and in domestic affairs.

A number of scientists worked on the Japanese problem and of these one group was the Foreign Morale Analysis Division in the Office of War Information. The OWI sponsored the Division in cooperation with the Military Intelligence Service of the War

---

* (1) Menninger, W. C. *Psychiatry in a Troubled World; Yesterday's War and Today's Challenge*. (New York: Macmillan) 1948.

(2) United States Office of Strategic Service. Assessment Staff, *Assessment of Men; Selection of Personnel for the Office of Strategic Service*. (New York: Rinehart) 1948.

(3) Samuel Stouffer, and co-workers, *Studies in Social Psychology in World War II* (Princeton: Princeton Press) 1949.

43

Department General Staff. The Division operated as a service for the State, War and Navy Departments, the Office of Strategic Service and for outposts in Asia and the Pacific. The staff numbered thirty people, when the unit was fully developed, and consisted for the most part of men and women trained in cultural anthropology, sociology, and psychiatry rather than as experts on Japan. There were, however, a number of persons in the Division who had knowledge of Japanese language and culture and in addition consultants were available who had specialized on Japan or the Far East.*

The Foreign Morale Analysis Division grew out of an earlier project that had been sponsored by the Navy and the Department of the Interior to make studies in a Japanese Relocation Camp. A team composed in part of Japanese Americans had been trained so that they might aid with social-science techniques in the military government of Japanese areas. When this plan failed, largely because of a Navy rule against accepting Japanese Americans into the service, the core of the team became part of OWI, and from this nucleus the Foreign Morale Analysis Division developed.

The Division's field of interest encompassed all the psychological and social factors pertinent to the Japanese capacity to put forth their best effort in war. The work consisted in sifting, classifying and interpreting current intelligence data. These included: prisoner-of-war interrogation reports; captured diaries, letters and official documents; reports from neutral observers in Japan; Japanese newspapers and periodicals; and radio broadcasts. In addition, background descriptions and analyses were prepared from prewar sources such as novels, histories, travel and anthropological books, movies and interviews with Japanese living in the United States.†

---

* For a detailed statement of the Division personnel, see Appendix A.
† An example of a report of this nature is *The Chrysanthemum and the Sword*, by Ruth Benedict (Boston: Houghton Mifflin) 1946.

A Case History in Applied Social Science

The essential characteristics of the research were two: a conceptual frame of reference and a method of continuous operation. In regard to the first, all analysis was based on a limited number of assumptions concerning the nature of man derived chiefly from psychiatry, psychology and cultural anthropology. With reference to the second, there went forward in accordance with the assumptions a continuous "processing" of the intelligence data as it arrived daily. The processing was analogous to the constant sifting, classifying and recording of observations that take place in a weather bureau where reports are received from many stations. The files thus assembled constituted the basic material utilized in further analyses and published conclusions on particular topics.

The nature of the material with which the Division had to deal made it necessary to rely heavily on the basic assumptions regarding the nature of man. Although the intelligence data were informative, they were unavoidably fragmentary and incomplete. Controlled observations were impossible and statistical methods could be used only to a limited degree. In consequence, the Division employed its basic assumptions as a paleontologist uses his concepts in reconstructing an extinct animal from a few teeth and a piece of bone.

In the following chapters there will be described the principal findings of the Division for both the Japanese armed forces and the civilian population at home. These will be compared with information secured afterward. A brief account will also be given of the basic assumptions and the method of analysis.

The presentation is not a summary of the total work of the Division, but only of certain aspects.

CHAPTER II

JAPANESE MILITARY MORALE

I

In March, 1944, when the Division first began to function, the toughness of Japanese morale was a major problem for the Allies. Of particular importance was the question: Can Japanese soldiers be induced to surrender in significant numbers and to give information of value?

There were many men in top command and policy-making positions who felt that Japanese morale was a solid wall of uniform strength which nothing could destroy except the actual killing of the men who displayed it. Every Japanese soldier was regarded as an ideal fighting machine — fearless, fanatic, obeying instantly, something not quite human that looked only for an opportunity to die for the Emperor.

This kind of estimate was not limited to those who had little actual knowledge of the Japanese. Some men who had spent twenty to thirty years in Japan supported the picture and, acting as expert advisors, asserted that the Japanese did not fear death and were anxious to commit suicide.

These attitudes also appeared in newspaper stories of the time. In an interview with General Romulo by Anne Hagner in the Washington *Post* on March 2, 1944 it is said:

"The creed of Shintoism is that every one in the country belongs to one family with the Emperor as the supreme father. As one Japanese feels, so does the other. . . . Our great productivity here is diverted into many channels — the war, civilian goods, black markets. But whatever the Japanese has is only for the war — he is trained to live with nothing."

46

A Case History in Applied Social Science

An Associated Press article in the same paper on March 11, referring to Los Negros Island, said:

".... When they failed to crack the line ... the Japanese took their own lives rather than admit failure.

" 'One Jap officer jumped on a bunker directly in front of us,' said a private, 'waving a Jap battle flag in one hand and a sword in the other.'

" ' "Kill all the American dogs," ' " the officer shouted. 'Then he plunged the sword into his own stomach.'

" 'I saw one group of a dozen or so Nips gather in a circle in a clearing after we had thrown them back,' said another private, 'then each pulled the pin on a grenade and held it against his chest. All were blasted to death.' "

Although some policy makers and military leaders felt that it was an overestimation of the enemy to suppose that all Japanese would behave in accordance with these striking examples, the views of those who regarded Japanese morale as virtually impregnable tended to prevail.

There were probably many reasons for this, but two seem prominent: rebound from an earlier underestimation of the Japanese, and fear that there might be a slackening of the American war effort. The latter was particularly evident after the fall of Saipan and the resignation of the Tojo cabinet in July, 1944.

The question of the strength of Japanese morale was an important one since it had bearing on how best to conduct the war and which to choose among numbers of possible plans. If the morale of the enemy was everywhere, and under all circumstances, of the extraordinary character depicted, and if no useful number of troop surrenders could ever be expected, then it would be necessary to prepare for long fighting that would be extremely costly in American lives and other resources. Every isolated garrison would have to be exterminated no matter how hopeless its situation. There would be the painful process of taking Japan foot by foot with endless mopping up behind the lines wherever there were Japanese left alive. Prisoners of war would be exceedingly rare and the few who were captured would be of no value as sources of information, either because they were atypical and hence unreliable or because of an adamant attitude of non-cooperation. Psychological warfare would be useless both for softening resistance and for securing the surrender of soldiers.

II

As a result of its first studies, the Foreign Morale Analysis Division concluded that, in spite of the fact that the enemy's military morale was exceedingly high, it was not of uniform consistency and had weaknesses which could and did become worse when circumstances were adverse for the Japanese. As early as April, 1944, the Division stated that prisoners could be captured in significant numbers and that such prisoners would provide reliable and valuable information — information which would, among other things, throw more light on the nature of Japanese morale and on the changes occurring in it as the war progressed.

Looking back now, these conclusions seem obvious, but at the time, as may be imagined from what has been said about prevalent attitudes, the practice was to reject both the possibility of taking prisoners and their utility if captured. One officer who was an important expert advisor in the War Department said flatly that trying to get morale data from prisoners of war was a waste of time and money.

Reports have since accumulated to show that Japanese morale had weaknesses and that it did decline under adversity.* Japanese troops gave themselves up to capture first as a few isolated individuals or in handfuls, then by hundreds and finally, toward the end of the war, by thousands. Although far more German

* Based on a review of all available intelligence reports as of June, 1946; due to security regulations exact sources may not be specified. This restriction also applies to other general statements in the present chapter.

troops surrendered in combat than did the Japanese, Germany as a nation fought until dismembered, whereas Japan stopped the war while still a relatively whole and functioning country.

Reports from all theatres represent the Japanese prisoner of war as cooperative and reliable to an extraordinary degree. They gave military information, described the morale in their units, criticized our psychological warfare techniques and undertook to produce better leaflets and broadcasts which we used again and again to our profit. Perhaps most important of all, they often returned to their own lines and persuaded hard-pressed troops and isolated units to surrender.

III

These primary conclusions of the Division regarding Japanese morale and troop surrender were accompanied by a number of other points. For one thing, it was concluded that, as in any other large aggregate of human beings, there was a wide range of personality types among Japanese troops. At one extreme there were men who never possessed very good morale, and at the other men whose personalities enabled them to display the kind of morale generally attributed to the Japanese and to fight even under the most terrible and prolonged situations of stress. Intermediate between these two types were a large number who, to varying degrees, could show good morale for a time, but who would yield to the pressure of sufficiently severe circumstances.

There were also indications in the intelligence data that different groups of Japanese varied in their morale, or at least in important aspects of morale. For example:

Navy morale was higher than army morale.

Soldiers recruited from the country had higher morale than those from the cities.

The less sophisticated had more confidence in victory than the more intellectual.

49

Human Relations in a Changing World

When morale was broken down into component factors it was found that among nearly all Japanese troops some of these factors consistently supported high morale while others were changeable or operated generally to lower the capacity to fight.

Factors contributing to high morale were:

Faith in the Emperor, and in the divine power and way of life he symbolized.

Faith in victory.

Faith in the rightness and justice of the war as a defense against "Anglo-American imperialism" and as necessary to avoid "economic enslavement."

Faith in the top leaders, military and political.

Faith in the Japanese people and their spiritual strength.

Factors contributing to low morale were:

Discomforts and weakness from physical hardship, disease and malnutrition.

Lack of faith in Japanese weapons, planes, equipment, supplies and productive capacity as compared to those of the Allies.

Staleness, weariness with the war, desire to go home.

Lack of confidence in news and information.

Some of the morale factors were relatively stable while others would deteriorate in the face of prolonged adversity and eventually lead to lowering of over-all morale.

Factors most resistant to shifting lower were:

Faith in the Emperor and the divine power and way of life he symbolized.

Faith in the rightness and justice of the war.

Faith in the Japanese people and their spiritual strength.

A Case History in Applied Social Science

Factors which showed a tendency to shift progressively lower were:

Faith in victory (changing to despondency over campaigns and battle reverses).

Faith in Japanese weapons, planes, equipment, supplies and productive capacity as compared to those of the Allies.

Faith in leaders.

Staleness, weariness with the war and desire to go home — growth of willingness to become a prisoner of war.

Conclusions regarding the range of personality types to be found among the Japanese soldiers and sailors have been validated from many sources both during and after the war. Similarly, the patterns of strong and weak factors influencing morale have on the whole run true to form. About some, such as confidence in victory, attitude toward the Emperor, and lack of confidence in Japanese weapons and equipment, there is no longer room for doubt. However, since it was never possible to carry out a systematic investigation of each of the morale factors, others must be regarded as "probably" true rather than "proven." The least well established of any of the early statements of the Division are those regarding the differences between such various groups as Army and Navy, or urban and rural recruits.

The general pattern of changing Japanese morale was first pointed out in material derived from the New Guinea campaign and became more pronounced in succeeding actions. The Division predicted that under increasing military pressure the morale of the Japanese in the Philippines would go through a cycle similar to that displayed in New Guinea, but that it would happen much faster. This turned out to be the case.

IV

If Japanese morale were vulnerable, it was important to decide what steps the Allies should take. Keeping up the pressure of war was, of course, the main point, but there was also the possibility of using psychological warfare.

In regard to the value of this operation, opinion among those who controlled policy was divided — just as it was in regard to Japanese morale. Long before the Division came into existence, there were many persons with strong convictions as to the value of psychological warfare putting their ideas into effect for the Army, the Navy, the OWI and the OSS. On the other hand, there were, both among the commanders in the field and among the policy makers in Washington, many men of influence who either doubted the value of such work or actively opposed it.

The Division, being sponsored by those who did believe in psychological warfare, was asked to make analyses that would help in a program to promote surrender among the Japanese. The position of the Division for this purpose was strategic rather than tactical, since it was located in Washington with an overall view of data coming in from the theatres. However, even for strategic analysis, its opportunities for handling this problem were limited, since it lacked experience with field situations, opportunities for firsthand observations under combat conditions and control over the gathering of the material it had to use. This handicap was severe and it was never overcome despite constant effort to get personnel into the field. As a consequence, the conclusions of the Division on psychological warfare were general and somewhat fragmentary. They yielded little that was new, but acted to confirm some current concepts and to oppose others.

The basis for the conclusions was the analysis of Japanese morale that has just been outlined plus more specific studies of reactions to Allied propaganda. A summary of the principal findings as of September 1, 1944, follows:

1. Some prisoners had been influenced toward surrender by Allied leaflets, broadcasts and loud-speakers. The total number was not

A Case History in Applied Social Science

great, but considering the training of the Japanese soldier, the circumstances of propaganda dissemination and the limited opportunities for surrender, the results must be considered of value. Indeed, the response was actually higher than advertising psychologists generally expect in terms of sales from an advertising campaign. It was suggested that a greater yield could be had if the program were intensified.

2. Many data indicated that considerable numbers of enemy soldiers who did not surrender nevertheless had their fighting efficiency significantly reduced by psychological warfare.

3. There was indirect evidence that the Japanese soldier was becoming more responsive to psychological warfare. For example, the Japanese military authorities showed increasing concern about its influence.

Assuming that psychological warfare could make a difference, some conclusions were advanced as to the best techniques to employ.

1. *Situation*

A. Isolated units were more vulnerable to propaganda than large masses of troops.

B. The sound of the human voice as conveyed by public-address systems speaking directly and using familiar turns of phrase had special opportunities for being persuasive and convincing as compared to leaflets.

2. *Propaganda Form and Style*

The form in which propaganda themes were cast was often as important as the content. The Japanese were very sensitive to calligraphy, to small points of style, to errors in grammar and pronunciation on loud-speaker broadcasts. A certain word could create a great stir for or against the propaganda, while another which from the Allied point of view seemed to mean the same thing could leave them unmoved. Thus the choice of words in expressing a theme could insure or prejudice its utility.

A familiar example was the use of Japanese words for "surrender" which were very offensive to the enemy. On the other hand, the same meaning expressed in some such phrase as "negotiating for resumption of peaceful conditions" was often quite acceptable.

As a consequence, as much care was needed regarding *how* things were said as was given to *what* was said.

3. *Content of Propaganda*

A. Propaganda themes which dwelt on lack of coordination in the Japanese forces, failures of reinforcement and support, lack of accurate information, blundering and cowardice on the part of officers, lack of food, lack of weapons and supplies, and a hopeless military position, were subjects concerning which troops usually felt uneasy when in a losing position.

(At the present time these points seem so obvious as to be not worth mentioning, yet at the time, they were in considerable dispute. It was frequently asserted that they did not apply because "you must remember that the Japanese are different from the people of the West.")

B. Themes relating to larger issues such as the meaning of the war, the deception of the Emperor by the military clique and the appeal to building a new and greater Japan after this war produced few results. Still less effective were attacks on Japanese moral and political ideology or the presentation of the advantages of the democratic way of life.

C. To hard-pressed, front-line troops, local news was more interesting and moving than world news.

(Points B and C may also appear obvious now, but they were strongly rejected by some policy makers who felt it was the mission of psychological warfare to argue, reason and persuade the Japanese of their error and who expected that this would weaken their faith and contribute to surrender.)

D. Nostalgia themes were useful in weakening fighting efficiency and could be successfully produced by appropriate Japanese music, poetry and pictures.

E. It was of first-rate importance to convince the Japanese that prisoners were not maltreated or tortured. It was worth while to make them understand that they would have an opportunity to work and would not be forced to live, as many pictured it, "idly on the enemy's charity." It would be still better, if it could be done truthfully, to tell them they would not have to go back to Japan unless they wished, but could settle in Allied countries.

F. No theme could be given unqualified recommendation. The local situation and timing had always to be considered.

Over and above these findings, the analysts came to the conclusion that the most important single point connected with obtaining surrenders was the necessity of convincing Allied troops and local field commanders of the value of prisoners and of training men in the technique of securing them. Without this, surrender propaganda was a waste of time, since it could not overcome the effect of witnessing the fact that men were shot when they tried to give themselves up. Our evidence indicated that this happened time and time again and that many of the desperate holdouts and *banzai* charges of the Japanese were based to a significant extent on the conviction that the Americans would not take them prisoners and that their choice was merely between two different kinds of death. Treacherous behavior on the part of some prisoners was no doubt a reason for the attitude of the American troops, but this did not alter the fact that it resulted in stiffening enemy resistance and made fighting more costly.

At a later date during the winter and spring of 1945 the analysts strongly advised the policy makers against employing attacks on the Emperor or the imperial institution in psychological warfare. It was believed that such lines would at best be wasteful and could well harden enemy resistance. On the other hand, the analysts thought that the Emperor might be turned to good use in lowering resistance if the enemy were told that the decision regarding his fate after an Allied victory would be up to the Japanese themselves—in short, announcing and making plain the policy which was actually followed after the war.

V

Reviewing now these early conclusions regarding psychological warfare, a number of things are evident.

The general point that propaganda could be produced which would aid in lowering Japanese resistance and in promoting surrender has been substantiated by experience in all theatres. However, as far as the question of the best types of message and technique is concerned, no studies were ever made on a sufficiently broad scale to permit the establishment of definite conclusions on most points.

Nevertheless, heading a list of well-supported items is the conclusion that it was not profitable to attack the deep-seated beliefs of the enemy. The Emperor was the focal point in this connection. It was found throughout the war that no matter how morale deteriorated in other respects, in this faith and belief the Japanese soldier remained steadfast. It will be remembered that at the end, when the Japanese Government was preparing to surrender, the only question asked the Allies was the fate of the Emperor.

The corollary to avoiding attacks on deep-seated beliefs is the point that it is profitable to pay attention to the current and changeable factors concerning which the enemy troops have major misgivings when suffering reverses. Most important of all, if the aim is to secure surrender, is the use of psychological warfare as a means of showing the enemy soldier a way by which he can escape from terror and strain and approaching death to safety, and, at the same time, retain his self-respect.

This is a point to which, as already noted, there was much

objection. It was believed instead that the Japanese did not mind hardship and death and so could not be influenced by appeals to self-preservation. The evidence of the war indicates, however, that indifference to suffering and death was a Japanese ideal which a limited number of men achieved, but it was not characteristic of the mass of troops to such an extreme that urges toward self-preservation were extinguished.*

* Interesting points of comparison with this chapter may be found in Edward A. Shils and Morris Janowitz' "Cohesion and Disintegration in the Wehrmacht," *The Public Opinion Quarterly*, Summer 1948.

CHAPTER III

JAPANESE HOME-FRONT MORALE

THE central questions about Japanese home-front morale were much the same as those that have been described for the military. Similarly, among our policy makers, the opinion prevailed that this morale was for all practical purposes indestructible.

There was, however, one difference: the opinion was more uniform. In the issues that have been discussed regarding the psychology of Japanese soldiers, there were some voices on each side. In the case of the civilian morale, almost none of the policy makers or experts with whom the Division had contact believed that the Japanese might have difficulty in keeping up their fighting spirit. The accepted picture was the stereotype of fanatical and suicidal resistance and it hung like a spectre over planning and discussion. The policy directives for psychological warfare were all based on the assumption that the Japanese population and leading groups were suffering no significant decline in their will to fight.

Without losing sight of the capacity of some Japanese for extraordinary valor, the Division early felt that such high morale was probably not characteristic of all Japanese under all circumstances. During the latter part of 1944 analyses showed increasing evidence that Japanese home-front morale, while still formidable, was nevertheless deteriorating in a number of important respects.

By January 5, 1945, the indications were strong enough to warrant presentation at an OWI meeting for preparing the weekly directive. The Division reported at this time that the Japanese home front seemed to be "full of tensions and dissatisfactions" and that it was likely that "something was going to happen," either "a blowup of some kind," or else "a decline into a state of chronic inefficiency." The specific points made were:

The Japanese are being worn down by severe physical discomforts and privations, by bad war news, and by the upheavals from evacuations;

Some types of people (such as students, factory workers and Christians) are being treated as scapegoats and blamed for falling down in the war effort;

Campaigns are being carried out to whip up spirit, using such devices as claiming fictitious victories and pointing to the Germans as examples of what the Japanese should be able to do;

In the political scene, there is widening of cleavage lines and an increased turnover in men occupying important posts.

This report had little effect except to anger some of those responsible for planning the OWI directives and arguments were advanced to show that the political turnovers were without significance. Nevertheless, in succeeding months, the indicators of progressive decline in Japanese civilian morale continued to increase. By the end of March it seemed very likely that the OWI (and other) policy makers were working in terms of a largely false picture of the home front.

The principal conclusions of the Division were:

1. A significant number of Japanese think that the Allies will win and consequently they are disposed to pay attention to what we tell them — an attitude quite different from people who still believe in their own victory and one that gives special opportunities in psychological warfare.

2. There is widespread apathy toward the war effort;

3. But there is very great fear of what the Americans will do when they land. It is therefore important to reassure the Japanese and try to prevent them fighting vigorously from terror.

None of this, of course, implied an opportunity for slackening in our war effort. It concerned only opportunities for psychological warfare.

Throughout the spring of 1945 there were many discussions with policy makers on these and related points and by May a report had been prepared. Since much of this seems merely common sense now in the light of hindsight, it is worth noting that at the time the OWI Japan Section in the office of the Deputy Director for the Far East held up the report's publication and required that it be toned down.

The report on home-front morale was finally brought out as of June 1, 1945. A condensation follows, matched with appropriate excerpts from a report by the U. S. Strategic Bombing Survey based on information secured in Japan after the war. The Division's report is reproduced in full in Appendix B, while the Bombing Survey report is available at the Government Printing Office.* Appendix C provides some notes on the Survey and its relationship to the Division.

It should be said that since the Survey report was not prepared with the idea of checking the Division, it is organized differently. As a result there is a certain amount of awkwardness in comparing the two. The general sense, however, is clear and, due to the danger of distortion, it has been thought best not to extensively reword either report for the sake of matching. Some condensation has, however, been carried out.

Report of the Foreign Morale Analysis Division

The Japanese people are suffering markedly from:

1.† STRESS RELATED TO SUBSISTENCE, WORK AND SHELTER
Food is deficient in quantity and quality.
Work is characterized by long hours and few days of rest. Salaries

* *The Effects of Strategic Bombing on Japanese Morale:* Strategic Bombing Survey, June, 1947, Washington, D. C., Government Printing Office.
† Numbers refer to sections in original report not all of which are represented here.

and wages are consumed by inflation, forced savings and high taxes.

Migration to industrial centers has caused overcrowding and related housing problems. These difficulties have been intensified by bombings which have not only destroyed buildings directly, but have also made it necessary to tear down structures to create fire-breaks, to evacuate people from urban centers and to decentralize industry.

2. STRESS RELATED TO HEALTH

The general health of the Japanese people is deteriorating. There is malnutrition and lack of medical personnel and facilities.

Post-War Report

As the war continued, the supplies of fish and rice fell seriously and almost uncontrolled inflation permitted inequities to develop in the distribution of the limited amounts that were available.

The net result of this situation, the mass of evidence shows, was widespread undernourishment, nutritional disease, social conflict, and depression of the will to resist.

Report by the Foreign Morale Analysis Division

3. STRESS RELATED TO SOCIAL DISLOCATION

The number of men in the army, the men and women who have moved to participate in war work and the evacuations have resulted in severe dislocation of the normal Japanese family and community patterns.

Post-War Report

See page 67.

Report by the Foreign Morale Analysis Division

4. STRESS RELATED TO WAR NEWS

The Japanese know that their army is losing; that their navy has not been able to keep the supply lines open, nor United States task forces away from Japan; that their country is being severely bombed; that they lack a strong air force; that invasion is imminent; and that the West is superior to Japan in material strength and technical knowledge.

Post-War Report

. . . As Japanese defeats began to accumulate in the latter months of 1943 . . . and still more in the early months of 1944 . . . the bad news became impossible to suppress . . . the facts filtered through to the homeland and were reflected in public attitudes.

Some Japanese knew from the beginning of the war of the tremendous superiority of the United States in physical resources, industrial plant, and skilled man power. As the war continued, many more came to realize or at least suspect the fact.

Report by the Foreign Morale Analysis Division

In response to these various types of stress, the following conditions prevail:

1. While there is no evidence that any significant number of Japanese have lost confidence in the purpose and rightness of the war, many have doubts about victory and a considerable number already feel that Japan cannot win.

Post-War Report

Analysis of an important component of morale, confidence in victory, indicates that once the decline set in, in the latter part of 1944, morale cracked at an ever-increasing rate.

. . . while Saipan was a shock to the home front, really widespread depression and apprehension came after the Philippine Campaign.

On 10 July, 1945, the "Thought Police" issued a secret report, the result of a survey of public reactions . . . on the loss of Okinawa on 25 June. The major conclusion seems to be that, "the publication of Okinawa's fate has apparently given rise to no special trend in public thought." The reason for this, according to the report, was that morale was so low anyway, and Okinawa's loss only added to the defeatist feelings.

A Case History in Applied Social Science

A cross-section sample of the population was asked by the Bombing Survey, as one of the items in the questionnaire:

"As the war went along, did you ever begin to have doubts that Japan would win?" If the answer were "Yes," then the respondent was asked, "When was that?"

Using these answers it was possible to chart the total percentage of Japanese who said they had doubts about victory at successive stages of the war. The result is shown on Chart I. A similar curve for the question, "When did you first feel certain that Japan could not attain sure victory?" is shown in Chart II.

The Bombing Survey sums up its conclusion by saying:

Obviously, what happened to a critical component of Japanese morale was not a sag, nor a decline; it has something of the characteristics of a crack-up.

Report by the Foreign Morale Analysis Division

2. In the event of defeat, most Japanese expect to be enslaved, starved and physically mutilated.

Post-War Report

Probably most important . . . at least as the war went on, was fear of the consequences of defeat. The propagandists, throughout the war, instilled in the Japanese a fear of the dire consequences of an American victory, until the overwhelming mass of them expected anything from enslavement to annihilation. . . . To the question, "During the war, what did you think would be in store for you and your family if Japan lost the war?" almost three-fourths of the responses were in this vein. As a woman munitions worker in Hagi said:

". . . I thought that it was better to be dead than to be captured. I hated to die suffering. I thought that it would be better if we died together happily."

GROWTH OF DOUBTS OF VICTORY (1)

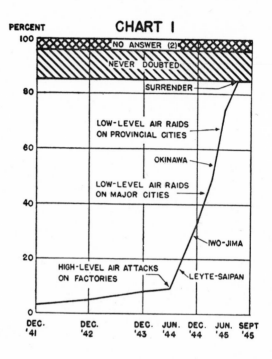

PERCENT | CHART I

100 — NO ANSWER (2)

NEVER DOUBTED

80 — SURRENDER

LOW-LEVEL AIR RAIDS
ON PROVINCIAL CITIES

60

OKINAWA

LOW-LEVEL AIR RAIDS
ON MAJOR CITIES

40

IWO-JIMA

20

HIGH-LEVEL AIR ATTACKS
ON FACTORIES   LEYTE-SAIPAN

0

DEC. '41   DEC. '42   DEC. '43   JUN. '44   DEC. '44   JUN. '45   SEPT '45

(1) More specifically, this chart is a presentation of total percentage of Japanese who said they had doubts of victory, at successive stages of the war. The chart is based on answers to the following questions: "As the war wore on, did you ever begin to have doubts that Japan would win? When was that?"

(2) This category includes persons who gave no answer or whose answers were irrelevant.

64

GROWTH OF CERTAINTY
THAT JAPAN COULDN'T WIN (1)

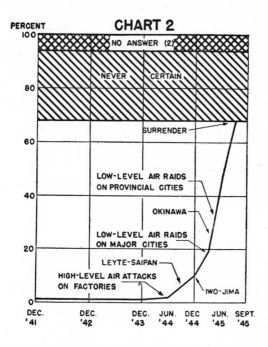

(1) More specifically, this chart is a presentation of the total percentage of Japanese who said they were certain Japan couldn't win, at successive stages of the war. The chart is based on answers to the following questions: "When did you first feel certain that Japan could not attain sure victory? When was that?"

(2) This category includes persons who gave no answer or whose answers were irrelevant.

Human Relations in a Changing World

Report by the Foreign Morale Analysis Division

3. There has been no weakening of attitudes toward the Emperor and the Imperial Institution, but for all other leaders, from the Cabinet down to neighborhood air-raid protection units, there are both satisfactions and dissatisfactions, with the latter mounting.

Post-War Report

Parallel to [this] . . . faith in spiritual resources was the Japanese obedience to and faith in the Emperor. While 37 per cent of the Japanese were definitely critical of their leaders' conduct of the war, and 60 per cent criticized home-front leadership, the Emperor remained practically immune from criticism; he was above and beyond any schism between people and leaders.

A well-informed community leader in Kyoto observed: "Throughout the whole war, the attitude of the people toward the Emperor did not change, for they regarded him as the father of the people and symbol of all that is good and great in Japan. Toward their other leaders from the prime minister down, the attitude of the people changed greatly. At first the people were proud of and greatly trusted their leaders, but as news of the war reverses began to leak through, and as cabinet changes took place, the confidence of the people in their leadership was rudely shaken and finally utterly shattered . . . the people themselves were not fully united in the latter part of the war."

Report by the Foreign Morale Analysis Division

a. The trend toward social disorganization and hence disorganization of the war effort is seen in:

Hostility between urban and rural people, the city dwellers feeling that the peasants are hoarding and falling down on production, while the farmers feel that those who live in the big towns are the cause of heavy taxes, lack of fertilizer and low prices for country produce. There is also an influx of city people into the country as a result of evacuation, and these are a strain on rural housing and subsistence facilities.

A Case History in Applied Social Science

Post-War Report

Evacuees had a most unsettling effect upon the communities in which they sought refuge. They went everywhere, spreading news of disaster and eating into the meagre resources of their hosts.

Their leaving [home] resulted in disorganization of family life, and the abandonment of passive defense against bombs in the communities from which they came. . . .

In nearly all the communities which received evacuees, the commonest complaint of the people was the increased black-market activities and the consequent rise in the price of commodities. The people blamed the black market upon evacuees who, they charged, being rich, were willing to pay high prices to obtain goods otherwise unavailable.

Even had organizational efficiency remained at a high level, this vast migration would have been a calamity. But the very scope of the evacuation dissolved organization, already under heavy strain from the physical results of bombing. The combination was disastrous.

Evacuation, then, was bad for the morale of the evacuees, bad for the morale of their hosts, and bad for the morale of those whom they left behind. It materially disorganized the economy and the social life of the entire country.

Report by the Foreign Morale Analysis Division

b. The Koreans, who have been imported for labor, are feared and suspected of plotting against the Japanese.

Post-War Report

Rumors and recrimination regarding a scapegoat minority such as the Koreans rose especially sharply.

Report by the Foreign Morale Analysis Division

d. In politics, cleavages between different factions are becoming more evident. These political moves indicate not only scheming and

67

counter-scheming but also dissolution of solidarity, hostility between cliques, lack of clarity as to aims and methods and, above all, a roughened sea of rising public fear, hostility and confusion.

Post-War Report

Soon after Tojo's fall in July, 1944, the IRAA (the single political party that replaced all the previous political parties when they were officially abolished) was beginning to deteriorate. . . . The basic trouble had, of course, been the lack of truly popular support. . . . There was, furthermore, a good deal of internal conflict. The factions and feuds among the old parties which the IRAA was supposed to eliminate, reappeared in its midst. There was, for instance, bitter rivalry between the IRAPS and the Youth Corps.

Report of the Foreign Morale Analysis Division

h. There are a small number of radical secret societies operating below the surface who would like to see the Allies win because it would discredit the ruling groups and give themselves a chance to develop political power.

Post-War Report

There are indications of the existence throughout the war of a fairly coherent organization, at least among party Communists. . . .

Report of the Foreign Morale Analysis Division

i. The Government and the public generally blame each other for the war situation. The people accuse the Government of bungling, interfering, red tape, lack of trust in the people, concealing information and economic muddling so that the food situation is desperate and the black markets are uncontrolled.

A Case History in Applied Social Science

Post-War Report

Despite vigorous control measures, the incidence of both overt subversion and rumor-mongering showed a distinct increase after March, 1945. According to one Special High Police report of July, 1945:

"Recent rumors, scribblings and [other] manifestations are numerically increasing. . . . They say that the Japanese war leaders, or the leading circles, are responsible for the decisive battle against Japan proper, for intensified air raids, shortage of food stuffs, acute inflation, etc. . . . This indignation against the ruling class was shown in criticisms of military strategy and misrepresentation of the attitude of military circles. Others speak ill of government measures and government communiqués. They explicitly assume a hostile attitude toward the government circles. Some others dare to speak of class antagonism."

A report on Japan's fighting capabilities as of early June, prepared by Suzuki's chief cabinet secretary, Hisatsune Sakomizu, arrayed the grim complex of forces which were recognized by a goodly part of the ruling group and which were forcing them to sue for peace. . . . Sakomizu's report, called "A Survey of National Resources as of 1 to 10 June, 1945," stated in part:

"The ominous turn of the war, coupled with the increasing tempo of the air raids, is bringing about great disruption of land and sea communications and essential war production. The food situation has worsened. It has become increasingly difficult to meet the requirements of total war. Moreover, it has become necessary to pay careful attention to the trends in public sentiment. . . .

"Morale is high, but there is dissatisfaction with the present regime. Criticism of the government and the military is increasing. The people are losing confidence in their leaders and the gloomy omen of deterioration in public morale is present. The spirit of public sacrifice is lagging and among leading intellectuals there are some who advocate peace negotiations as a way out."

This statement is typical of official Japanese statements on morale. . . . No one would dare to admit openly and generally that things were as bad as they were. However, in the detail of reports, the intended impression would be conveyed. Sakomizu's own testimony to Morale Division interrogators was that he took a dim view indeed of public morale.

Report by the Foreign Morale Analysis Division

5. Emotionally, five trends can be distinguished:

a. Some people are inspired to greater effort by the difficulties.

b. Some people show variable activity in which they seek by trial and error some escape from their stresses but stick at no one thing for long.

c. Some people are angry and aggressive toward others in Japan and blame various individuals and groups for the predicament the nation is in.

d. Some people are panicky and prone to hysterical outbursts, flying from one extreme to another.

e. Some people have become apathetic, slowed down, imbued with defeatism and concerned only with their own personal needs.

It is difficult to say which trend is the most prevalent at present, but there is some reason to infer that it is apathy.

Post-War Report

Such practices as labor hoarding and "pirating" by companies, paying "black-market" wages to entice workers, absenteeism among workers and production "blocking" by disgruntled workers prevailed. Labor-management disputes were never eliminated. Intraplant conflicts between conscriptees and old workers existed, and many war workers resented being forcibly removed from trade and service occupations or light consumer-industry jobs. Furthermore, in most instances wages were inadequate to meet the real cost of living in a black-market economy.

A national security report, dated August, 1945, makes this statement concerning the trend of labor morale:

". . . . after the big raids [from March on] the . . . majority of workers in [the bombed] areas disengaged themselves from production and became very interested in their own self-preservation. This behavior . . . is gradually deepening the tendency toward defeatism and the trend is following a course which warrants attention to the preservation of peace."

While the drastic reduction in the food supply helped to undermine confidence in leadership and intensified the cleavage between the "haves" and the "have-nots" among Japanese civilians, the consequent competition for the necessities of life, together with heightened nervous tensions and mounting difficulties brought on by air raids struck at the nerves of individuals. As the war progressed, people began to distrust each other more; they became ruder, more selfish, more short-tempered and more inclined to pick fights. In answer to the question, "Did the people's attitudes and conduct toward each other change during the war?" almost half the responses indicated growing tension among the civilians.

A middle-class housewife of Ogaki expressed herself this way:

"Yes, definitely — everyone became inconsiderate. Stores didn't extend services; riding trains and streetcars was a mad commotion. I think the people became irritable due to lack of food. They are always hungry and dissatisfied and naturally they try to blame their suffering on someone."

Report by the Foreign Morale Analysis Division

Looking to the future (as of May, 1945) it seems that:

There will long remain many energetic and determined Japanese in all walks of life, particularly among the military, who will wage a desperate last-stand fight. This will be countered by a determined effort on the part of other people to save Japan from devastation by ending the war. The people who do this will be those who see more advantage in an integrated, if defeated Japan, than in a crushed and disorganized Japan. They will be made up of political realists from the court, of the less extreme militarists (especially in the Navy), of bureaucrats and of men with industrial and business interests. They will not for the most part be liberals. They will seize as much power inside Japan as they can grasp and will try to drive a hard bargain with the Allies. On the other hand, they will strive to control the last-ditch fanatics and will evolve formulae in terms of recognized Japanese values that will permit the ending of the war.

Post-War Report

As a political force, morale found its opportunity for expression in the existence of factions within the controlling group . . . fissures . . . gradually widened as reverses occurred. A faction emerged which had more to lose by continuing the war than by surrender.

In mid-April, Admiral Kantaro Suzuki had been named Premier, and had been given definite instructions to "bring the war to a conclusion as quickly as possible."

The important thing to note about this group of peacemakers is that there was nothing essentially democratic about their behavior. . . . Their efforts were definitively and literally conservative. They represented a privileged class of the population who saw in the continuation of hostilities a threat of destruction to their status and privileges. In the first place, because of the military situation, they feared that carrying on to the point of invasion and the final battles would result in the disintegration and disappearance of the system through which they profited.

Report by the Foreign Morale Analysis Division

The downward trend in Japanese morale may take a long or a short time before it reaches a point that makes possible the termination of the war. The military pressure brought to bear will be the principal controlling factor. Assuming that the military pressure is sustained, the psychological and social tensions now handicapping the Japanese will continue to mount in severity until they actively cripple the Japanese war effort. This may take the form of extreme social chaos, but it is more likely that those leaders who wish to stop the war will be able to secure control, most probably through the Emperor.

A Case History in Applied Social Science

Post-War Report

By the early spring of 1945 the peace group had considerably broadened its influence. Further elements of the naval top command had been won over, the closest advisers of the Emperor had been influenced and access gained to the Emperor himself. Secrecy was still important, however, as the army radicals and the lower echelons of the Navy were still strong in their refusal to admit the bankruptcy of their policies. . . .

It is not appropriate in this place to detail the complicated maneuvers involved in the denouement. It is sufficient to state through Premier Suzuki, that

"When the Emperor took his active role in politics at the end of the war, it was because the Premier . . . had been able to lead the Government up to a point where it could be left to the Emperor to make the decision."

In general summary, the post-war report states:

After the loss of Saipan, their morale began to disintegrate. The process was one in which an accumulation of prolonged war weariness, social unrest, increasing consumer shortages (especially food) and a succession of military reverses weakened the will to resist. Then air attacks brought direct and immediate pressure on large segments of the population and morale abruptly went into a decline.

The striking characteristic of Japanese morale during the war with the United States, therefore, was not so much its steadfastness, but rather its extremely steep climb during the period of initial victories and its precipitate fall at the end.

Since there is a widespread belief in the United States that the atomic bomb was *the* cause of Japanese surrender, it might also be supposed that this event produced deterioration in Japanese morale. It is of interest therefore to report the findings of the Strategic Bombing Survey in this connection:

Human Relations in a Changing World

The level of confidence was quite low in Japan well before the time of the atomic bombing. Under these circumstances, the announcement of a new and devastating weapon was merely added to the already eloquent evidence of national weakness. In Japan, as a whole, military losses and failures . . . were cited twice as frequently as the atomic bomb in inducing certainty of defeat. The general air attack was nearly three times as important in this respect. Consumer deprivations, such as food shortages, were also more important.

The atomic bomb had more effect on the thinking of Government leaders than on the morale of the rank and file of civilians outside the target cities. It cannot even be said that it was the atomic bomb which convinced the leaders who effected the peace that surrender was necessary. The decision . . . had been taken in May, 1945. . . .

Nor can it be said that the atomic bomb persuaded the top leaders of the group opposing surrender to change their opinions. After the bomb was dropped, voting in the Supreme War Guidance Council still remained divided as it had been before, with the War Minister and the two Chiefs of Staff unwilling to accept unconditional surrender. However, as the Bombing Survey says:

There seems little doubt . . . that the bombing of Hiroshima and Nagasaki weakened their inclination to take strong measures against the peace group. . . . The atomic bombs hastened surrender, but did not themselves provide the major motive.

The report of the Foreign Morale Analysis Division ended with a series of recommendations for psychological warfare based on its findings and these may be found in Appendix A. They are omitted here because they are not of central importance in this presentation, because they are lengthy and because they are difficult to check for validity.

As noted earlier, the Division's report fell short in expressing

74

A Case History in Applied Social Science

the Division's conclusions, due to modifications that were imposed. Actually, by June, although nothing was known of the atomic bomb, it was expected that the Japanese would very soon make real overtures for peace and this was expressed in verbal statements to policy makers and others. A number of the members of the Division together with some other workers in the same field when participating in a panel discussion under the auspices of the Office of Strategic Services estimated that the war would be finished some time between July and the end of September if no major change occurred in our military activity or State Department policy.

The Strategic Bombing Survey concluded:

From its studies of Japanese resources, military position, and ruling politics, the Survey estimates that the Government would have surrendered prior to November 1, 1945, and certainly before the end of the year. . . .

. . . Japan would have surrendered even if the atomic bombs had not been dropped, even if Russia had not entered the war and even if no invasion had been planned or contemplated.

CHAPTER IV

METHOD OF ANALYSIS

I

As PREVIOUSLY noted, a number of basic assumptions derived from psychiatry, pyschology, and anthropology underlay the work of the Foreign Morale Analysis Division. Space does not permit discussion of each of these assumptions, but they will be listed in order to suggest their content and range; and two will be selected for more detailed treatment in order to illustrate meaning and use.*

Basic Assumptions

I. There exist psychological uniformities common to all the tribes, nations, and "races" of human beings.

II. Each psychological uniformity has a range through which it varies; some variants are characteristic of particular groups of people and as such form a part of their culture.

Uniformities that are important in morale analysis are presented in Assumptions III to XIV.

III. All people are disturbed by these general types of stress:

1. Threats to life and health;
2. Discomfort from pain, heat, cold, dampness, fatigue, and poor food;

---

* These assumptions are adapted from a longer list previously published in an analysis of human behavior under stress. See Part II, and Appendix, *The Governing of Men,* by Alexander H. Leighton, Princeton University Press, 1945.

3. Loss of means of subsistence, whether in the form of money, jobs, business or property;

4. Deprivation of sexual satisfaction;

5. Enforced idleness;

6. Restriction of movement;

7. Isolation;

8. Threats to children, other family members and friends;

9. Dislike, rejection and ridicule from other people;

10. Capricious and unpredictable behavior on the part of those in authority upon whom one's welfare depends;

IV. When the above types of stress combine in the following three forms, they are by that fact additionally disturbing:

1. Frustration of expectations, desires, needs, intentions or goals;

2. The dilemma of conflict between mutually incompatible desires and intentions ("ambivalence" or "multivalence");

3. Circumstances creating confusion and uncertainty as to what is happening in the present and what can be expected in the future ("disorientation").

V. All people have a tolerance-for-stress threshold.

VI. Among all tribes, nations and "races" of human beings, individuals vary greatly from one to another in the level of this tolerance-for-stress threshold.

VII. When the tolerance-for-stress threshold is exceeded, all people respond with some *combination* of the following psychological patterns:

1. Integrated and efficient action directed toward overcoming the source of stress;

2. Random, trial-and-error activity, implicit and overt;

3. Suspiciousness, hatred, hostility, destructive action often directed at substitutes rather than at the actual causes;

4. Apathy, withdrawal from effort to cope with the situation actively.

VIII. All people everywhere have systems of belief which influence their behavior and which are in part:

1. *Logical,* based on experience and reason;
2. *Cultural,* based on the pressure of other people's opinion;
3. *Personal-emotional,* serving to satisfy the aspirations and allay the fears of the individual.

IX. The beliefs which people hold range from the transient and changeable to the deeply ingrained and relatively unchangeable.

X. The most deeply ingrained and unchangeable beliefs are those predominantly rooted in 2. and 3. in Assumption VIII.

XI. The systems of belief (or "cultural concepts") of any tribe, nation or "race" influence their tolerance to stress, and the predominant forms the reactions to stress (Assumption VII) will manifest.

XII. All changes in psychological patterns, including those occurring in response to stress, require time and may be delayed or hastened by influences intruding between the beginning of a change and its conclusion.

XIII. If morale is defined as *the capacity of a group of people to pull together consistently and persistently in pursuit of a common purpose,* then it is dependent upon preponderance of the following factors:

1. The faith of each member of the group in the common purpose;
2. The faith of each member of the group in the leadership;
3. The faith of each member of the group in the other members;

4. The organizational efficiency of the group;

5. The health and balance of emotions in the individuals of the group.*

XIV. In analyzing any particular situation, the following items are a basis for evaluating the nature, validity and the approximate strength of the above morale factors:

1. Frequency of reference;
2. Ratio of positive and negative references;
3. The multiplicity of sources;
4. The nature of the sources.

(Assumption XIV is doubtless obscure, but it will be more fully described in the next section.)

II

Assumptions XIII and XIV are selected for further discussion and explanation, since they bear most directly on actual operations.

On the basis of the intelligence material available to the Division, there was no way to study directly over-all morale. However, utilizing Assumption XIII as a conceptual tool, it was possible to study and follow changes in the five morale factors and from these to estimate the nature, relative strength and the changes occurring in over-all morale.

Estimates of this sort must have some standard for comparison and it was consequently decided to use the Japanese themselves as a base line. This was in contrast to a common method of estimating enemy morale where the rule of thumb was to ask whether a given symptom of morale was higher or lower than

---

* Assumption XIII is modified from "A Working Concept of Morale for Flight Surgeons," Alexander H. Leighton, *The Military Surgeon*, Vol. 92, No. 6, June, 1943.

a corresponding element among ourselves. If it seemed the same or better than with us, it was considered good morale.

The Division felt that this was a serious error because the state of morale among ourselves was usually not adequately known, no account was taken of differing cultural influences and differing circumstances, and very often the two elements or factors being compared were of quite unlike significance.

For instance, evidence of complaining by the Japanese against government leaders was dismissed by one policy maker as indicating nothing significant about morale because in American we also complained about our leaders. Such a view did not take into consideration cultural differences regarding what could be said publicly about leaders in the two countries. It is well known that in Japan, especially under the influence of "thought police," one did not readily speak against those in authority. The view likewise neglected the totally different circumstance that we were winning the war while the Japanese were losing it. When a nation feels it is achieving success, criticisms of leaders may amount to little more than "blowing off steam" and have little effect on morale as here defined. On the other hand, when a war is being lost and the people feel themselves in a tight spot, criticism of leaders has very serious implications for the capacity to pull together toward the common goal. Furthermore, the view regarding American criticism of leaders was not based on any knowledge of its prevalence or its rise and fall during the war, with circumstances. Finally, there was no consideration given to whether this complaining on the part of the Japanese represented a change in their behavior, and if so, whether toward more complaining or less.

The Division took as its chief base line in estimating Japanese military morale the results of a careful study of all the morale factors during the New Guinea campaign. Morale factors revealed in later material or from other areas were considered higher or lower in accordance with divergence from the New

Guinea picture. Many other comparisons were also made, but in all cases significant differences were in terms of matching Japanese with Japanese.

Assumption XIV deals with ways and means of evaluating the morale factors and includes frequency of reference, ratio of positive and negative responses, multiplicity of sources and nature of source. Precision was obviously impossible, but it was thought that approximate accuracy could be achieved, comparable with that which has to be employed for important decisions in numerous human situations, such as clinics and law courts. The information might not be sufficient to satisfy the intellect, but it would be enough for action — to use Clark-Kennedy's paraphrase of Kant. At the very least it was certain that the available data could be carefully analyzed and its contents known, in contrast to the usual method of skimming and guessing.

1. *Frequency of reference*. The number of times a given item was mentioned in data covering an area or time period was assumed to be of significance. For example, if there were more frequent expressions of fear of defeat found among prisoners taken in the latter part of the New Guinea campaign as compared with those captured in the early days, it was assumed that this probably indicated a change of feelings.

2. *Ratio of references*. With each morale factor it was possible to have many shades of attitude from strongly positive (tending toward high morale) to strongly negative (tending toward low morale). Thus, in the attitude toward victory there could be a range from high confidence to a feeling of certain defeat. It was therefore decided that the important thing was not only the absolute number of references to high-morale items or the opposite, but also the proportion. For instance, at one time 30 per cent of the prisoners taken in a given area might express confidence in

victory and then later the figure might drop to only 10 per cent. This did not in itself show a decline in a positive feeling about victory since it could be the result of less questioning on the subject by interrogators. Such would be strongly indicated if the references to fear of defeat dropped from 20 per cent in the first instance to zero in the second. If, on the other hand, the references to fear of defeat markedly increased while the references to confidence in victory were dropping off, this would point to a real change of attitude.

The ratio of positive and negative factors, therefore, was considered of more importance than the absolute count in estimating strength, weakness, or change in any morale factor.

3. *Multiplicity of sources.* In addition to frequency and ratio of reference, the number of different sources from which the same kind of information came was considered of significance. Flagging confidence in victory was considered more certain if it were reflected not only in prisoner-of-war interviews, but also in captured diaries, personal letters, official military reports, comments by neutral observers, and in anti-defeatist home-front propaganda.

4. *Nature of source.* Weight was also given to the nature of the source from which an item of information came. For example, information regarding desertions in the Japanese army from a single source might be given as much or more weight than many references in prisoner-of-war reports or diaries, if that source were a captured letter from the Vice-Minister of War addressed to theatre commanders and marked "top secret."

On the basis of Assumptions XIII and XIV, a system was set up for processing all the intelligence material that came daily to the Division's hands. This data, from sources tapped by the War Department and the Office of War Information, had already been scanned and selected so that most of it contained some information of a psychological or sociological nature. Since the quantity of material was great in proportion to the size of the Division some sampling had to be employed.

The prisoner-of-war interrogation reports were coded and data dealing with morale factors and background information were reduced to punch cards which could be sorted and tabulated by machines. In addition to this, however, extracts were made from the reports and filed in two systems, one dealing with the morale of the *fighting forces* and the other with the *home front*. These systems were based largely on Assumption XIII, with subdivisions and special headings under the five morale-factor categories, but there were in addition other headings derived from the other assumptions listed and from purely practical considerations related to the way the data came in and to the kinds of questions the Division was most frequently asked by its superiors and by other organizations.

Aside from the interrogation reports, other types of material employed (captured diaries, letters and official documents, reports from neutral sources, Japanese periodicals and newspapers and the radio) were also examined, extracted and filed in the two systems, *fighting forces* and *home front*. Punch cards were not used except in the case of newspaper material where a small-scale experiment was made in tabulating trends.

Through this "processing," the material was broken down into categories. This first step represented in effect a preliminary analysis and prepared the material for more intensive and more specifically focused analysis. Chronological order and groupings according to areas (Philippines, New Guinea, Burma-India, etc.) resulted in the files becoming a constantly growing series of information bins, in each of which trends appeared as the material accumulated.

The more specific and intensive analysis consisted in selecting a question (such as attitude toward surrender or suicide) and then studying and comparing relevant data brought together from various bins and interpreting the results in terms of the assumptions.

To summarize: (a) The Division started with general assumptions (I to XIV) regarding man and his culture; (b) applied these to various intelligence data bearing on the Japanese in order to select and organize the information; and (c) further employed the assumptions to reach conclusions on specific points concerning Japanese military and civilian morale.

A detailed account of the method is given in Appendix D.

CHAPTER V

EXAMPLES OF ANALYSIS

I

THE PROCEDURE that has been outlined involved a blending of information, theoretical concept and common sense. However, it would require a book-length report to explain each of the conclusions that has been mentioned and to describe the employment of all the basic assumptions set forth in Chapter IV. In consequence, attempt at further clarification will be limited to a few illustrative examples.

II

In Chapter II, p. 48, it is stated that the Foreign Morale Analysis Division concluded that Japanese Military morale was "not of uniform consistency and had weaknesses which could and did become worse when circumstances were adverse for the Japanese." This was contrary to a prevailing view, which held that Japanese morale was to all intents and purposes "impregnable." The Division's conclusions arose from the following considerations:

1. If morale is of the nature set forth in Assumption XIII, and if Assumptions III, IV, VI and VII (Chapter IV) are valid, then it follows that at the present stage of human evolution there can be no such thing as "impregnable" morale for any large group of people. Under severe and prolonged stress of war, some combination of the reactions specified in Assumption VII must occur. Of these, Items 2 (random activity) and 4 (apathy) are incompatible with uniformly high morale as postulated in Assumption XIII.

2. When prisoner-of-war interrogation reports were examined with these assumptions in mind, patterns of psychological reaction were apparent which fitted the theoretical expectations. For example, there was suspicion and hostility directed at officers and at other units of Japanese. These tended to lower the morale factors, "faith in leadership" and "faith in the other members of the group."

Tabulations of references by prisoners of war to all morale factors made possible estimates of prevalence and the ratio of positive and negative elements (Assumption XIV, 1 and 2).

3. Translated portions of 250 captured diaries were surveyed and compared with the prisoner-of-war data in order to check by means of a different source (Assumption XIV, 3). This material could not be readily treated with quantitative methods, but a qualitative and descriptive analysis revealed the same patterns that were present in the interrogation reports and confirmed impressions regarding prevalence and intensity. Eventually, translations from 314 diaries were accumulated, of which 20 were of good length and completeness.

4. Finally, captured official Japanese documents came to hand which revealed their own morale problems (Assumption XIV, 4). These, together with the diaries and the prisoner-of-war reports, further confirmed the expectations and gave more detailed information regarding the specific forms the trends were taking among the Japanese and the circumstances associated with them.

The procedure can be further illustrated by a medical analogy. General medical theory would lead one to expect that disease in a given community is correlated in a general way with sanitation and one might anticipate broadly which types of illness would be most prevalent if one knew that sanitation was bad and getting worse. On receiving additional, even if scattered, fragments of information about the community from a number of different sources, one would be able to confirm the general expectations and fill in some detail regarding the specific sorts

A Case History in Applied Social Science

of diseases present, their extent and severity and whether they were increasing or decreasing.

III

Turning now for purposes of further illustration to a more specific issue,* it has been stated (Chapter II, p. 50) that one of the factors supporting Japanese morale was "faith in the Emperor and the divine power and way of life he symbolized," and that this, in contradistinction to some of the other morale factors, did not tend to shift lower under the stresses of prolonged war, either among the Japanese military or on the home front. It was also said (Chapter II, pp. 55-56) that the Division advised policy makers in psychological warfare against attacks on the Emperor. Instead, it was suggested that enemy resistance might be lowered by appealing to this belief and making clear that the Emperor would be treated along those lines which have since been carried out in practice.

To explain these findings, it is necessary to say a little more about Assumptions VIII, IX and X.

The statement that beliefs often have a logical basis (Assumption VIII, 1.) means that they may stand in part on observation combined with reasoning. This is true not only of thought in Western civilization, but of all human thinking. The Eskimo and the jungle native in their hunting and the Japanese peasant in his planting have hundreds of beliefs that are supported by experience and reasoning.

The cultural, "non-logical," components of beliefs (Assumption VIII, 2.), in contrast to reasoning and direct observation, come from the precept and example of one's fellows and the pressure of their opinions. Beliefs that are predominantly of

---

* This section was written in collaboration with Morris E. Opler and appeared under the title, "Psychiatry and Applied Anthropology in Psychological Warfare Against Japan," in *The American Journal of Psychoanalysis*, Vol. VI, No. 1, 1946.

this character are the "facts" which in any society "everybody knows" without proof or demonstration. He who raises questions about them is made to feel either a fool or guilty. In reality, these beliefs may or may not be true and they may or may not have significant logic in their structure. Their particular quality is their social and cultural nature.

That the world is flat, that it is a crime against God to use anesthetics, that swine are unclean, that holy water has power to bless, that corn pollen will make a man healthy and lucky, that vitamins are what we all need, that cannibalism is evil, that free competition will solve the world's economic difficulties, that Communism will save mankind—all these are examples of beliefs which exhibit a large share of the cultural component.

The personal-emotional support for belief systems (Assumption VIII, 3.) has to do with the emotional balance within the individual, the satisfaction of aspirations and the control of anxieties and inner conflict both conscious and unconscious. Beliefs which are mainly supported by these factors are those which involve ideas that enable the individual to feel easier about something which would otherwise produce an unpleasant or intolerable state of emotions. This process has been most clearly demonstrated in mental illness and personality maladjustments. Psychiatrists commonly find that a delusion, a compulsive ritual or a neurotic symptom is retained by a patient in defiance of all reason because of the emotional satisfaction it supplies. However, this kind of function on the part of a belief is by no means confined to the psychotic or the maladjusted. It is part of the equipment with which all people make their way through life.

Assumption X (dealing with changeable and rigid beliefs) may be elaborated by saying the systems of belief that are most strongly held are those that deal in basic values, the nature of the world, the character of the supernatural, and man's place in both. Although influenced and, within limits, modified by reason, they are widespread in the culture, are profoundly emotional rather than logical, and are felt with certainty, rather than thought through. They have close ties with the roots of human motive and the sense of being protected amid the storms of the world. They enable people to act together in common understanding and with a feeling of mutual belonging where otherwise there would be confusion and strife. They protect from devastating doubt and provide a sense of compensation for such adverse influences in life as man's awareness of the inevitability of death and the loss sooner or later of all things held dear.

The rational content of such beliefs is not nearly so important to their strength as the degree to which they fulfill these functions. During stress, human dependence on some beliefs to satisfy these needs has a tendency to become greater, at least for a time, and may be affirmed even at the price of life itself, as by the martyrs who went to the stake for their convictions.

If these assumptions are true, it should be possible to estimate the strength of a system of belief, not by its logical soundness, but by examining its cultural prevalence and the degree to which it functions in the personal-emotional balance of most individuals in the society.

As already noted, almost all references to the Emperor from every source were expressions of faith, devotion, loyalty and conviction as to his importance. Some examples from prisoner-of-war interrogations are as follows:

"From childhood on I was taught that the Emperor is of divine origin and that if capable I may become the Premier of my nation, but never could I be Emperor."

"The Emperor is the father of the whole nation, a living god."

"The prisoner saw two Japanese soldiers worn out with wounds and hunger. One of them called to the section leader and asked to be killed, as he could not keep up with the retiring force. He asked that he be remembered to his family and said 'Long live the Emperor

(Tenno Heika, banzai!).' The section leader then shot him through the head."

"The prisoner stated that the morale in the unit was very high in spite of their hopeless situation. All the men were deeply instilled with the spirit of undying loyalty to the Emperor and were resigned to their fate."

"A good many people will unhesitatingly fight an invading army, even with nothing more than bamboo poles, if the Emperor so decrees. They would stop just as quickly if he so decreed."

In a diary was found this entry:

"In order to do our best for the Emperor, we must deny ourselves and our families. One's faith then becomes a thing exalted in the world. We achieve immortality by casting aside our petty temporal lives and becoming a member of the Fraternity of the Spirits of Dead Heroes. Our spirits and bodies are not merely our own; they are rather for the gods who created the world to use and dispose of. We live by the grace of the Emperor. For people who live in this belief, life is worth while, living has a purpose."

A poem from a diary:

> "The shield of our Emperor's domain, this Iwo Jima,
> Upon our honor we hold this ground,
> We, the Defenders."

It should not be supposed from these quotations that every Japanese died willingly with "Long live the Emperor" on his lips. The Division's records revealed that many called for their mothers or other loved ones instead. Nevertheless, the number of references to the Emperor at a time of reverse, last effort or self-destruction indicates that he was important in Japanese morale.

Considering these findings in the light of Assumptions VIII, IX and X, it was evident that belief in the Emperor was so

A Case History in Applied Social Science

widespread among the Japanese as to constitute a cultural type of belief strongly reinforced in any one individual by the sheer pressure of his whole society (Assumption VIII, 2.). It would be impossible to reject it without being outside almost all the ideas and value systems that are Japanese and, since most Japanese are not members of any other society, this would mean a kind of isolation (Assumption III, 7) that few human beings can stand, except psychotics and extreme mystics.

However, the symbol has also wide latitude in the way it can be interpreted and this permits personal-emotional functioning in many people who, as individuals, are very different from each other. A close scrutiny of Japanese comments on the Emperor and a checking of these against the point of view of the speaker revealed that to the expansionists and militarists he was a strong war leader bent on liberating the East from Western domination; to those who were or became opposed to war, the Emperor was steadfastly a man of peace deceived by the warmongers in Japan; to the partisans of democracy, he was a democrat at heart; to the simple and uneducated he held supernatural powers; to the sophisticated he represented the highest ideals of Japanese culture (Assumption VIII, 3.).

The structure of the attitudes which exist in the Japanese family are another source of faith in the Emperor symbol, which combines both cultural and personal-emotional factors. The rigid hierarchy and other restrictive aspects of the Japanese family have often been described, but less often stressed and just as important is the sense of security that also exists in this unit and the strong feeling of belonging. The Division's information indicated that the Japanese father is not so much the autocrat who demands as he is the recipient of honors which others strive to give, in part at least, because they feel their own worth in this giving. When failures occur, it is not so much the father who punishes the offender as it is the other members of the family group; all together feel the adverse opinion of the neighbors.

The child who grows out of this into adult life is ripe for a counterpart in the larger society. He finds it in the Emperor who is endlessly spoken of as the Father of his People. Each individual can give to the Emperor and feel that this giving contributes a worth-while purpose to life (Assumption VIII, 3.).

Through all of what has been said runs the religious aspect of the Emperor symbol. Here, as in the case of the Emperor's "real intentions," there is much room for interpretation so that he can fulfill the needs of very different sorts of persons, including Christians, Buddhists, and those who belong to Shinto sects. However, the distinction between religion and everyday life, that is so formalized in Western thought, is much more fluid in Japan as in other parts of the East. The filial respect and devotion noted above shade off into religious devotion to dead ancestors who are considered to be watching over their descendants. All men are potential deities to be revered after their death, but the greater the man, the greater the god he will be. The Emperor, with his line of ancestors from the founders of the nation, has the greatest potential of living men. Because of his frequent ceremonial communication with the departed imperial ancestors he is a symbolic bridge between the living and these mighty dead of the past. This parallels on a grander scale the ties between living and dead maintained in each Japanese household before its family shrines.

The Emperor symbol therefore plays a major role, not only as a bond between the living members of Japanese society and as a repository of national ideals, sense of worth and hopes, but it also links the living and the dead as one people and to each living Japanese assures a place in the afterlife.

Thus, the Emperor belief is deeply rooted both in the culture and in the personal-emotional system of aspiration and security of most individuals (Assumption VIII, 2 and 3.). A man who might otherwise be lost in a chaotic universe, and be appalled by his own littleness, helplessness and temporariness, can find meaning and security in believing he is a part of something far greater than himself that spans the natural and the supernatural worlds (Assumption VIII, 3.).

In such a situation, it is evident that increasing adversity would tend to throw more reliance and faith toward the Emperor — at least for a time, and probably for a long time, since he constitutes a type of support for which it is very hard to demonstrate failure.

Beliefs in the righteousness of the war and in the Japanese way of life were of a similar nature, in that they too ran deeply into the aspiration and security sense of the people concerned.

It is easy to point out that the Emperor belief is not only "non-logical," but embodies actual contradictions. How, for example, can the Emperor be supremely divine and yet fooled by advisers who are, by Japanese admission, ordinary rascals? To raise this kind of question is merely to stress a characteristic that is common to many systems of belief. Western thought has struggled to reconcile ideas of an all-powerful God and the existence of evil, of free will and predestination. Although these rational points can be the source of endless dialectics, and can play a part in schisms, they are not where the main strength of a belief lies. The latter is in its cultural force and in its meaning and function in the emotional life of men.

Attacking the Emperor with the means available in psychological warfare seemed at best wasteful, since arguments in leaflets stood little chance of penetration. One cannot effectively attack with logic that which is not logical. At worst, it seemed probable that such efforts would serve to remind people of their belief and its resources and hence tighten their grip and increase the support from this factor at a time when other factors were giving way. There could then be renewed determination and the feeling that death would be preferable to submission before an enemy who vilified the values that were the foundation of existence. It would seem better to lose one's life than to lose hope.

Human Relations in a Changing World

Although it is hard to find in our culture any exact parallel with the Japanese feeling for the Emperor, the difference is one of degree and mode of expression, rather than of kind. Most of us have symbols in which we believe with a firmness which resembles that displayed by the Japanese. With us, however, these beliefs are not so widely shared, and differ in many respects from one group of people to another. Nor, as a rule, do we combine so many different elements in one symbol. However, "The American Way of Life" has some resemblances in having cultural prevalence together with strong personal-emotional ties, and often means very different things to different individuals, e. g., a Quaker and a member of the Ku Klux Klan.

IV

In concluding this chapter, some remarks on the current situation are necessary in order to avoid conveying a false impression. What was true during the war does not necessarily obtain now.

America no longer has the problem of psychological warfare against Japan, but there is the task of fostering a peaceful way of life in that nation. The Emperor is still there, still functioning as a symbol in the lives of the millions, and is now given credit by many of them for having saved Japan by stopping the war. An understanding of his cultural and psychological significance remains important.

However, even though belief in the Emperor is still strong and even though the indications during the war were that little or nothing could be done to shake this faith, it does not follow that change is impossible. On the contrary, it seems likely that the emotional upheaval resulting from defeat and the need of new orientation, the presence of American troops in Japan, and the conscious efforts of American officials to influence the Japanese through press, radio, movies and educational reform will combine to have an effect. America is now in a position to bring pressure to bear which may result in changes at both the cultural and the personal-emotional levels in the lives of vast numbers of Japanese. This is a very different situation from that which existed when we were outside Japan hurling in both leaflets and bombs.

The fact that change will occur, however, and the fact that it will take place largely as a result of American influence, does not necessarily mean it will be in accordance with our aims and expectations. That is still a different matter.

PART III

THE USE OF
APPLIED SOCIAL SCIENCE

INTRODUCTION

THE ACTIVITIES of the Foreign Morale Analysis Division are obviously but a tiny part in the total of social science. A much wider range of concepts and techniques have been applied to a great variety of problems, and in many instances, even during the war, much more precision was achieved than in the case of the Division.*

Furthermore, looking to the present and future, the work of Division has little direct bearing on Japan or on psychological warfare. Conditions in Japan have changed and any social-science approach to its problems would require new observations, measurements and analysis. As for psychological warfare, the speed and extent of destruction in future wars will drastically reduce the opportunity to do work of the sort that has been here described.

The implication that matters is the possibility that the understanding of human behavior can be illuminated by science and that through increased understanding there is increased opportunity for control. Acceptance of this point of view has to be more than theoretical. There must be action in the form of systematic observation, analysis and prediction. It is not enough to recognize that social and psychological forces exist, but there must also be recognition of the fact that like other natural forces they result in a process of constant change. There must be constant examination to determine which combination of many possible forces is at work at particular times and in particular places, which direction the process of change is taking and the range within which it can be altered.

* See footnote, p. 43.

Moreover, in a democratic society, the fruits of such work must not remain as knowledge restricted to transient administrators nor to powerful groups that try to set national policy. It must permeate the educational system and the journals of the nation so that the citizens who select and criticize the government — and whose accumulated prejudices strongly influence policy — may exert pressure that is realistically geared to the needs of the situation rather than merely an emotional release.

The opportunity ahead is a double one: to press forward in discovery, and to apply what is already known. *Discovery* in social science has far to go before it matches the other sciences and before it can provide tools which will surely solve the problems raised by their advances. The question of *application* has scarcely less magnitude, since even today the gap between the known and the actually used is enormous. Nevertheless, if knowledge can be carried far enough, fast enough — and accepted widely enough — there is hope of preventing disaster and contributing to better living.

In the remainder of this book an attempt will be made to outline some of the problems to which work like that of the Division can be applied, some difficulties in application which must be overcome, and finally a few observations on the relationship between social science and human values.

CHAPTER VI

PROBLEMS OF TODAY

I

THE PREVENTION of war and the promotion of workable relationships between nations is the most pressing need.

A necessary ingredient in satisfying this need is knowledge of other nations. Accurate descriptions are required of the predominant opinions, attitudes and beliefs of the people in each, descriptions which state the facts in so far as they can be discovered without being colored by what we may hope, fear, or want to think. In addition to description, it is necessary to know which beliefs are strongly held, their causes, and their relationship to the basic social, psychological, biological, and economic balance of the people. In addition to beliefs and attitudes, there are similar questions regarding the social organization and institutions of nations. We need, in short, knowledge of both form and function.

Some readers may feel that we already know these things, and, certainly, a vast amount has been written by travelers, journalists, and scholars about the habits and attitudes of many nations. While some of this is valuable, much is inaccurate and highly colored with a bewildering array of viewpoints. Not the least impelling source of distortion is the desire to make the writing above everything else thrilling or entertaining. Comparatively little is based on scientifically oriented observation and analysis. Much more work has to be done before there will be social and psychological knowledge of nations sufficient and accurate enough for use in the present world situation.

Human Relations in a Changing World

Most important of all, such knowledge is not something that can be obtained once and the matter considered settled. It must be constantly up-to-date because change is ever taking place. The early identification of trends provides toe holds for encouraging movement toward cooperation between nations and for counteracting drifts in the opposite direction. Observation and analysis, therefore, must go forward systematically and continuously.

The point, of course, is to understand the behavior of any one nation in relation to other nations. "Understanding," as used here, does not mean intuition and is not limited to sympathy. It means a grasp of causal factors derived by a process based on science. Such understanding should enable us to distinguish more accurately between the behavior that is possible for a country and behavior which we as a nation might want that country to adopt, but which is impossible given its situation and particular cultural patterns. Within the range of behavior that is possible for a country, we should also be able to distinguish the easy and probable from the difficult and improbable. In particular, we should be able to guage better the effect of our own policies and actions and whether they produce the results desired or call forth responses that make worse the situation we wish to see mended.

A central question in the matter of national attitude and belief is the way the members of any given nation perceive the members of another. Generally, the people of one nation — and the United States is no exception — harbor stereotyped images of other nations, starkly simple and exceedingly inaccurate. Yet these images are the basis upon which people feel for or against other nations, interpret their behavior as villainous or good, judge their actions, and judge what they themselves as a nation should do in relation to the others. It follows, of course, that if the images are false, the resulting course of action can hardly ever be adequate.

The Use of Applied Social Science

It may be objected that the policy-making process is beyond the reach of the public. In a sense this is true, but to a large extent it is not, for the diplomat is often influenced by widespread, but poorly founded, attitudes among the people of his country. During the war a man who occupied an important policy-making position in the government told me that he was certain that if we succeeded in convincing the Japanese people that we did not intend to attack the Emperor it would materially reduce their will to resist, but that we could never attempt such a project because of the attitude of the American people. While it may be doubted that the policy maker's estimate of the American people was correct, supposing the reasons had been presented to them, his behavior nevertheless illustrates the point that those who make policy are influenced by what they believe to be the attitudes of the people. Even in non-democratic nations public opinion always exerts at least some limiting effect.

It must be added, however, that while the image which a diplomat holds regarding another country is usually more complex and often closer to reality than the popular stereotypes, it may still be far from an adequate picture of the social and psychological forces at work. In these matters he is almost wholly guided by traditional political and economic concepts, personal experience, impressions, guesswork, and intuition. He, too, has need of more accurate images of nations.

As with other beliefs, we should go further than merely recognizing images; we should explore their cause. This would mean more than simplistic and partial explanations such as "due to propaganda," "due to Communism," due to international conspiracy, or due to the machinations of some leader or group. It would mean understanding antecedent events and the current cultural, social, psychological, economic, and related factors — somewhat as the belief in the Emperor was analyzed (Chapter V, pp. 90-95), but with much more adequate information.

To face this matter of images squarely and accept the facts

would require a change from prevalent habits of thought where all considerations are overshadowed by whether we like or do not like what others think about us. In the case of adverse opinions, our customary recourse is to retaliate in some form, rather than to understand.

In relations between people it is now generally accepted that retaliation cannot be counted upon for satisfactory results. In a community, good relations between neighbors depends more on understanding and action rooted in that understanding than on retaliation.

To illustrate further, at a very simple level, when a psychiatrist is treating a patient, it sometimes happens that the patient is extremely insulting. In such circumstances the psychiatrist will restrain his natural impulse to punch the patient on the nose and will try to find out why the patient feels that way. The reason for this reaction is that the accumulated experience of the profession shows that when you punch patients on the nose you do little to advance the treatment. If such punches helped patients, they would be commonly practiced, since they would be much milder than some forms of treatment patients now undergo, for instance, electric shock. The experience is, however, that retaliation puts a stop to further treatment. There is cancellation of the physician's opportunity to help the patient improve his relations with people. On the other hand, when the physician learns why the patient has such an unfavorable impression and traces out some of the causes, he often finds he has arrived at the center of some of the patient's deepest conflicts and difficulties. Inquiry gives an opportunity for therapy and adjustment which involves successful changing of the patient's images and attitudes.

The problem of relations between large groups of people, such as nations, has many differences from the problem of relations between individuals, and yet there is the same principle of images, true and false, of causal factors, and the desirability of finding out, rather than resorting to naïve retaliation.

In addition to the images that other nations may have of us and we of them, there is the problem of discrepancy between reality and the images we have of ourselves as we move and act in relation to other nations. We have idealized pictures of ourselves and we have guilty pictures, and both are possibly as far from reality as are the distorted impressions other nations often have of us.

False images of ourselves as a nation produce barriers to understanding our position in relation to other nations and the consequences, particularly the indirect consequences, of our acts. Thus, we may think we are being cooperative when actually we appear weak. Or, on the other hand, what seems to us a demonstration of reasonable firmness may strike another country as an overt act of hostility requiring immediate retaliation. What we suppose is a generous effort to give support may be angrily treated as an attempt at exploitation. We are confident that we will never, without provocation, attack any nation with atomic bombs and so we discount the threat element in our possession of the weapon, while other nations with a different view of us never forget it.

When difficulties arise, we have a tendency to write off the behavior of another country as unreasonable, as due to peculiarities of its innate nature, or as the product of evil leaders with evil intentions. Other countries in their turn do the same regarding our behavior. Such conclusions may, at times, be just in terms of certain premises, but the trouble with them is that, just or not, they are a dead end. They do not lead to solving the problem. They lead to giving up, or to one of the well-established patterns of hitting back. There is no blindness like the blindness of self-righteousness. Inquiry and cool thinking with adequate perspective habitually cease to function at the time they are most necessary. In their place comes back talk, heightened emotions, hair-trigger readiness, misinterpretations and the taking of positions from which pride makes retreat impossible.

The nature of the various types of images that have been mentioned, their comparison with reality, and the identification of causal factors are attackable problems. Until some headway is made, international relations must always be in danger of decisions based on fantasy.

II

While understanding of causes and effects in human attitudes is prerequisite to mutual adjustment between nations, through providing new and wider premises, there is no reason to hope that this is enough. One cannot escape from the existence of conflicting interests. Adversaries can be aware of the causes in the behavior of each other and still remain adversaries, like two dogs after the same bone. However, the nature of the interests that conflict is another area where expansion of knowledge and its application can be pressed with some hope of finding ways of resolution.

For example, there is a prevalent belief that nations inevitably, by some instinct, struggle for power, and that they show this in military, political, and economic activity. Yet, one has only to look at Switzerland, Sweden, and many other countries in the modern and ancient worlds to find exceptions. Anthropology and history afford numerous instances of peoples who live or have lived without an apparent urge to dominate other groups. Therefore, while recognizing competition for power as common and important, we do not need to accept it as inevitable or inherent in nature but can study the causes of its presence and its absence.

It is also necessary to think of conflicting interests as arising from sources other than an itch for power. The question of the relationship of stress and suffering to a nation's potential for aggression, whether directed inward in revolution and civil

The Use of Applied Social Science

war, or outward in attack on others, is a critical matter. In Chapter IV, pp. 76-77, in Assumptions III and IV, a number of types of stress are outlined. It is pointed out that when these exceed the threshold that can be tolerated, one common result is active hostility, and that the potential for this action is increased as other modes of seeking relief fail. If this sequence constitutes a universal principle of human behavior, then the reduction of stress throughout the world becomes one of the essential steps toward peace. It opens as a major problem for social science, the estimation of stresses and the devising of ways and means for their reduction.

The reader may say that the idea of populations under stress becoming a liability to other groups through active hostility is already well recognized and is, for example, an underlying consideration in the European Recovery Plan.

Although this is in part true, the principle is generally obscured by other matters or treated gingerly, as if it were not quite real. Very often it is set aside, in order to consider whether the people of another nation "deserve" aid. This introduces a different frame of reference and bears on the questions previously outlined regarding the images and fantasies nations have of each other.

There can be many false assumptions and much misinformation underlying judgments on what constitutes "deserving" and "undeserving." On the other hand, if a cause-and-effect relationship between stress and hostile action is appreciated, it no longer appears always advisable to insist on the absence of hostility before stress is relieved, nor to recall past hostile behavior as a reason for present refusal of help. To do so is a little like insisting that a patient be free of symptoms before you give him treatment. Furthermore, to pick and choose the "deserving" rather than those who have need fails to keep in view the aim of reducing stress in order to reduce the world-wide potential for war. Indeed, it leaves under stress many of those with greatest need because they are closest to open hostility.

To use another medical simile, it is as if public-health measures in a community were regarded as a generous gift from the authorities to the "deserving," but denied to the uncooperative, the uninformed, the prejudiced, and the delinquent, thus missing the central aim of reducing the sources of infection that threaten the whole community.

So far we have been considering populations and countries as if they were composed solely of adults, omitting, as is commonly done, reference to the children. When one does consider the children, it is evident that by no manipulation of reason can they be held "undeserving" or accountable for the conditions into which they were born, or for the behavior of their elders. Yet these children are not only suffering from stresses, but are reacting to them and building habit patterns and belief systems in which hostility, aggression, and hate can be permanently ingrained. These traits will stamp their future societies.

Children in millions are now growing up throughout the world, from China to the slums of Europe, under the conditions of frightful stress. They are growing up twisted by these conditions, and one day they will meet our children.

It must be concluded, therefore, that although the causal relationship between stress and aggression is sometimes mentioned, it is not fully recognized nor carried over into action. One has only to look at the distribution of the national budget to see that this is so.

On the relatively rare occasions, when the principle is appreciated, it is by and large only for some kinds of stress. Starvation, for instance, can be perceived as a cause for riots, revolutions, and invading other people's land. But the effects of exposure to idleness, to lack of satisfying work, to low esteem and ridicule, to frustration, to uncertainty, and to other items listed in Assumptions III and IV (Chapter IV) that have to do with the way people feel, are usually ignored by those who are not themselves undergoing these stresses at the time. There are now tools available wherewith science can push far in discerning and estimating these less obvious, but no less real, sources of stress, and there is every reason to expect such skills can be much more highly developed.

A full realization of the importance of relieving stress would not lead directly to a solution of the problem, even if agriculture, engineering, transportation, and other technical matters were adequately handled. There still remain additional difficulties that come from human factors.

Food may be taken as an important instance. It is common knowledge that people in many parts of the world do not have enough to eat and it does not require social science, applied or otherwise, to point up this need. According to the figures of the Food and Agriculture Organization of the U.N., over half the world's population was markedly undernourished before the war. Up-to-date figures are not available, but there can be little doubt that they would show conditions to be more severe, with both slow, chronic starvation and recurrent, desperate emergencies.

Modern technologies make the elimination of starvation a practical possibility, at least for the existing number of people in the world. Agriculture provides improved fertilizers, plant-breeding procedures, the use of "hormones" and methods of preserving and storing food. Present-day transportation facilities offer amazing opportunities in distribution. To set all this going, however, the eating and cultivating habits of millions must change. Yet these people are as wedded to many of their customs as is a Catholic or Baptist in our society to his denomination, or a Southerner to the Democratic Party, or a Vermont farmer to the Republican Party. The reason for this rigidity, in addition to the inertia of habit, is that complexly entwined in the customs and assumptions that have to do with food and its production are loyalties, ideas of status and religious and ethical feelings. Altogether they form systems of belief which are exceedingly resistant to alteration, like the Japanese belief in the Emperor.

Human Relations in a Changing World

The problem is difficult but not impossible. It is evident, however, that even when the goal is clear and the technologies are available, progress cannot be made until the social and cultural aspects are understood and methods worked out for adjustment.

To return to the subject of hostile action, having noted that stress is important, it must be added that it is probably only one of the major factors. It is necessary to consider also the possibility that hostile action may arise among people who are not under stress, or at least not beyond any reasonable threshold that can be postulated.

It is popularly believed that almost all people have a "natural" tendency to be destructive and would be so if not held back by legal and other such restraints. This view in some form is shared by numbers of social scientists. Freud regarded the "death wish" as one of the fundamental characteristics of human nature. This is obviously a serious matter requiring full investigation at both the social and the individual levels. In the meantime, it is premature to reach definite conclusions and one should beware of simple, fatalistic interpretations. It may well be that people who are under little stress have a surplus of energy or spontaneity that has to be spent and that this often takes a hostile, destructive form. This does not, however, mean that it *must* take such a form. It is possible that aggression of this type may turn out to be more subject to rational control, more trainable, more easily sublimated and put to constructive use than that which arises willy-nilly from the pressure of stress.

However, one thing is certain, whether it is a matter of reacting to stress or of expressing spontaneity, the long-run behavior of any nation is always toward trying to meet the needs of the people who compose it. There is no stemming this. A nation is a society and such is the nature and function of societies. The chance for adjustment lies in the fact that for every need there is a range of possible remedies. The range varies from nation to nation and it is not unlimited, being for each made up of culture, social institutions, economic resources, existing interdependencies with other nations and such influences. But it is a range, nevertheless, and therefore provides some alternatives and some flexibility. This is the opportunity and the hope for developing mutuality between nations. To achieve this, both the needs and the possible range of adjustments have to be known.

It is inevitable that such adjustment will mean an adverse change in some aspects of life for some segments of the population in some nations. The world food situation previously mentioned may be taken as one of many examples. Relief of this particular stress means more even distribution of food and, consequently, those who have surplus resources must be prepared to reduce them, at least temporarily.

It is probable that the control of most other types of stress will require similar sacrifice. This is part of the price of preventing war and has to be realistically faced and thoroughly understood. This is "the blood, sweat and tears" of peace.

Science can aid in determining what adjustments are necessary and show ways and means for their accomplishment. It can help estimate the price of prevention and indicate how it may be distributed. It can supply what is now missing when the behavior of nations is interpreted purely in terms of economic motivation and political plots.

III

Some aspects of a number of world-wide problems that have to do with workable relations between nations have been outlined. It seems appropriate to follow this with brief reference to a number of related matters that are outstanding on the domestic scene. Each of these is significant in its own right, but each has additional importance due to its indirect effect on our potential for peace or hostile action and on increasing or decreasing our range of possible adjustments.

Human Relations in a Changing World

What is commonly called "race relations" is particularly important since a great deal of national life is made up of relations between the majority and minorities and between the various minorities themselves; and because of problems raised by a people who try to fulfil a democratic way of life and make numerous exceptions at the same time.

The necessity for improvement in race relations — where cultural, psychological and situational differences are much more crucial than biological factors — is obvious to most people, however violently they may disagree on the remedy. There are 123 national and many times that number of local organizations in the United States spending millions of dollars working to improve race relations. One cannot question the intelligence and sincerity of most of these groups. The fact remains, however, that greater results are needed and that progress, if it exists, is far, far short of what is necessary for a healthy society.

The problems in race relations are in many ways but special cases of the same problems that have been described in the international scene. Here, too, there are questions of systems of belief, of contrasting social organizations, of stereotype images, of fear, of conflict, of hostile action, of stress and of spontaneity.

Although the United States is one of the most fortunate countries in the world as far as standard of living is concerned, it contains large groups who do not have enough to eat, who do not have adequate shelter, who are forced to live under crowded conditions, who cannot adequately protect themselves from disease and who cannot secure sufficient medical aid when they become ill. With these physical conditions go the other types of stress, the impact of which is equally important — idleness, anxieties about children and family members, rejection and ridicule, being at the mercy of apparently arbitrary authorities — all adding up to frustration, uncertainty, and confusion (Chapter IV, Assumptions III and IV).

Altogether these stresses can and do result in behavior that is

The Use of Applied Social Science

neither rationally controlled nor constructive for the national welfare. Furthermore, the numbers involved are significant, for they include the urban slums of the great cities, the rural slums of the South, both white and Negro; the Spanish Americans in the Southwest and the Indian groups scattered over the United States and composing together with the Eskimos almost half the population of Alaska.

These people do not have an adequate place in the society of the United States and the effect of that maladjustment hurts them and hurts the nation. As with the starving and destitute outside the United States, so these people within have children who are growing up with the imprint of their condition on them to react violently or to become apathetic burdens.

A basic problem among all kinds of people in the United States is the question of what is happening to the family. What are the repercussions of the housing situation? What of the divorce rate? There are comments almost every day in press, in radio, in books, and in sermons on a prevailing restlessness and rootlessness that characterizes people in these times. Much of this can be laid to the existing social and economic pressures and uncertainties, but some seems to have its origin in the kind of upbringing and conditioning received by the oncoming members of the society. The family is a fundamental unit in a society and the strength and capacity of the whole is profoundly tied to it.

Are more children developing in unstable emotional environments and if so what are the effects of this upon them — and upon our future?

Present-day relations between industry and labor concern not only these major groups but ultimately all consumers. Those involved are not nations nor are they set apart as minorities within nations, but the social processes do again embrace systems of belief, contrasting social organizations, stereotype images, fear, conflict, hostile acts, stress and the adequate expression of spontaneity.

Human Relations in a Changing World

Government policy and government action present another constellation of problems. Almost everyone has been aware at one time or another of government action that did not fit human nature. Petty regulations that irritate the citizen are common, but there are far more serious situations in which the services of agencies vital in the lives of millions are rendered inefficient and the public is injured. One cannot estimate the exact total in human misery and death, but there can be little doubt that it has magnitude. Most of this is not through stupidity nor through intentions that are indifferent to the general welfare of people. It is due to the lack of understanding of cause and effect in social and psychological terms. Governments could serve the needs of people more accurately and more adequately and could create fewer non-human and inhuman laws, policies and practices. This applies to treatment of their own personnel as well as the nation at large.

The domestic use of atomic energy is expected to cause far-reaching changes. Most technical advances in civilization have brought both new opportunities and extensive miseries. Some of the troubles have been temporary, as when new machines make old methods obsolete and throw men out of work, and much of this disappears when the new technical development is adopted by society. Other problems, however, have not been solved and so exist chronically at the heart of labor issues, in the overcrowding of urban areas, in the unwieldiness and inhumanity of large industrial organizations, in cycles of depression and in numerous other pinches of civilization. Devastating disruptions, partial adjustment, with leftovers leading to accumulating, ongoing problems — this has been the history of the industrial revolution.

On this there will soon be superimposed tremendous new sources of physical power. The immediate and long-term impact on society will undoubtedly be vast, and the indirect effects will run far beyond what can now be easily pictured in the imagination. As the automobile was a major factor in transforming the

The Use of Applied Social Science

roads, changing the landscape, bringing the countryman to the city and the city man to the country, enlarging suburbs, altering courtship patterns, and in hundreds of other ways affecting society, so on a much greater scale will the advent of atomic energy alter our habits, outlook, and social institutions.

In view of past experience, in view of what is known about the social and psychological nature of man, and in view of the existing research tools and methods, it is not necessary to walk into this situation altogether blindly. Some, perhaps even most, of the oncoming difficulties can be foreseen and made generally known. Here, too, a price will have to be paid in terms of effort and sacrifice to meet the new situation, but the price does not have to be exorbitant. Benefits can be achieved sooner and the effects of maladjustment reduced if understanding and democratic planning in human terms match legal and industrial planning.

Finally, there is the question of conflicting social and political ideologies. Must these always be treated without perspective and without wisdom, without grasp of the processes at work? Must we continue under new names the processes that underlay the battles between believers and unbelievers — between the Moslem world and Christendom, between Protestant and Catholic, between Big-endians and Little-endians?

A belief like Communism could be approached in the same manner that the belief in the Emperor was investigated by the Foreign Morale Analysis Division, but with far more thoroughness. What needs does this system of belief serve, what part is logical, what part non-logical, what part personal and emotional? What is its function to individuals and what is its function in society?

Of coequal importance are the same questions applied to the systems of belief that are anticommunist.

These are but examples. There are numerous other conflicting ideologies of importance in national welfare. Unless we understand these as symptoms of social process and thereby come to perceive and control the process more effectively, there is no chance of breaking the spiral of ever-increasing blow and counterblow.

CHAPTER VII

DIFFICULTIES OF APPLICATION

I

In the last chapter, some problems were outlined for which help may be found in the methods of social science, including those employed by the Foreign Morale Analysis Division. Although the work of the Division represents only one approach, it seems appropriate to examine its achievements and failures in securing the utilization of its findings, since these may have bearing on the effectiveness of similar work in the future.

We shall begin with the achievements, although they are hard to estimate. As will be demonstrated presently, the failures are plain enough, but where the Division's conclusions were in harmony with policy or operations it is not always possible to separate cause and coincidence. Government aims and actions, even when supposedly coming from an autocrat, actually stem from conscious and unconscious drifts of widespread attitudes, from numerous opinions and considerations and from the interactions of many people. It happens, therefore, that no one can identify all the elements that shape policy or its end result in things done.

However, granting the difficulties of appraisal, it seems probable that the Division served to substantiate some of the OWI and War Department policies together with their underlying assumptions, and acted as a brake on others. Toward the end of the war it was very likely instrumental in a number of policy changes.

To give some examples, early analyses supported those who wished to use psychological warfare as a means of inducing surrender and substantiated some underlying assumptions regarding the nature of Japanese military morale. There was also support for more particular policy items, such as insistence on strict truthfulness in the leaflets and radio broadcasts directed at the enemy.

The Division acted as a brake on a tendency in some members of OWI to assume that they could, during the war, with leaflets and broadcasts, "change the Japanese way of thinking" through logical argument and "break down their institutions" (such as "form of government" and "Shinto practice and belief") by "proving they are wrong." In particular, the Division was one of a number of restraints on a recurrent urge to attack the Imperial Institution and through this symbol the greater part of the Japanese system of moral and spiritual values. As noted in Chapter V the Division opinion was that regardless of what one might feel personally concerning the assets and liabilities of the Imperial Institution, such an attack, if it had any effect at all, would serve as a stimulus to morale. It seemed unwise to mix psychological warfare with political reform in circumstances where they were incompatible and dangerous to the war effort.

On the positive side, the Division concluded that there were changes occurring in Japanese home-front morale from the latter part of 1944 on, which predisposed a portion of the population to pay attention to certain kinds of statements from the United States. After more than six months of discussion and urging, policy directives shifted emphasis from political and ideological argument to such matters as the inevitability of American victory, the disaster of prolonged war, the gains of peace, the fact that the United States was against militarist leaders, not the people of Japan, and similar messages bearing on the live concerns of the Japanese. By this time, however, it was the end of July, 1945.

In addition to direct suggestions for psychological warfare policy, the Division's work provided information and analytic interpretations for many other kinds of planning in which it was necessary to know as much as possible about what the Japanese were likely to do. There was a wide distribution of reports to all

The Use of Applied Social Science

the agencies and activities in Washington which were concerned with Japanese psychology, to the outposts overseas and to the British.

It is impossible to be specific in regard to the way in which these reports were useful, but there are a number of indicators which suggest interest in them. For example, they were said to be the principal reason why the OWI backed the development of the Division and the reason for the support and cooperation received in the War Department.

Report writers in the Government commonly gauge their success, at least in part, by how far up the hierarchy their work is read. Taking this for what it may be worth, some of the Division's productions reached not only the chief of OWI, but also the Chief of Staff of the Army and the President. Several brief reports were written for publications limited in circulation to cabinet members and those of similar rank. While this does mark interest, it is obvious that it provides no real clue as to the manner in which the analyses were valuable, nor to what extent.

In the Pacific and Asiatic theatres portions of reports were reproduced or summarized and disseminated widely. Indeed, parts appeared imbedded in some publications after having lost all indication of their source, but clearly recognizable because word for word the same.

Another function performed by the Division was that of teaching. Staff members participated in panels or gave lectures for OSS and other organizations and in OWI contributed to a series of three brief courses for a small number of Army and Navy military government officers who were being prepared for public-relations work in occupied areas.

The end of the war cut short a plan developing in one branch of the War Department to train men in psychological warfare, with emphasis on the importance of producing surrender among enemy troops. The Division was informed that this scheme had come about largely as a result of its work.

Human Relations in a Changing World

Turning now to the failures, a major item was inability to have the Division's findings adequately considered in the policy decisions it was supposed to be serving. Most policy makers were either unaware of social science or else skeptical and mistrusting. In the limited number of instances in which policy makers were encountered who had an interest in the activity, it usually emerged sooner or later that what they really wanted was evidence to support a course of action to which they were already deeply committed.

When the Division found that Japanese troops could be influenced toward surrender, there was agreement and enthusiasm on the part of policy makers who had all along been advocating psychological warfare. The reports of the Division were widely read by them and the contents used in speech and writing to support and justify their program. As previously noted the Division was given more funds, staff, office space and other such benefits. On the other hand, those who were opposed to psychological warfare found many opportunities for critical comment and objection.

When the Division reported that Japanese attitudes toward the Emperor were not weakening as the war went along and that propaganda attacks on him were useless and dangerous, these findings did not fit with the views of many policy makers in psychological warfare. The suggestion that we tell the Japanese of our intention to leave the Emperor's fate in their hands was still more distasteful. Numbers of those who had been supporting the Division's work were committed to an anti-Emperor program and they quickly fell away as admirers. Concurrently, however, new friends appeared among those who had for some time been convinced that the Emperor should be let alone. Some of these were people who did not have any particular interest in psychological warfare, but they became attracted to the Division when they found it issuing reports that supported their ideas.

The Use of Applied Social Science

Finally, when the Division concluded that Japanese home-front morale was declining, there were apparently few policy makers who were already convinced of this. As a result, policy directives in psychological warfare lagged behind the changes occurring among the Japanese people and were altered only when the war was almost over.

The possible importance of these matters is indicated in the biography of Henry L. Stimson, then Secretary of War. According to Stimson, the Government estimate in July, 1945, was that the Japanese would be capable of major fighting "until the latter part of 1946, at the earliest." Some consideration was given to making a statement about a tolerant policy in regard to the Emperor in order to weaken Japanese resistance, but an opposed decision was finally taken. This, it seems, was partly because "during the war years high American officials had made some fairly blunt and unpleasant remarks about the Emperor, and it did not seem wise to Mr. Truman and Secretary of State Byrnes that the Government should reverse its field too sharply; too many people were likely to cry shame." There was also a fear "lest Japanese militarists argue that such a statement was the first proof of that American fatigue which they had been predicting since 1941."

Looking back in 1947, it appeared to Stimson that "these fears had been based on a misreading of the situation" and that "history might find that the United States, by its delay in stating its position, had prolonged the war."*

Returning to the work of the Division it was found that when its conclusions reflected the prevailing ideas and beliefs of an important group of officials in the government, its reports were circulated widely and to the top. On the other hand, reports of a contrary nature had a limited circulation and traveled upward in the hierarchy only so far as the first line of disagreement.

* Henry L. Stimson and McGeorge Bundy, *On Active Service in Peace and War* (New York: Harper and Brothers), © 1947. PP. 619, 626, 628 and 629.

In neither instance — that is, favorable or unfavorable reaction by policy makers — was there any judgment of the validity of the findings based on inspection of the data or on having the soundness of the premises checked by other social scientists. No policy maker or policy maker's representative ever consulted the files of data in the Division for such purposes. Yet these files constituted a continuously growing encyclopedia of current information in regard to Japanese morale which for scope, arrangement and easy access was not to be found anywhere else.

Related to difficulties in securing the acceptance of results were failures to secure opportunities to improve the quality of the work itself. In spite of constant effort, the Division was never able to send any of its personnel overseas and into combat zones. Firsthand knowledge of the conditions under which front-line psychological warfare teams operated would have greatly improved the shaping of reports to their needs and would have made more appropriate and convincing the advice given the policy makers in Washington. It was hoped that analytic groups similar to the unit in Washington could be set up in the war theatres for the purpose of servicing the command there with faster and more immediate analyses of local changes in Japanese morale. Such theatre analytic units might have maintained a regular exchange of information and data with the Division in Washington and thereby greatly improved the latter's effectiveness.

To point up the importance of this, it is necessary to recall the extent to which opinion about Japanese behavior among many top policy makers was based on guess and hunch in place of information that could have been obtained, and its analysis.

The Division could also have had contact overseas with those who interviewed prisoners and sifted captured documents. As a result, the questions asked and the documents selected for translation and circulation might have been consistently relevant to morale instead of showing excessive variability according to the

The Use of Applied Social Science

interest and knowledge of different interviewers and translators. Immense improvements in morale analysis would have occurred had material been gathered specifically for its needs.

In addition to improving quality, such field contacts might have speeded the transmission of information to the point where analysis was carried out and thereby cut down on the inefficiency that arose from common delays of one or more months.

Just as the flow and exchange with the theatres was never loosened, so barriers remained between the Division and other intelligence organizations working in the United States. As a result, data was missed that could have been usefully processed by the Division, including a number of particular captured documents and interrogation reports of special importance. Due to the nature of the Division's files and the system of "processing" (Chapter IV) such material would not only have improved and better confirmed the Division's findings, but would itself have gained significance through being matched with the rest of the data in the files. It was a case of each organization having a portion of a jigsaw puzzle, but failing to bring them together. Through both OWI and the cooperating branch in the War Department continued effort was made by the Division to resolve these obstructions and to develop sharing rather than hoarding of information, but without result.

A related inability was the failure to secure access to any of the many thousands of Japanese prisoners in the United States. Although these men had been captured for some time, questioning them would have materially reduced guesswork in regard to certain kinds of psychological and cultural information about Japan and the Japanese military forces and would have provided opportunities for cross-checking some conclusions. This could have been done without violation of the Geneva Convention in letter or spirit for, as is now well known, many prisoners were willing and reliable informants. The only problem would have been the setting up of special segregation areas for cooperating prisoners so that they would not have to return to the mass of the camp and be at the mercy of more recalcitrant characters.

A major failure had to do with military government. This concerned not only the Division, but more particularly the unit developed in the War Relocation Authority from which the Division evolved.

At the time the social science work in the Colorado River War Relocation Center for Japanese and Japanese Americans began at Poston, Arizona (in 1942), there was no unified organization for occupied area government in either Army or Navy. It was obvious, however, that such a function must emerge, and it was also obvious that it would be of considerable importance. Immediately, during the war, it could contribute by stabilizing areas behind the fighting lines and thereby reduce the force necessary to control such regions. From the long-range point of view, it was a test of American principles in dealing with people of other cultures, in sponsoring self-government and, through these means, making a contribution to peace of some durability. Regardless of what arrangements were made later, military government would, it seemed, have the task of laying the first foundations of the transition from war to peace and this could be either a good or a bad start with aftereffects lasting far into the future.

One help in such a situation is constantly up-to-date information regarding the culture and psychology of the people administered, their ways of doing things, their needs and the types of stress they are enduring. Moreover, advance information, however complete, is never sufficient. Within a week of landing, the social and psychological factors are altered so that initial plans are bound to misfit unless also altered to meet the changing conditions.

With these ideas in view, it was the purpose of those who sponsored and those who participated in the research at Poston to develop both the techniques and a social science team that

The Use of Applied Social Science

could be absorbed later into military government. The plan was to establish a nucleus of workers who would know how to gather the appropriate information, analyze it and report the result in a suitable form. As experience was later gained in occupied areas, the numbers of these analysts could be increased through in-service training and members kept ready for advancing into new areas as the war progressed.

There was, for a time, considerable interest in this plan on the part of individuals in the Navy, but those who made the final decisions eventually rejected it. It was because of this closed door in military government that the research team originating in Poston went into OWI and turned to the analysis of intelligence material, a related though quite different field from that originally envisaged.

The effort to participate in military government did not stop with the creation of the Foreign Morale Analysis Division. It continued throughout the war with OWI backing. However, nothing was achieved except for minimal teaching and informal participation in the drawing of plans for social analysis that were not adopted.

Today, by contrast, the Navy has not only spent large sums of money for applied research in the Pacific islands, but is also letting substantial contracts to universities for basic research in human relations. Similarly, the army in Japan is developing some applied social science, though still on a very inadequate scale, for guidance in relations with the Japanese.

From all this it appears that the Division's problem of application had a number of facets: the opportunity to work, the materials necessary in the work, cooperation from related government activities, and, finally, getting the results understood and used as nonpartisan in origin and context. Each of these affected the others and all together created a condition in which end results in use, although not insignificant, were minimal compared to need and opportunity.

There still remains to mention the most outstanding failure: lack of contact with the decision to drop the atomic bomb. Former Secretary of War Stimson has said that it was decided to drop the bomb because, for one reason, as late as July, 1945, there was "as yet no indication of any weakening in Japanese determination to fight rather than accept unconditional surrender." *

It is evident from what has been presented here that as early as May, 1945, the Division had concluded that the Japanese determination to fight was seriously undermined and most of the essential points later made by the Morale Division of the Strategic Bombing Survey were explicitly described at that time. The first indicators of the downward trend had been noted as early as January.

The Division was not alone in having these opinions, as has been mentioned in Chapter III, page 75. It has come to light recently that by the end of May, Joseph C. Grew, former Ambassador to Japan and at that time Acting Secretary of State, was also convinced that the Japanese were ready to stop the war on our terms provided the right political moves were made. He believed that the Emperor was the key to the situation and that the war could be ended if the United States made it clear that we were not going to demolish the Imperial Institution. However, as has been noted earlier, our Army and Navy authorities felt that the time was not yet ripe for such a declaration.†

Setting aside these developments, it might be argued that the Division's findings, in May, 1945, while suggestive, were hardly sufficient to serve as a basis for conclusions that bore on so weighty a decision as dropping the atomic bomb. This is conceded, but with the added observation that despite numerous deficiencies the findings were better based on available knowl-

* *Ibid.*
† *Ibid.*, and a personal communication from Mr. Grew together with the privilege of seeing a part of his personal journal.

edge than estimates about Japan which were actually employed. The important point, however, is the fact that the findings were suggestive, strongly suggestive. As such they could have been followed up and put on a firmer foundation by overcoming the numerous difficulties in securing information and achieving communication that have just been described. The methods, the materials, and the personnel existed and could have been brought together in a project that would have shown results and either established or refuted the Division's contentions. Such a venture would have been infinitesimal in size and expense compared to other activities related to the atomic bomb.

As it was, the difficulties with application prevailed and Mr. Stimson very likely never heard of those findings by the Division that had bearing on the matter.

III

That the social sciences can develop so as to be of significant help in the kinds of problems we face today is a reasonable possibility. That they will do this quickly enough to make a difference in the present trend toward disaster is a matter of doubt. That the discoveries of social science, if they were so developed, would be used is still more unlikely. The experience of the Division with policy has been given in broad outline, but it is not a special case or an isolated instance. Numbers of its members had in the past encountered the same problems while working in various branches of the Government. Other social scientists who have engaged in work that has bearing on policy report similar adventures.* One man who headed a morale study that was a giant compared to the Division said:

"You always get one of two requests: to show that some policy

---

* For examples see editorials and articles in *The Journal of Social Issues,* Vol. III, No. 4. This number is devoted to the subject of "Social Research in Political Decision."

the executive has already decided upon is badly needed; or, to show that some policy the executive is already employing is working well."

In another part of the Government it was a popular saying that,

"The administrator uses social science the way a drunk uses a lamppost, for support rather than for illumination."

The difficulties of application continue today. There has, of course, been progress. The understanding and acceptance of social science at present seems vast if compared to what it was before the war, but it is scarcely noticeable if compared to current needs and the pressures of time. The episode at Bogotá in 1948 is one recent example of how we are still lacking in these matters. The potential for a disturbance such as occurred there during the Inter-American Conference does not spring up suddenly and it is not invisible. A very crude type of social science could detect it. Indeed, in this instance, the chief of the Central Intelligence Agency, Rear Admiral Hillenkoetter, is reported in the press to have told a House Subcommittee on April 15 that he did notify the State Department before the meeting, but no use was made of his findings.

It appears worth while, therefore, to look at some of the causes behind the difficulties. If we can, through past experience, foresee the pitfalls, we may be able to avoid continually falling into them.

CHAPTER VIII

THE SOCIAL SCIENTIST

I

ALTHOUGH the views expressed in this and the succeeding chapters are in general terms, they are based on particular experiences in the Division together with some observations made in other government branches before, during and after the war. They do not, of course, pretend to scientific analysis nor to comprehensiveness, but are rather a set of impressions picked up in the course of work.

The first point is that social science is new and because of this newness, people do not know what to expect. There is no generally recognized body of past experience and accomplishment whereby men can perceive the possibilities in the present and so look to the future. Policy makers, therefore, and other leaders in government have little to guide them. Even in those cases where individuals are acquainted with and well disposed toward social science, they still must reckon with the attitudes of others not similarly persuaded but upon whom they are dependent for authority, for funds and for support. These are their superiors, their peers and their staff in the executive branch of the Government, and the Legislature, the editorial writers, the columnists and the voting public.

The newness of social science, however, produces more difficulties than can be explained purely as a direct result of inadequate information and reasoned caution. There is resistance to innovation as such, with powerful, nonrational social and psychological factors at work, factors that have to do with culture and with personal-emotional relationships.

Human Relations in a Changing World

History is full of instances in which new knowledge and promising fields of endeavor have been neglected or fanatically fought in defiance of reason (though not without rationalization). It was so with the fact that the earth is not the center of the universe, the principle of organic evolution, vaccination, the laws of genetics, the concept of natural causality in human behavior, the existence of bacteria, the need for sterile techniques in surgery, the treatment and prevention of syphilis, the invalidity of stereotyped concepts of race, the intellectual equality of women with men — and many more, all treated at one time with derision, or like the Jackdaw of Rheims, cursed by bell and by book. That lemon juice would prevent scurvy was demonstrated in 1753 by James Lind, a British naval surgeon, but it was forty-two years before it was adopted by the British Navy and one hundred and fourteen before it became regulation in the Merchant Marine. Dr. Simpson of Edinburgh, a leader in the development of anesthetics, was for a time rewarded by contemporary society with public denunciations as "a shame upon Edinburgh," "a blasphemer, a heretic who utters words Satan has put in his mouth." His colleagues and his fellow citizens turned against him and charged him with being a charlatan and with immorality.

Instances of resistance to innovation can be pointed out at times and places that are nearer to hand than those just given. It might be thought that in the military services the obvious need to keep ahead of all potential enemies with new and better weapons would create an atmosphere of seeking. Perhaps this is true today, though it would be well not to be too sure. At all events, until yesterday slowness in the adoption of new opportunities was the rule as demonstrated in the case of the airplane, with Billy Mitchell as the martyr symbol of that struggle. Regarding the atomic bomb Einstein has said: "The professional soldiers who today talk so much, so loudly, with such arrogance, displayed at the outset a skepticism which often acted as a brake.

The Use of Applied Social Science

The bomb undoubtedly could have been discovered two years earlier."

While the military are generally among those sub-groups in a society that tend toward extremes of conservatism, we need not single them out. Behavior of this sort is found to a considerable degree in all parts of a society and among all societies. What we face here is the existence in ourselves of that which we note among primitive or backward people in their holding to traditional crops and traditional methods of cultivation despite undernourishment and the availability of more effective methods.

Social science, as a new activity, receives the usual weight of these nonrational as well as the rational forms of resistance, but due to some special features there is additional difficulty. In the first place, the findings are hard to demonstrate and are therefore at a much greater disadvantage in appealing to reason than was the case with lemon juice, anesthetics or the military use of the plane. For understanding most demonstrations in social science, a specialized background of information and perception is necessary. Moreover, the demonstrations are usually time-consuming and require a great deal of concentrated attention.

More important than the obscure aspects, however, is the fact that the results of social science are particularly apt to carry obvious implications for social change, which is to say, for altering the commonly accepted goals and ways of doing things. The most deep-going values are involved, the hopes, fears and the whole sense of understanding the world and one's place in it.

Because of all this, social science, in so far as it deals with problems that are significant for application, must be exposed to grave difficulties. The truths it discovers are ever liable to stir people profoundly, now those to the right of center, now those to the left, now those in the center itself. Men and women of conservative tendencies are disturbed by the fact that many social-science findings point strongly to the need for conscious changes in society to meet those that are happening anyway and they think of social science as something akin to socialism, or even more radical political creed. On the other hand, those who do advocate radical social change are provoked when science fails to confirm the particular formula to which they subscribe.

II

The quality in social science of being new affects both the policy maker and the social scientist. Since this book is written from the latter's point of view, it seems fitting to begin with some examination of ourselves. What obstructions to use that might be remedied does the social scientist create? Does the experience of the Division high-light some errors that could well be avoided in the future?

To begin with, the social scientist is often unaware of the best way to serve the policy maker. He may work on questions nobody asks while neglecting others that are important for application; he may tackle significant questions but produce the results too late; he may deliver the results on time, but expressed in a manner that fails to show relevance for policy and action; or he may run to another extreme and try to make policy himself and so reach beyond his competence. All these and more are easy mistakes that come from a number of common sources.

One such source, which seems to be growing less as it is more understood, is a failure to grasp the policy maker's point of view, his position, the demands on him, and the limitations within which he has to operate. Some of the first social scientists employed in the Government to help deal with people of non-Western culture illustrated this. What they recommended was often fitting as far as the non-Western people were concerned, but not adjusted to the culture and social organization of the government branch doing the work. These social scientists evidently did not realize that they were dealing with a problem of relations between two groups both having social organization and systems of belief.

Not infrequently we have as social scientists been reluctant to work on questions raised by policy makers when they appeared to us as trivial or actually meaningless because based on false assumptions. Granting that policy makers sometimes waste their research staffs on transient trivia, or interfere in professional and technical aspects, it remains a fact that we go too far in being on guard. In consequence, we miss opportunities to understand the policy maker's point of view and to work from the question as he sees it through to something that has meaning to both of us. Very often a policy maker's question that may appear at first fruitless can be made to serve as a satisfactory (if not the best) approach to more fundamental matters.

The work in the Poston Relocation Center provided a useful lesson in this regard. At the very beginning the Director asked me to find out how he should handle a small but unruly group of men, "the old bachelors," who had formerly been itinerant farm laborers. With the problem still before me of getting to know the whole camp of some 20,000 people this seemed incidental and superficial, a question brought up merely because it happened to be the Director's worry for that day. It appeared that tackling it would delay getting at those main dynamic forces in the camp which had to be understood before any real work could be accomplished. Consequently, I did not pick up the Director's question.

A year and a half later, after something had become known about the Center, it was evident that if I had begun with this unruly group and proceeded in a thoroughgoing manner following all the important interconnections, I would have come rapidly to one of the main dynamic forces of Poston and would have gained a fairly comprehensive picture of the others. It could have been a first-rate problem with which to begin.

Human Relations in a Changing World

There are times when social scientists become so involved in the uncovering of new knowledge or in theoretical problems that they ride clear away from the context of applied work. There is often no doubt of the long-term, intrinsic value in the aims, but the policy maker cannot be expected to underwrite research on just any lead the social scientist may elect to follow. It is natural for him to point out that there are other appropriate settings for free-ranging basic research and to insist on relevance — relevance, moreover, in which the yield is not indefinitely postponed.

Too much enthusiasm for social-science theory sometimes leads to attempts at making policy rather than providing material for policy and to claiming much more for the science than it has yet available. Such overreaching is frequently evident to the policy maker and arouses strong misgivings. We shall get further and more surely avoid shipwreck if we follow Locke's sailor and realize that at present our rope is not long enough to fathom all the depths of the ocean, but that it can reach to certain bottoms and give reliable information about them.

Taking a long time to move from a question asked by a policy maker to an answer delivered by the social scientist is inherent in the nature of the work. All social-science research, whether applied or basic, is time-consuming just as it is expensive, and everyone concerned has to be reconciled to this. However, there are at least two major opportunities for increasing speed. One is to reduce unnecessary embellishments of procedure such as will be discussed presently in connection with scholarly fashions and rituals. The other is to anticipate what the policy maker will want to know and to set up machinery in advance for making observations, collecting data and giving it a preliminary analysis. The Division's system of "processing" (Chapter IV) accomplished this, in part, and it ultimately became possible to give a fairly solid answer — at least all the available data — to the general who telephoned in the morning and wanted to know by afternoon some such item as Japanese attitude toward their officers on all fronts. The crude beginnings made by the Division along these lines could be greatly developed and increased in effectiveness.

The problem of making the findings of social science clear and understandable is rooted in the existence of two very different ways of thinking, as will be discussed in the next chapter. However, just as is the case with the time factor, an inherent difficulty can be reduced when more attention is given to it. The war made everybody conscious of the great need for clear expression and better communication. Although there are still instances of unnecessary obscurity, the danger is probably now of going to the other pole and oversimplifying. One can become so engrossed with making something which is complex understandable that he ends with the false assertion that it is simple. Moreover, a desire for clarity can shade into a desire to be pleasing which similarly obscures actuality and leads to a falling off of scientific quality. An overemphasis on the acceptable by the social scientist sometimes succeeds in securing recognition for a time, but in the long run loses out when it becomes evident that the pleasing reports happen not to be true.

An extreme striving to be pleasing sometimes leads to abandoning social science for a superior kind of clerking. This consists in an orderly and energetic collecting of facts, but unenlivened by concepts and without attention to process and dynamics. Reputable social scientists wishing to appear practical to practical men have thus sometimes jettisoned that which should be their major contribution because afraid to appear theoretical.

There is also the danger of becoming merely opportunistic and flitting from practical problem to practical problem without any long-range consistency or coordination. This is particularly likely to happen when theory is allowed to go overboard altogether, and as a result no contributions are made to science from the chances for experiment that are present in applied work.

Human Relations in a Changing World

On the whole, the Division did not suffer from trying too hard to be popular; in fact, we might be criticized for not going far enough in this direction. We did, however, tone down and understate our conclusions in an effort to find toe holds of agreement. This possibly helped at the time, but it is doubtful if it was good long-range policy. At any rate, we paid for it eventually by having a weaker record with which to show the results of the work.

III

In the foregoing outline of some of the reasons social scientists do not meet the needs of policy makers, a difficult entanglement has been skirted which must now be squarely approached. Those of us who attempt to apply science to social and psychological problems are often in a position similar to the doctor who rigged up a set of mirrors and took out his own appendix — though it is hoped our motives are more reputable. The man or woman who analyzes human relations is himself in the midst of human relations and a part of his society and culture. In consequence, his incisions and explorations touch his own quick sources of confidence, doubt, fear, aspiration, and his sense of values. As a further consequence, feelings and emotional convictions irrelevant to scientific purposes are ever liable to intrude and warp both observations and interpretation.

To these sources of bias within the scientist must be added the shifting pressures exerted by other members of society who favor, ignore or scorn his findings not through reason alone, but also through hope, fear and resistant traditions. These pressures from others are the more powerful since they play on the predispositions of the scientist and thus easily thrust him from his course.

The chances for excursion into error are enhanced by the common lack of opportunity in studies of people for controlled experiment through which conclusions can be established, modified, or eliminated. On the other hand, there is rich opportunity for slipping into rationalization and erecting those scaffolds of argument that mount brilliantly further and further from the foundations of fact and which have always been enemies to scientific progress.

The field is, therefore, full of uncertain areas and the scene of clashes of opinion, of dogma, and of changing theories which rise and fall in waves of fashion.

These difficulties should sober any offhand approach to the subject, but they warrant neither despair nor rejection of investigation. They are matters to be taken into account and mitigated through constant awareness and attention. This means that he who works in the science of human relations must strive to maintain vigilance over his own emotions and sentiments in order to keep them in their place and to prevent conclusions leaping along inviting lines of intuitive conviction and thus outdistancing disciplined observation and systematic thinking.

The problem is, of course, common to all sciences but in none is it so troublesome as in the human sciences. The restraint is neither easy nor pleasant, and it may be terrifying. The person who takes his implements to study the nature of belief, for example, is dissecting the tissue of his own sense of security and it may be necessary for him to have powerful convictions regarding the wholesomeness of the fruit on the tree of knowledge.

It is superfluous to say that in practice we fall short, often far short, of the ideal. In applied work, the deviations we can make from the scientific process are many and the policy maker is often quite aware of them. He may see very well, when it happens, that the social scientist is blinded by his desire to find his own theory is correct, or that the group to which he belongs is better than another, or that what it is personally profitable to do is scientifically justified, and so forth.

Human Relations in a Changing World

In government, as in industry and other large organizations, the struggle for power and status with which the social scientist is necessarily in contact is one of the most treacherous areas. We easily become defensive or offensive in issues which are really struggles for position and hence become more wound up in proving ourselves right than in finding out what is right.

In order to cope with this problem at the Relocation Center, the research unit, called the Bureau of Sociological Research, had the following as part of its policy:

"In giving statements, the Bureau must attempt to avoid getting involved in controversy, or taking sides. Above all, it must refrain from any attempt to propagandize or maintain the correctness of its own stand.

"The Bureau must avoid becoming a competitor with any group of persons in any issue whatever. It must not take pride in the acceptance of its suggestions. The point for attention is whether or not in the long run the suggestions turn out to be correct, not whether they are accepted."

At Poston it was possible to stick to this fairly well, although there were times when there were severe temptations and pressures. On the whole, the administration understood the point of view and supported it.

When the Division was formed in OWI and the War Department, it was my intention to pursue the same policy. It must be confessed, however, that the departure from the ideal in this case was great. In the course of time and by degrees I succumbed to the feeling that I faced a choice between being ineffective and fighting. As a result, we became more and more embroiled in a struggle only too typical of the factional disputes and rivalries that clog the operations of government.

To illustrate, there was a dispute with a policy-making group over the significance of the apparent splitting of political factions in Japan. This dispute hinged on the question of the Division infringing on the prerogatives of the policy-making group in offering comments on Japanese politics, not on the validity of the conclusions. The opposed group felt the Division "should stick to morale studies," while the Division felt that the leadership patterns were an integral part of morale. Actually, the policy group and the Division both commanded different areas of knowledge and concept, with the former having by far the better grasp of Japanese political structure. Pooling of the two points of view could have produced a much more penetrative analysis and more detailed understanding of the situation. Competition for exclusive prerogatives, however, made this impossible.

Having pointed out failures in collaboration, due to status and prerogative struggles, the question may be raised as to what kind of relationship is desirable between a unit such as the Division and the policy makers. The Division never took the position that it should be responsible for creating policy. We conceived our function to be the production of conclusions from our data and from our frame of reference that would have bearing on the questions before the policy makers. Such conclusions would then have to be considered together with those coming from other sources quite outside the province of our work. These sources would include such matters as the over-all policy of the Government, the sub-policies of different Departments and Offices, the practical possibilities in terms of men, money and materials, legal considerations, the attitude of Congress, the attitude of the public, and many more. After comparing and considering all such items, the policy makers would decide what to do, which might or might not be in harmony with the Divisions conclusions.

For example, the Division might decide that if Japanese prisoners of war were settled in Allied countries with assurance that they would never have to return to Japan and that if this fact could be brought home to the Japanese troops, then there would be a great increase in the number of prisoners taken. The policy maker, on the other hand, might decide against making this into a program, not because he thought it was untrue, but because the immigration policies of the Allies made it impractical.

In our experience, however, when policy makers made decisions contrary to the findings of the Division, it was frequently with the assertion that they did so because the findings were false, not because of other considerations. The Division reacted by pressing for more adequate consideration of its conclusions and this ultimately led at least to the margins of trying to form policy.

Another form which the struggle for status takes is the crossing over of social scientists from their own field to that of administration. Although there are many who sincerely believe that this is admirable for increasing the effectiveness of social science, it is my opinion that such is not so. The loss of men into administration (other than the administration of scientific projects or education connected with science) further reduces an already inadequate force and resembles spending capital instead of interest. During the war there were numerous temptations to leave one's field. Indeed, it was the common experience of a social scientist that if he succeeded in converting an administrator from hostility or indifference to interest, shortly thereafter he would be offered an administrative position. Many men did leave social science to be administrators, and many of these performed excellent service as citizens and as men with superior endowments. But they did not contribute to social science any more than a physicist would have contributed to applied physics had he turned to running a Red Cross supply depot.

The reason often given for such transfers was that as administrators the men could do more to advance social science than they could in a strictly professional capacity. It was my observation, however, that once having assumed administrative duties they quickly became embroiled in so many other matters that they rarely did more for social science than show a benign attitude and put in a good word now and then where it helped.

The Use of Applied Social Science

This had value, of course, but considerably less than social scientists remaining in their own field, reinforcing each other and demonstrating worth through accomplishment. Furthermore, regardless of the reasons given, it looked very much as if the renunciation of social science in favor of administration actually reflected a lack of confidence in the field, a lack of confidence in oneself, or both. This also occurred to some administrators and policy makers who felt that "this so-called science must be second-best in the minds of the people who profess it if they are ready to leave for administrative jobs, often not very important administrative jobs."

I once heard a social scientist who had become an administrator say something of this order when talking about a recent promotion: "Now when I say that every representative of the United States shall use the word 'cooperate' rather than 'support' in referring to our relations with Turkey, by the next morning, everywhere all over the entire world, 'cooperate' comes into use."

His eyes were shining as he spoke, and we have to recognize that this is heady liquor, but it is surely poor and transient compared to the work of attempting to enlarge the store of human wisdom.

Crossing over into administration has another implication besides the reduction of man power, group force, and accomplishment in social science. It has a disturbing effect on administrators. Even though administrators do themselves advocate such transfers when they feel the need of able executive assistants, nevertheless, in the long run, they will be more antagonistic and inclined to scuttle social-science projects. This is because when social science is not performing a defined function in an organization, but seems rather a bridgehead by which men get into administration, then existing administrators who might be displaced are on their guard. It is inevitable that many will refuse to help applied research lest they awake some morning to find themselves out of their jobs and the social scientist ensconced. Most things point to the conclusion that the more the social scientist sticks to his task, the better for the field as a whole.

IV

The fact that the social scientist is himself a part of the processes he studies has still other protean forms. A word more may be said about the fashions and rituals to which allusion has already been made.

Blindly following rules, doing what others do just because they do it, and striving to be in the social swim of scientific circles rather than concentrating on the nature of a particular problem and its goals, all of these are at times enormously wasteful of time, effort and money. From the very beginning of science there has been a tendency for scientific activities to revert to scholasticism and dogma, like cleared land becoming overgrown with scrub. In applied science (as contrasted to basic), where one is not striving primarily toward discovery, practices can rapidly become routine, full of deadwood and out of touch with new opportunities. When it becomes more important that things look well than be well, there is inevitable loss in ultimate results.

Classification and the systematic arrangement of categories are particularly seductive. They have their place in science, of course, but they can easily get out of hand, become ends in themselves and detached from relevance to dynamic process and actual problems. Moreover, scholarly perfectionism is often vastly impressive to the layman who easily mistakes it for thoroughgoing science, as Conant points out in *On Understanding Science.*

Statistical and mathematical procedures, to take another instance, carry with them some of the aura and prestige of the physical sciences. They, too, impress laymen and give those who employ these techniques a sense of dealing in "hard facts." Without wishing to detract from their great intrinsic value, it is evident that they can be exceedingly treacherous because of the false sense of accomplishment that comes from unerringly following out the approved procedures, and from the ease with which interpretation can be made to appear factually demonstrated by figures.

To give an example: the same set of questions were asked two matched groups of Negro soldiers, but in one case the interviewers were white men and in the other Negro interviewers were used. The results showed that with a Negro interviewer more answers derogatory to whites were received. It was asserted, however, that the figures demonstrated that when a Negro interviewer is employed, *more truthful* answers are obtained. The figures, of course, show nothing of the sort, but presented in this way they tend to hide the interpretation and hypothesizing that had been injected. In reality there is no way of knowing whether or not the Negro interviewer got more truthful answers regarding attitudes toward whites than did the white interviewer; all that is known is that they got different answers. It is merely assumed that because they were more derogatory they were closer to the truth. It is just as plausible to suppose that a Negro soldier when talking to a Negro interviewer would tend to conform to a group pattern and overstate his hostility.

The purpose here is not to assert or deny regarding the kind of difference interviewing by white or Negro makes, but merely to point out that the figures alone do not demonstrate the conclusion. Interpretation and assumption enter covertly at a critical point.

Another perfectionistic tendency is one that may be called "obsession with exceptions." In academic training, the critical faculty rates high, sometimes to the detriment of originality and creativity. An extreme of this infects social science as a rejection of any proposition as soon as a negative instance can be demonstrated, or even the probability of such an instance. This can only appear among people who, on the whole, have no responsibility for action, but they may for a time carry it over into applied work and be greatly hampered. If medical clinics were run this way it might be that there would be fewer mistakes, but there would be no treatment of patients at all. The doctors would sit around paralyzed by their own discussions which proved that no line of treatment could be right because of evident exceptions and instances to the contrary.

In applied work, and indeed in all science, the aim has to be the securing of the best data possible; the use of it to the full with realization of the limitations; and judgment not only by relevance to theory, "goodness of fit," or the fulfillment of rituals, but also by results. What works? What leads to reliable prediction? Demonstration by outcome is better than demonstration by canon law.

These remarks are not intended to approve sloppy work, but to note that there is an opposite pole consisting in perfectionism, and a tendency to follow fashionable practices uncritically. All this is human, of course, and characteristic of group activity, but that does not preclude it from being wasteful nor does it mean that it cannot be improved.

V

A further characteristic of human social behavior that affects the efficiency of social scientists is the existence among us of divisions in the ranks. Part of this is probably necessary for growth and development since many of the great discoveries in science seem to have their roots in controversy. To an important degree, however, disunity is a source of delay in growth and a hindrance to application.

The splits follow differences in theory, arguments about what is applied and what is "pure" science, quantitative methods as

The Use of Applied Social Science

opposed to qualitative methods, conflict between groups that are competing with each other for status, and differences arising from the fact that social science has grown from many diverse origins, such as history and psychology, and that virtually all questions are frontier problems.

The intramural difficulties sometimes make us appear grossly inconsistent and uncertain and it is not surprising that the policy maker and the public often wonder if we know what we are talking about. This can lead to refusing to give trial to applied social science, or to a cautious attempt by the policy maker to avoid mistakes through calling on representatives from all the different schools of which he is aware. This course may prove worth while when it is a question of general advice, but when it is a matter of getting under way with actual work, it is likely to resemble the progress of an automobile that has wheels of four different sizes.

Most of these difficulties between groups of social scientists are sufficiently obvious so that it is not necessary to discuss them at greater length. However, there are two points that do warrant further consideration.

Traditionally, the training of graduate students fosters competition rather than teamwork and each man ropes off a ring where he can put on his performance without interference from his fellows. Name, credit and a piece of work that is all your own are matters of paramount importance. This kind of individualism is part of the Great Man tradition, the monolith who gathers around him a band of disciples, and as such it has produced great men and has been a part of great discoveries. However, it has been evident for some time in the physical sciences that most of the significant problems are of a nature that require so many observations, measurements and interrelated investigations from so many individuals and so many different kinds of individuals that the Great Man pattern cannot cope with the opportunity and the need. Social science has now come to the same point. Most of the worth-while work that lies immediately ahead involves problems which cannot be solved without large teams working on them. There has to be modification of the traditional importance of doing work that will carry one's own name and only that name. Those who strive to become monoliths are forced to work either on very small problems as scientists, or on large problems as philosophers.

It is my opinion that in the present stage of social science, social philosophy and speculation is not one of the foremost needs. We live in a wilderness of possible and probable but untested theories and we are not too badly off for technical methods. The greatest lack is in the breaking down of existing theories into hypotheses that can be tested by existing methods. Work of this type does not appeal to the person educated in the monolithic tradition. He would rather create new theories or invent a new method. During the war, one social scientist who acted as an idea man to a policy maker told me frankly that he was not interested in work that involved checking and validating conclusions. He said, "I would rather have many lightly validated hypotheses than one hypothesis with sound validation."

There is, of course, a time for this sort of thing and there is always room for some of it, but the pressing need at present is for teams with spades.

The second general point of this section is that just as there can be too much emphasis on theory, so too there can be too much emphasis on method. One sees sometimes a technique created or adopted and then used for all problems, or almost all, sometimes with extravagant claims. One is reminded of a golfer insisting on playing an entire course with a brassie. This tendency fits well into the monolithic pattern, but it is essentially a technician's approach, the approach of the maker of instruments, rather than that of the scientist. For the latter, the problem is the center of concern and all methods are brought to bear that may be fruitful.

CHAPTER IX

THE POLICY MAKER

I

Since policy formation is handicapped by many factors besides insufficient application of social science, it seems advisable to note briefly at the outset, for the sake of a balanced view, some of these other major influences.

Men and women engaged in making policy, whether the level be high or low, are always subject to determinants not of their own choosing. These include law, protocol, budget, personnel, interlocking with other policies, lack of time, and the opinions of fellow government officials, the legislature and the public. As a result, it is not uncommon for matters that really have nothing to do with a particular policy issue to force on it a shape which none of the policy makers concerned thinks wisest or best. Policy making in practice is largely a matter of improvisation, of doing the best you can with what you have and, as in other aspects of life, this is seldom ideal.

In addition to the limitations of the external situation, there are the human limitations of the individual policy maker in matters of character and intelligence. There may be bad and stupid men in policy positions. However, there is no need to dwell on these aspects since they are the common frame of reference with which critical evaluation is approached. Although they have their importance, they cannot by themselves lead to much understanding or to permanent improvement. "Bad" situations attract or manufacture "bad" people; and until the defective social process is itself altered, the pinning of guilt and the removal of one individual serves chiefly to make room for another of the same stamp.

There will be more on this subject later in the chapter when the "functional" concept is discussed. For the moment we shall leave the topic by merely noting that "looking out for number one" spans an arc of behavior that connects on one side with deliberate rascality and on the other with unconscious drives toward personal advancement at all costs and that it includes conduct that is socially condoned and even admired. It is equally necessary to realize that there are numerous policy makers who are by every accepted standard intelligent, sincere, honest and extraordinarily self-sacrificing. Such qualities, however, are evidently not enough, for these men no less than their opposites produce policies that are not adjusted to human nature and, like psychological King Canutes, they too tell human tides not to rise.

Therefore, although much of what follows is critical, it should be understood as aimed at practices and situations and not at individuals or groups. Furthermore, it should also be understood that pointing out needs for improvement is not the same thing as pointing out fault in a moral sense. From one point of view, the really extraordinary thing is the degree to which policy makers have accepted social science despite the difficulties and uncertainties; but from another point of view it is clear that given the needs of the times this is not enough.

II

One of the reasons policy makers do not utilize social science is that they look for demonstration and proof in terms that are not appropriate. The Division, for instance, was never able to "prove" a single point at the time policy decisions were being made. It dealt in probabilities and approximations that had varying degrees of reliability, resembling in this, as in some other aspects, weather prediction. Substantiation only came with the unfolding of events and the accumulation of additional information long after the time for fixing policy had passed.

The Use of Applied Social Science

This kind of situation is common in social science. When "proof" or an opportunity for prior testing is lacking, findings have to be judged by the way they are derived. In order to make such an evaluation, one must possess at least two essentials: the data and the concepts that give the data meaning. As is commonly the case, these indispensable ingredients were only partially known to the OWI policy makers and in consequence they judged the Division's findings from an inadequate basis. As has been noted previously, although the data was available it was not examined. There were probably a number of reasons for this, but one at least was lack of the concepts. Without them, the data could have little meaning and little value.

It is to the concepts, therefore, that we shall first direct attention. What is meant by concepts, or principles, has been described in Chapter IV. These were, of course, available to the policy makers no less than the data, in as much as they were often presented by the Division. However, it takes more than statement to make concepts come alive, particularly for busy people who do not have time to listen carefully and digest thoroughly and who have not been prepared by previous education and experience.

In place of social-science concepts, the policy makers had concepts derived from such fields as politics, international affairs, the Far East and Japan. This knowledge embraced much that was valid and significant about human behavior, but it dealt in special aspects rather than the total picture that was important for morale analysis.

The concepts of the policy makers were also derived from their own psychological theories. It is likely that most of them would have repudiated "theory" and said that they were dealing in "hard facts" with "common sense." Nevertheless, theories they were, of a rough-and-ready, rule-of-thumb variety. Every person has a lore he believes regarding the behavior and motives of other human beings, a lore which he has been storing since childhood and by which he interprets what is happening. Some of it comes from individual experience and some from patterns in the culture. If he has been successful enough to be a policy maker, he is very likely to be strongly convinced that most of his ideas are right. Furthermore, since there is high esteem in our culture rendered to those who "know people" he will jealously guard his reputation as a judge of men.

The policy maker's concepts include much truth, as a rule, but they also include notions, prejudices, vestigial cultural patterns and sentiments that are based not so much on fact as on further-ing hopes and reducing fears. That common sense can be as wrong as any other kind is clear enough; it was once common sense to suppose that the world is flat. No one can afford, of course, to throw it overboard altogether, and it is a useful base to keep in mind as one progresses with the elaboration of theories. However, as observed by Adolf Meyer, one of its strong advo-cates in psychiatry, common sense requires to be "systematically checked by orderly comparison with organized technical experi-ence."

The concepts derived from the scientific approach to human relations differ from "practical" theories in that neither the experience of an individual nor the prevalence of an idea among people generally is accepted as a warrant for truth. The social scientist is fallible enough, as has been discussed at length, but he does strive to build his concepts on systematic work by many investigators who have carried out observation, experimentation and analysis and produced results that check and supplement each other. The concepts are not the final word, but they are usually more comprehensive, complicated, subtle and closer to reality than the "common-sense" theories.

To illustrate, the following is an approximate statement of a policy maker's concept: The older a custom or a belief held by a nation, the greater its strength and capacity to resist change. Social science concepts would confirm the idea that new customs

The Use of Applied Social Science

or beliefs are likely to be unstable for a period of time, but would deny that this is necessarily of long duration in terms of years or that antiquity *per se* is an indicator of strength and durability. The view would be, rather, that it is not the *real* age of a custom that counts, but the *beliefs* of the people regarding age. If it is in their cultural pattern to set a high value on antiquity, and if they think a particular custom is old, then this will add to its staying power. However, even this cannot be used to evaluate strength unless consideration is also given to a whole complex of factors that have to do with the *present situation* and the role of the custom in the current needs, aspirations and anxieties of the people.

The Japanese Emperor may again be used for demonstration. Those who believe in the causal effects of great age were impressed when scholarly research seemed to show that much of the Japanese attitude and behavior toward the Emperor had come about since the Meiji Restoration in 1868. They concluded that in consequence the belief in the Emperor must be much weaker than anyone had hitherto imagined. To the social scientists, on the other hand, it was the supposed history of the Imperial Institution rather than the actual history that was significant in this connection.

Another illustration in a different context may be found in the common belief that man is innately lazy and prone to do nothing unless prodded by the threat of punishment or lured by specific reward, like a donkey with a carrot before his nose. This permeates much thinking in editorials and at policy levels in industry. Yet the weight of evidence from careful study is on the side of assuming that work is one of the enjoyed and rewarding human activities and that most people under normal conditions actively seek it. On the basis of this concept, refusal to work cannot be accepted as a natural if immoral state of affairs, but must be regarded as an abnormal condition for which causal factors exist. This view would lead to remedies that are quite different from the exhortive or punitive programs that often arise from the first concept.

III

The conceptual differences between the policy maker and the social scientist extend much further than certain contrasting assumptions about individual and social behavior. At the bottom there appear to be two antithetic systems of thinking.

In both scientific thinking and policy thinking there is the employment of definition, of categories, of facts, of basic assumptions, and of logic, in order to arrive at conclusions or to explain human behavior.

In the scientific approach, facts, observed events, and ascertained information play a dominant role. Logic is used, of course, but as a bridge between those facts already known and those being discovered. In itself, logical elaboration does not rate highly as a means of establishing a conclusion. It is rather a way of arriving as efficiently as possible at points where tests can be applied by direct experiment or by experimental observation. Brilliance of argument is important only if it leads to such tests and is supported by them. Reasoning that has very long spans between piers of supporting facts is regarded with skepticism and is not heavily relied upon.

In policy making, however, the conclusions are supported by a structure of logic that extends dangerously high on its mixed foundation of facts and basic assumptions. It is vast in proportion to the facts employed. Frequently the facts are insufficient to form any part of the foundation, and are fastened on the superstructure here and there for illustration. Much importance is attached to neatness, brilliance, persuasiveness, dramatic quality, and even to the sheer mass of logical elaborations.

The history of science has shown repeatedly that such endeavors — and I refer here to the insufficiently supported scientific bridge as well as the policy maker's structure — can be monuments of error due to the omission of pertinent but unknown facts. As Francis Bacon has pointed out, this is inevitable because even the most intelligent mind cannot construct in imagination the complexities of nature from a few premises. Some things are always left out unless there are frequent "helps" by checking back to nature with direct observations.

Customarily, the thought sequences that go into policy making are formally presented as if rooted in fact and developed in an orderly manner from assumptions to conclusions after the fashion of Euclid. If one watches the process, however, it is usually apparent that the practice is in the reverse order. The "conclusions" come first from roots that are not always clear but which lie in the personality, social situation and culture of the policy maker. From such "conclusions" a rational framework is built downward in search of foundations in facts and in commonly held beliefs. This is illustrated by the policy maker who said, "We are pressed for time this morning and must decide this matter at once; tomorrow we can figure out the reasons."

The policy-making process has some similarities to the scientific procedure of forming hypotheses, but is different in the emphasis on "proving a point" rather than exploring and examining. Facts, ideas and concepts that do not fit the conclusions are ignored unless too obvious, or likely to be brought up in argument by opponents. As a result there is considerable development of skill in making wishful thinking plausible, giving it a legal or learned form, and making it forcefully persuasive. Much time is spent on the elaboration of ideas, on working up arguments for defense or attack, on building towers of syllogisms and in discussions that last days, rather than in a systematic effort to collect and analyze all available data and to achieve conclusions through induction.

There is a story of two medieval scholars who argued for thirty years about the number of teeth in a horse's mouth without ever looking at a horse. Modern policy makers are not exactly like the medieval scholars who totally avoided looking in the horse's mouth. They give consideration to the idea of looking at the horse, but hang back afraid that the result might not come out in their favor and people would "jump too quickly to unsound conclusions." If someone else looks at the horse and finds that a policy maker's view is correct, approval results. If on the other hand it is reported that the policy maker was wrong, he will bring his rational battery into play and say that this means nothing because only one horse was examined, and he might have been exceptional, and that it would be necessary to look in the mouths of 10,000 horses in order to show proof and have the "hard facts." Meanwhile, since policy based on the number of teeth cannot wait pending the extensive research this would require, or since there are no funds to finance it, or because Congress and the American public would not approve, the policy maker is forced to go ahead and make his decision on the basis of the original idea of five teeth or fifty teeth rather than rely on the dubious findings of the man who has looked in the mouths of one or two horses.

In addition to the heavy reliance on rational elaboration, there is in much of the thinking that goes into policy an assured and absolute tone in regard to the validity of the conclusions. This is part of "selling" the idea and getting evidence to make a case. But since scientific appraisals and interpretations are by nature tentative and searching they do not do well in the atmosphere of a court, where contending parties are trying to win rather than discover the truth. Even the fundamental assumptions useful as starting points are regarded as only approximate and as abstractions which may be in error when applied to particulars. It is only by this attitude that the scientist can make progress in knowledge. Because of it, however, the findings of science are apt to appear weak and uncertain to the policy maker. If the scientist attempts to strengthen his position by turning to argument and asserting absolutes, he is very likely to damage his particular abilities and become merely another contender. The only tenable position for the social scientist is one like that of the expert witness called by the court to give information and opinion without being attached to either side and without fear of either side.

It must be admitted that the scientist presented has been idealized for the sake of contrast. As indicated in the previous chapter, he only too often displays the kind of thinking that has here been attributed to the policy maker. This is especially likely to happen when he participates in policy formation and becomes identified with a plan. Such failures, however, do not alter the fact that the scientist has at least a different ideal pattern and has also had some practice in its exercise. Nor does it alter the fact that, by and large, he gets closer to truth when he is being a scientist than when he is wandering off in other directions.

IV

Much of what has been said thus far may be summed up by describing the policy maker as having more in common with rationalism than empiricism, of being more inclined to Plato than Harvey or Newton. This observation is not limited to men with a scholarly background, for the "practical man" can be exceedingly rationalistic in supporting his conclusions with points of law, rules of administrative procedure, economic and business theories, or popular notions about human behavior. The contrast between rationalism and empiricism carries with it a related factor of major importance. This is the common absence of a *functional* view of human behavior on the part of the policy maker. Since this lack is a major source of numerous misconceptions that have far-reaching practical consequences in human affairs, it is worth pausing to consider the meaning of function as used in this special sense.

The concept of function has been borrowed by certain social scientists from physiology. In the latter field it has to do with asking such questions as, What is the role (function) of the heart or a gland in relation to the whole body? As applied to anthropology, Radcliffe-Brown puts it this way:

> The concept of function . . . involves the notion of a *structure* consisting of a *set of relations* amongst *unit entities*, the *continuity* of the structure being maintained by a *life-process* made up of the *activities* of the constituent units.

If, with these concepts in mind, we set out on a systematic investigation of the nature of human society and of social life, we find presented to us three sets of problems. First, the problems of social morphology — what kinds of social structures are there, what are their similarities and differences, how are they to be classified? Second, the problems of social physiology—how do social structures function? Third, the problems of development — how do new types of social structure come into existence?

By the definition here offered "function" is the contribution which a partial activity makes to the total activity of which it is a part. The function of a particular social usage is the contribution it makes to the total social life as the functioning of the total social system. Such a view implies that a social system (the total social structure of a society together with the totality of social usages, in which that structure appears and on which it depends for its continued existence) has a certain kind of unity, which we may speak of as a functional unity. We may define it as a condition in which all parts of the social system work together with a sufficient degree of harmony or internal consistency, *i. e.*, without producing persistent conflicts which can neither be resolved nor regulated.

Opposition, *i. e.*, organized and regulated antagonism is, of course, an essential feature of every social system.*

* Concept of Function in Social Science," by A. R. Radcliffe-Brown, *American Anthropologist*, Vol. 37, July-September, 1935.

The Use of Applied Social Science

Bronislaw Malinowski says: "The primary concern of functional anthropology is the function of institutions, customs, implements and ideas. It holds that the cultural process is subject to laws and that the laws are to be found in the function of the real elements of culture."[*]

Since this matter is difficult to realize on the basis of abstract terms alone, three illustrations are offered: the first is from animal ecology, the second from entomology and the third from medicine. Although drawn from non-social science fields because less entangled, they are nevertheless relevant.

Suppose that a naturalist is studying a wilderness area for purposes of conservation. He finds that the various plants and animals as they go through their life cycles of growth and reproduction exist in a state of complex interdependence. His attention is directed toward mountain sheep that are diminishing in number and also to the presence of wolves. Were he a sportsman or rancher, he would be likely to assume that the wolves were *the cause* of the reduction in sheep and to maintain this view with no little heat. The naturalist, however, does not stop with such a single idea. He observes, theorizes and tests his theories with further observations. He finds that the wolves kill the sheep but that they also kill numbers of other animals that are in competition with the sheep for the same food. He discovers that the sheep suffer from scarcity of food, from the washing out of certain chemicals from the soil due to erosion, from diseases and from the winter killing of lambs. In the end, the naturalist may find that the wolves are one of a number of serious threats to the sheep and that their reduction would help the sheep population. Or, he may find that the balance of nature is such in this particular case that the wolves aid the sheep more than harming them, by

[*] "Culture," in the *Encyclopedia of the Social Sciences*, Vol. IV. (New York: The Macmillan Company) © 1931.

A mathematically oriented discussion of functional dependence may be found in *Principles of Anthropology* by Eliot Dismore Chapple and Carleton Stevens Coon (New York: Henry Holt) 1942.

keeping down the number of animals that eat the same food. In either event, the naturalist sees multiple forces at work in a state of interdependence, rather than a single cause that fits like a key into a lock. Moreover, he does not take sides with sheep, wolves or other animals in such a way as to blind his understanding of how they are interdependent.

Suppose another naturalist is studying insects purely from an interest in advancing knowledge. If he turns his attention to bees he will find that complex interrelationship of individuals to make a hive that has often been described. There are the workers, the drones and the queen, each with patterns of behavior that aid the continued existence of the colony with a striking disregard for the well-being of any one individual. The drones are starved, mutilated and thrown out when their functions have been performed. Workers that arrive home with frayed wings or begin to fail in their productive capacity receive the same treatment. Even the queen, ordinarily surrounded by attendants who minister to her needs, is destroyed when infirmities begin to creep upon her. The naturalist will observe further that all this behavior does function with considerable efficiency to perpetuate individual hives and bees as a whole. He will make these discoveries in a spirit of finding out how it all works and without pronouncing judgments on the bees, without calling the drones "useless" or the destruction of damaged workers "wicked."

For the third picture, suppose a doctor is carrying out research on the cause of tuberculosis. His first goal is to understand the process, and he finds before long that he cannot regard the tubercle bacillus as *the cause* of the disease. It becomes evident that millions of people harbor the germ without developing any signs or symptoms of tuberculosis. The research physician must, therefore, study the reactions and interactions of glands, nerves, blood vessels, lymphatic system, and other organs and functions of the body in relation to the whole, to the tubercle bacillus and to other germs that might have a predisposing or immunizing effect. Nor is the list exhausted here, for it is also necessary to look into such matters as diet, light, nature of work and the possible presence of hereditary and psychological factors. The germ, it turns out, is only one of a number of conditions that must be present before tuberculosis occurs. At no time does the doctor get wound up in hating the germ and in weaving patterns of revenge into his research. He keeps his mind on the central aim of finding out what is going on so that remedial change can be introduced.

In these illustrations at least two common elements are evident. The first is an attempt to understand any item as part of a larger whole, as the product of multiple, interacting forces, rather than the result of a single cause that can be ferreted out like a detective uncovering a murderer. The second is that the forces are regarded as natural rather than good or bad. One's own hopes, fears, and ideas of what *should be* are set aside in favor of discovering what *is*. Whether the naturalist likes or dislikes wolves is not relevant to understanding their relationship to the sheep. The man who studies the bees may be himself a believer in democracy, fascism, or communism, but this must not be allowed to intrude itself into his reports about their social life and how it works for them. The physician does not permit belief in the wickedness of the tubercle bacillus to lead him into underestimating or overestimating its power, nor to neglecting all the other matters that are equally important in understanding and controlling tuberculosis.

Few people will quarrel with all this as long as it is confined to the natural sciences, but many difficulties arise as soon as these few and simple points are transferred to the study of human behavior and an effort is made to view society as the naturalist looks at the animal kingdom, the physician the functions of the body and the astronomer the stars. In place of such a view the policy maker, like most other people, has it ingrained in him from his early years to measure human affairs in terms of good and evil.

Starkly simple explanations are sought to the neglect of deeper understanding and hence opportunity for control.

In evaluating the work of the Division, there was constant danger from misplaced moral judgments and "explanations" of cause in terms of innate badness. From the fact that the Japanese were our enemies came a disposition to regard them as depraved and to use this to account for their behavior. Their bravery was "fanaticism peculiar to the Japanese," their devotion to the Emperor was due to lack of intelligence and lack of moral character, their ability to endure extreme physical hardship for long periods was evidence of sub-human qualities, and so on. There were many people who thought of the actions of the Japanese almost exclusively in terms of their moral and intellectual inferiority. Such people could understand neither the methods nor the conclusions of the Division. The only "scientific" explanation of Japanese behavior that would have appealed to them would have been the discovery of a deficient pituitary gland that caused moral idiocy.

This kind of thinking recurs continuously in all sorts of contexts. If war is threatened, if an economic depression descends, if unemployment appears, if Congress fails to pass the Fair Employment Practice Bill, if a strike takes place, if patients in a mental hospital are mistreated, if a child is found neglected, we always give far more attention to discussing the rights and the wrongs of the situation, in deciding who is to blame and in taking sides, than to understanding the forces that have brought it about and deciding what can be done to control them. If we can make somebody suffer for it, we are likely to go away satisfied, leaving the situation no better than before.

We are always looking for the villain instead of human beings going through the business of living as best they can, some helpfully and some destructively in their actions toward the welfare of others. Preoccupation with the search for the villain blinds us to the constellation of events past and present that gave rise to him. From the functional point of view, "what gives rise" is the question. Can we, through understanding the forces that produce villains, alter situations so that there will be less ground on which they can flourish?

Must we be forever content with trapping rats? Cannot we also stop up their holes and rid ourselves of the places that breed them? The world is getting too small for the luxury of villains and there is a widespread need for the physician's obsession with getting at causes and not tinkering with symptoms only.

These, then, are the implications of the functional view. By and large, they enter only a little into most of the thinking that gives rise to policy.

V

Related to the lack of a functional view of human affairs is a difficulty in seeing common qualities and common dynamic patterns when they appear in widely different contexts, or in strikingly different shapes. If one does not think in functional terms, it necessarily follows that he will not perceive how functions exist like recurrent themes in an enormous variety of different situations. Non-scientific thinking tends to generalize on the basis of gross similarities and differences of structure, not on similarities and differences of dynamic process.

Bacon made the point very clearly, writing 300 years ago when science was just beginning:

The heat of heavenly bodies and the heat of fire seem to be very heterogeneous; so do the fixed red of the rose or the like and the apparent red in the rainbow . . .; so again do the different kinds of death, death by drowning, by hanging, by stabbing, by apoplexy, by atrophy; and yet they agree severally in the nature of heat, redness and death.

❋   ❋   ❋   ❋   ❋   ❋

Human Relations in a Changing World

If anyone conceive that my Forms [Bacon's word for natural law] are of a somewhat abstract nature because they mix and combine things heterogeneous . . . he may be assured that he is held in captivity by custom, by the gross appearance of things, and by men's opinions. For it is most certain that these things, however heterogeneous and alien from each other, agree in the Form or Law which governs heat, redness and death; and that the power of man cannot possibly be emancipated and freed from the common course of nature, and expanded and exalted to new efficients and new modes of operation, except by the revelation and discovery of forms of this kind.

The nineteenth-century Scottish physicist, J. Clerk Maxwell, defined energy as "that which in all natural phenomena is continually passing from one portion of matter to another." This means that although energy has various forms such as mechanical, electrical, thermal and chemical, and appears in many different portions of matter, it is still energy.

Nowadays there is some recognition among many people who are not scientists that in the physical world the same dynamic force can operate in different contexts. It is accepted that you can find electricity in storms, in carpets, in nerves, in batteries and in generators and that it is all still electricity. It is also accepted that you can use that electricty to boil a pot of water and so convert the energy from an electrical form to heat and motion forms.

In matters related to living things, the principle of common functions is also recognized, but not so completely. It seems impossible that a jellyfish and a man can have the same ground plan, so great is their difference in appearance; yet they share metabolism, growth, reproduction, respiration, irritability, and much else. The physiologist who uses animals in his laboratory is frequently told: "You cannot generalize from guinea pigs to men because human beings and guinea pigs are altogether different." The person who says this probably takes vitamins when feeling run down and knows he would depend for his life on insulin if he developed diabetes — to point out but two of a vast number of discoveries to which animal studies have made essential contributions. The remark to the physiologist about guinea pigs is the result of gross appearance overshadowing the less visible functions so that "some differences" are mistaken for "everything different" and the "need for caution" is confused with "total rejection."

In the understanding and interpretation of human affairs, the dominance of appearance over dynamic principle is still more marked and in fact seems to stand about where the view of all nature stood at the time Bacon wrote. It is hard to accept the fact that anger in the neurotic, the psychotic, the administrator, the union leader, the rank and file, the businessman, the politician is still anger and that much can be learned by orderly comparisons. Similarly, it is difficult to believe that leadership among African natives, Navaho Indians, the CIO, and the National Association of Manufacturers, and in innumerable other settings, is still leadership and that what is learned in one setting has pertinence to the others. The manifest differences between a factory, an Indian tribe, a village and a psychiatric clinic obscure the common processes.

As a result, it was impossible for the Division to proceed very far in explaining the derivation of its findings. Talking to policy makers in terms of studies in a psychiatric clinic, in field work among primitives, or in the early development and training of children, instead of being convincing usually excited ridicule and disbelief that matters from sources apparently so far removed from the Japanese could have any bearing on the problems under consideration.

VI

There is one major exception to the previous statement that policy makers do not see common themes in widely different situations. Unfortunately, this exception is in the wrong direction since it consists in seeing plots where they do not exist or are of secondary importance. Groups of people, whether communities, nations, "races," or socio-economic classes are looked upon as if they were individual human beings with consistent conscious motives and completely coordinated actions arising from those motives. In reality, human societies act in response to many divergent forces, some coming from outside and some from within the group — some conscious, some unconscious, and many a mixture of both. The actions of numerous individuals and numerous subgroups in response to different situations and different motives are involved. Many people will agree verbally to this fact and even say it is obvious, but they still will not make policy in terms of it. Anthropomorphizing society — that is, thinking of groups of people as if they had the attributes of an individual man — is a costly error in determining policy. Speculation about plots and efforts to find one that will "explain" divergent behavior and make it all a part of a consistent scheme diverts attention from the social and psychological forces at work. The inconsistencies and disparate actions that spring from the different parts of any large group of people and from the existence of opposing trends, instead of being recognized for what they are and analyzed in such terms, are ingeniously interpreted to show the existence of a deliberate plot. The very habits of our language by which we refer to a nation as "she," use single verbs after their names and otherwise personalize them, or refer to a leader as if he were the nation itself, impel us toward this line of thought and expectation. Consequently, opportunities for understanding and remedy are missed while confusion and hostility increase.

In our frontier days (to take a simple example and one without current emotional involvement), if Indians raided a settlement at a time when a treaty was in existence the assumption would be that "*the* Indians" had broken the treaty and an attack in retaliation would be made on their nearest village. It was almost never considered that the scalping might have been done by some band from a distance or one that had not signed the treaty or by a few criminals who were outcasts among the Indians. Yet the latter was very often the case, and many an innocent Indian village was exterminated to the last woman and child by vengeful whites. The converse was also true. When outlaw whites raided Indians during a time of peace, the latter were equally quick to assume that this had been done by agreement on the part of all whites and they would retaliate upon a settlement that had no connection with the event.

During a strike at the Japanese Relocation Center at Poston, social science observers saw that the administration and the strikers both acted in response to a great many influences and that on each side there were groups who represented strongly different views and tendencies, ranging from uncompromising hostility to moderation. It was also evident that the existence of these sub-groups, and of others who took advantage of the situation for their own private ends, made over-all control in terms of any consistent line of behavior very difficult. Many, many things happened that were not part of any over-all plan, and what over-all plans existed on the two sides changed from day to day according to circumstances. Yet each side thought of the other as highly coordinated and deliberate and assumed that anything that happened was the result of a single scheme.

During the war people were forever explaining Japanese behavior on assumptions of extraordinary unity and one-mindedness. Granting that the Japanese have many patterns in their culture that do show more coordination of people than is commonly seen in urban American life, the extremes that were supposed by responsible policy makers were highly improbable in the light of existing knowledge of social interaction and variations in personality. After V-J Day some of those who were piecing together in Tokyo the wartime picture were astounded at the disorganization and conflict that was revealed. They were moved to remark that the reason we won the war in spite of the "snafu" from which we suffered was because the Japanese "snafu" was so much worse.

Nevertheless, explanations in terms of elaborate plots continue. One of the most distinguished of Far Eastern experts told me when we happened to meet in the early months of the occupation that "they" had issued a "directive" to all Japanese. He estimated that it contained the following orders:

1. Make a big play about food and try to convince the Americans that it has to be imported. This is necessary in order to avoid the social and economic changes that will occur if food is not imported.

2. Make a great show of cooperation in order to shorten the occupation.

3. Make a name for openness and good-fellowship by admitting your mistakes; but also point out that others have made mistakes too and we are all human beings together.

4. Drive a wedge wherever possible between the Allies.

5. Promote civil war in China by siding with Chiang.

6. Use the Japanese militarists as a lightning rod; get the attention of the Americans on them and off the rest of us.

7. By indirection, save the Emperor who will save us.

These orders were thought by this Far Eastern expert to constitute a careful, deliberate plan transmitted to all ranks with appropriate "schooling" in what to say to the Americans and how to say it. He seemed to doubt that the behavior of the Japanese we were observing every day was in any sense a genuine reaction or expression of feeling but thought it all took place in response to strings which "they" were pulling.

The functional concept would suggest that the above "orders" were in fact a partial list of many reactions on the part of Japanese as a result of their culture, past experience and current situation. No nationwide plot was necessary to explain the prevalence of the Japanese anxieties about food, their fear for the Emperor, their disillusionment with the wartime leaders, antipathy toward the Chinese Communists, and so forth. The fact that some of the moneyed classes might see advantages to themselves in these widespread attitudes and hence encourage them, did not mean that they "controlled" them. Consequently, laws, fines, or punishment of these classes or other supposed plotters could not, alone, alter the behavior described. The plot idea suggests a spurious consistency and long-range purposiveness in behavior that is at variance with nature; it induces overlooking of conflicting trends among the people and it obscures a functional understanding of the interacting forces that go to make up their overt behavior.

Today we continue with the same line of thinking. The enormous difficulty of producing coordinated human action is ignored, especially if we are thinking about people in another culture. We talk and reason about "the" Japanese or "the" Germans or "the" British or "the" Russians, as if they really were as they appear in the political cartoons, each a single man with schemes, good or bad according to whom they are for or against. There has been much puzzling and many ingenious explanations as to why the Russians say one thing in Moscow but do something else in Korea, Poland or Berlin. The puzzling and the explanations have, in most cases, assumed that whatever was done came about as a result of consistently rational if malevolent behavior on the part of all Russians from the politicians to the lowest private or consular clerk. Until the quarrel with Yugoslavia came out into the open, I did not see many news analysts suggesting what, from the social science point of view, was always the most likely explanation — that the Russians are many people, with many sub-groups and levels of leadership holding many different points of view and that their behavior, at least in this regard, is only a puzzle when we insist on looking upon them as if they were one man. We are too much inclined to accept their own propaganda about themselves and are misled into believing that a one-party label really means the elimination of contending groups.

Along this line it may be said further that as far as the Russian attitude toward the West is concerned, the probability is that there are three kinds of Russians: those rigidly hostile, who believe that the only course is to dominate the West, with war if necessary; those who believe that a cooperative solution can be worked out; and those who are in between and capable of moving to either of the extremes. Even this is an oversimplified picture, but if it is even crudely right, policy is needed that will move as many leading Russians as possible to the second attitude. While admitting all the difficulties, it can hardly be argued that our present course and national attitude constitute a force in this direction. It seems more likely to encourage all Russians to side with those who advance the first point of view. On the other hand, our policy is appropriate if we think only in terms of a nation that plots and schemes like an individual.

All this does not gainsay that some societies are more coordinated than others and that plots do exist. The point is that the plots, like the leaders, are a part of the social process. They need to be considered, but not exclusively considered, for they are determined by the prevailing social and psychological influences. As for coordination, even highly organized societies with strong traditional patterns such as the Japanese fall far short of being the integrated machine that is postulated in so many popular explanations of group behavior.

The history of man's understanding of the physical world is the history of progress away from an anthropomorphic view. Storms, floods, famines and epidemics of disease were originally thought to be due to spirits that had the loves, hates, vanities and disposition to revenge that are found in a person. No storm or fire happened as a result of interacting forces in nature. They were perpetrated by anthropomorphic beings that had schemes in mind. "Somebody does it deliberately" was the universal assumption, and explanation consisted in finding out who he was and why, in individual human terms.

When a plague hit the Greeks before Troy, it was because ". . . Phoebus Apollo . . . came down from the peaks of Olympus wroth at heart . . . and he let fly an arrow; and there was heard a dread clanging of the silver bow. First did he assail the mules and fleet dogs, but afterward, aiming at the men his piercing dart, he smote; and the pyres of the dead burnt continually in multitude." *

Those who first began to consider the forces of nature in other than anthropomorphic terms were treated as heretics and thought to be undermining the values that gave life meaning. Galileo is probably the best-known example and symbol of the pain and danger in the struggle. Yet, even among the scientific pioneers, the anthropomorphic view persisted at subtle levels. Three hundred years ago in academic centers of Europe, metals were said to have "spirit" and to "agitate with anger" when heated. Heavy objects were said to fall down because of "an appetite to rest and to conserve their nature in that place which is most proper for them." Gradually, however, by slow degrees, as science developed, people came to see, as Hobbes put it, the absurdity of "ascribing appetite, and knowledge of what is good for their conservation, which is more than man has, to things inanimate."

We have come at last to see storms, chemical reactions and other events in nature as forces acting according to natural law, not in response to the jealousies and whims of anthropomorphic spirits. In our thinking about the society of man, however, it yet remains to eliminate the naïve idea that large groups of people behave like individuals.

The realization that societies act in accordance with multiple forces that affect them within and without is not wholly absent from policy makers and their critics in the press and among

* Fr. Homer: *Iliad.* Tr. Lang, Leaf & Myers. Used by permission of The Macmillan Company.

the public. Indeed, the concept is often given considerable lip service. It becomes overwhelmed, however, when emotions are aroused, which is to say in virtually every significant issue. In its place appear interpretations and explanations based on the idea of struggle against evil men. There is little interest in understanding the evil, but instead this is taken for granted and all things are explained by it. The movements of nations and the parts within nations are thus reduced to the simple formula of a primitive myth, of a broadside ballad, or a Western movie, the "goodies" against the "baddies," "we'uns against you'uns."

It was in these terms, naturally, that most thinking was done about the Japanese during the war. It is in these terms that people think and plan in regard to strikes, or the behavior of the vested interests. What is John L. Lewis doing? What is the National Association of Manufacturers up to? How shall we stop the Communists? These are the questions with which people are familiar and on which they want action, not the forces that underlie and determine such symptoms.

A consequence of this kind of thinking, one that brings gnawing deterioration and quick havoc into human affairs, is the belief that the remedy lies in punishing groups of people for their behavior without understanding and dealing with the forces producing that behavior. False issues then develop around slogans like a "tough" policy and "no appeasement" with all the obscuring emotions these bring with them. Solving the problem easily becomes secondary to the satisfactions of releasing one's resentment.

VII

Inherent in the different concepts and different ways of thinking is the problem of words and what they mean. The policy maker and the social scientist employ some words that are strange and incomprehensible to each other. It has to be so, since concepts are represented by words and if one party lacks a concept then the words that symbolize it must be meaningless to him. Attempts by the social scientist to define and explain his words plunge him at once into the tangle of having to use other words that are also unfamiliar and requiring explanation and hence into the whole problem of differences in modes of thinking.

It is probable, however, that it is not the unfamiliar words that cause most of the trouble, for they, like the rattlesnake, at least give warning of their presence. The greater difficulty comes from the words that are familiar but to which the social scientist and the policy maker each attach different meanings. Thus, the two can easily begin a discussion under the impression that they are talking about the same thing and proceed to an impasse of disagreement, when actually there is not so much difference in opinion as a case of talking about two different subjects. For instance, one of the difficulties in the Division's attempt to present the decline in Japanese morale was due to the policy maker using the word "morale" as the equivalent of "courage," while the Division referred to "the capacity of a group of people to pull together consistently and persistently in pursuit of a common purpose." In many instances the Japanese showed both high courage and lowering cohesiveness so that the two sides of the apparent disagreement were equally correct.

The converse also happened: what seemed to be agreement in the beginning, due to using the same words, turned out later to be a situation in which widely divergent views were held. This sometimes led people into feeling that they had been double-crossed.

The Division tried to deal with the problem of words by taking pains with its reports, explaining points as they came up, striving for simplicity of expression and employing an experienced professional journalist as editor.

Simple English, however, had its dangers, especially when explaining the bases for conclusions, in contrast to the conclusions themselves. The latter were usually fairly easy to state briefly but the reasons for them rarely were so. In such a case one is easily lured into presenting a simple and plausible explanation that the policy maker will accept rather than a completely sincere statement which runs the risk of being incomprehensible and hence rejected. Simple English is not necessarily accurate English when the subject matter is complex.

It is obvious that the social scientist has responsibility for trying to make his work and its potentialities intelligible and that explaining and describing his concepts is part of this. The question may very properly be asked, however, as to how much effort the policy maker should make on his side. It would, after all, be impossible for him to become acquainted with every one of the professional systems of thought which serve him. The chief who has on his staff lawyers and engineers does not have to become a specialist in their fields.

This issue must be considered in relation to another: should the policy maker question the scientific soundness of the social scientist's conclusions? That is to say, apart from his undoubted task of examining their applicability, should he also, over and above the scientist's evaluation, make decisions regarding their degree of probability or validity?

Perhaps he should. But if he does question the validity of the social science conclusions and if he is not in a position to put them to some preliminary test, then he *must* make himself acquainted with the data and the principles upon which the conclusions stand. If he does not have time to gain such knowledge, then his course is to avoid judgments and accept the results. Otherwise, his questions and decisions cannot be other than hit or miss and obstructive.

There remains a more compelling reason than checking the social scientist as to why the policy maker should understand the concepts and the mode of thought that lie at the heart of the scientific approach to human problems. He needs them himself. Although scientific and lay thinking have been discussed for the sake of presentation as if they were separate, they shade one into the other. It is a question of more and less between two poles, rather than absolutes. In circumstances where the pressure of time, absence of information, and other factors force heavy reliance on rationalism rather than empiricism in reaching a decision, one can still be functional rather than vengeful or self-righteous in his outlook; the basic assumptions can be from the best-established principles rather than from folklore and rule of thumb.

CHAPTER X

PROBLEMS OF ORGANIZATION

I

So FAR, in considering applied social science, attention has been given to concepts, ideas and ways of thinking about human relations. Overlapping with this, but still distinct enough to warrant separate discussion, is the question of introducing this new activity into the structure of administrative and policy-making organizations. The problem is a little like adding a meter to a machine that has not been designed to receive it.

The matter is intimately tied to the nature of hierarchical structure and to competition for status, for among a number of primary prerogatives, the making of policy is one of the most important. It has been noted in the previous chapter that the policy maker, like the lawyer, tries to win his case. He does this because, again like the lawyer, his livelihood and career depend on it. It is by "putting over" a policy that men get higher positions.

Morris E. Opler has described this situation thus: "Not infrequently the policy maker tends to identify himself with the policy that he advocates and feels personally attacked when the social scientist, thinking of policy in instrumental terms, advocates a change. It is interesting that in politics or administration a change of policy often means a shift of personnel at the top. Yet a social scientist in his own work will use all sorts of means and 'policies' without any sense of failure or alarm."

"Another divergence in approach has to do with the respective attitudes of scientists and 'practical men' toward failure. To experiment is to confess that everything is not perfect and that aspects of a problem have not been solved. Therefore the scientist has no sense of fear or failure when he must try again or confess that something new must be attempted. The policy maker and administrator, on the other hand, may have the idea that everyone must be convinced all is going well under his direction or regime. . . . At ———, for instance, the administrators were unwilling to send in reports which hinted that everyone was not happy and contented with conditions. It made no difference how desperate the situation was or whether hell was going to break loose the next day. They wanted as long as possible to give the impression that they had absolute control over everything. In other words, the administrator tends to have a vested interest in proving that he has administered well and wisely whereas the social scientist has more of a vested interest in discovering just what is occurring." *

Policy making is a prerogative that is jealously guarded and to share it with others is to lose some of one's stock of prestige. It is in the monolith tradition and the conference table is often a kind of battlefield where one wins his reputation or loses it. Discussions about "what policy" sometimes only make sense if one realizes that the real issue is "whose policy." The promotion of collaborative thinking, the development of group participation on the part of all staff members, the building, in short, of an effective team so that the vast work can be accomplished that is necessary in creating an efficient and well-adjusted policy, these are secondary matters.

This pattern is not superficial, nor does it represent the behavior of merely a few people who are no better than they should be. It is deeply entrenched traditional behavior with innumerable formal and informal conventions for its operation, and it is very difficult for any single individual to escape from it. One is virtually forced either to be in the struggle or else drop out of policy making altogether.

* Personal communication.

Human Relations in a Changing World

The introduction of social science into this setting is a facet of the problem of cooperation in a competitive society. Science can exist in the policy-making pattern that has been outlined only as a technical instrument by which the policy maker finds the means for doing what he already wants to do. Such a narrow use can be good neither for science nor society and is open to grave abuses. Collaboration in a team is the only atmosphere in which science can grow since it is so heavily dependent on spontaneity. Under existing circumstances, not only is science hampered, but its discoveries and criticism are taken for attacks in the general struggle for prerogatives and policy makers react toward the scientists as they do toward anyone who threatens to take some of their territory away from them. This hostility is the more heated if, as is generally the case, the policy makers are in a state of war with several other departments above and below them in the Government. Under such circumstances, a unit in the staff that emerges with conclusions which favor the point of view of one of these "enemies" will not be regarded as scientists trying to get at the truth to the best of their ability, but as traitors to the organization busy about some horse trade designed to advance themselves.

II

Policy is not the only prerogative that gives trouble in the adjustment of social science. At least two others should be mentioned: the prerogative of area, or field of activity, and the prerogative of making interpretations as contrasted with mere fact finding.

The prerogative of area is founded on the idea that all activities in an organization can be divided into specific, clearly separated fields each dealing with different materials and that one must not trespass in another's field. This is in contrast to the scientific approach which requires that when one launches on a problem, he must explore all fields that are relevant and bring to bear all materials that show a yield.

The Division's situation in this regard has already been illustrated. The kind of material required in order to follow changes in Japanese morale has been outlined in Chapter V, where it was found that cross checks from multiple sources were of paramount importance.

Certain policy makers relied heavily on scanning the Federal Communication Commission's translations of Japanese broadcasts as a means of keeping themselves posted and getting ideas in regard to what was happening in Japan. When the Division turned to radio sources for some of its data, this was intensely resented. It happened because of the policy makers' preoccupation with exclusive spheres of influence over materials, instead of realizing that different kinds of analysts can use the same stuff for different purposes. They sliced the pie according to materials, not according to problems.

The most troublesome instance of jealousy over areas of knowledge came in connection with some of the experts on Japan. Men who had had missionary, journalistic or other experience in that country were inclined to feel that they alone were in a position to know how the Japanese behave and why. There could be no question that numbers of these men had an enormous wealth of experience and knowledge, much of it badly needed by the Division. For the most part, however, different individuals were acquainted with different aspects of Japanese life and often ignorant of others. Consequently, there was constant danger of giving offense to the expert by not accepting what he said as the whole truth.

This insecurity of the Japanese expert is an example of the ever-present insecurity of those with a reputation for intuitive judgment in the face of scientific method. It was in this context that the doctors of the period were hostile to the discoveries of Pasteur. Since this is a widespread and recurring human tendency, often unconscious in its operation, it is worth illustrating it with a story.

At the dawn of history there was probably once an artist in a cave-dwelling tribe who was respected by his fellow men because he had great skill in drawing circles. With a free hand he could draw them swiftly and when finished they seemed almost perfect. He was in great demand for circles were popular. One day he was approached by a fellow tribesman who said,

"Look here, this is something that will interest you."

He had two sticks tied together at their ends to make a crude draftsman's compass and he swung it in the sand to make a circle, a circle that was not almost perfect, but perfect.

"This will help you in your work," he continued to the artist, "you can make the circles even faster and better now. I also want your advice on the improvement of the design of this gadget and how best to put it at the disposal of the other tribesmen so all can benefit."

The artist considered the compass for a few minutes and then asked, "Can everybody draw a perfect circle with this?"

"Yes," said the inventor, very pleased, "anybody with a little training can make his own circles now."

The artist arose and went to the council of chiefs and denounced the inventor, presented a long and moving argument to show the superior quality of circles made by genius rather than by the compass, and finally urged a law that would protect the people from mechanically made circles and banish the inventor.

In regard to the prerogative of making interpretations, it may be noted that it is traditional in many parts of the Government to draw a line between "gathering the facts" and "making interpretations" based on those facts. The latter is reserved for the expert advisor of high level or for the policy maker. It is difficult to imagine accommodating any kind of applied science in such a frame, for data by themselves never produce a conclusion, nor even convey meaning. They have to be interpreted and it seems extraordinary to insist that those with the most experience in the subject matter should abstain. No one would expect a doctor to give a report to a patient's family on his blood pressure, temperature, blood chemistry, physical signs, and so forth, and then leave it to the family lawyer to make the diagnosis.

This analogy does not exaggerate what sometimes happens to science in government.

CHAPTER XI

RECOMMENDATIONS

1

THE CHIEF recommendation is, obviously, to apply the kind of work done by the Division in the service of peace. The Division was a very small unit, its materials were inadequate and its operations were often fumbling and poorly directed. Nevertheless, its findings suggest that there can be developed organizations capable of showing a high degree of precision in this type of analysis. It may well be that such units would ultimately bear little more resemblance to the Division than an adult does to an embryo, but at the very least there has been indicated a direction in which to go. Many other experiences with applied social science point to the same conclusion.

The goal would be the understanding of international relations and it could be approached through attack on the problems outlined in Chapter VI, sections I to III. There might be, for instance, a unit or units in the Federal Government that carried out the continuous collection and analysis of information on the causal factors underlying international animosities and international cooperation. These would include the customs, beliefs and trends of change in other countries, the images they have of us and of each other, the physical, psychological and social sources of stress, and the range of possible adjustments. An effort could be made to measure the pressures that can produce active hostility before they have gone so far; to state the human-relations planning that must accompany the economic, agricultural and engineering steps toward relieving world distress; to state the full range of direct and indirect consequences likely to

The Use of Applied Social Science

flow from alternative policies; to appraise, after our policies have been put into effect, the actual foreign reactions; and, finally, to estimate the cost of peace and survival and suggest how the best result can be obtained for the least expenditure in money, social disturbance, lives, suffering and grief.

Peacetime analysis would have vastly better materials with which to work than did the Division. There would be more and richer sources in newspapers, magazines, technical journals, fiction, drama, movies and radio. More than these, however, there would be opportunities for direct observation and interview by field workers living in the countries under study. The interviews would range from those that are highly individual and intensive to surveys of public opinion. It should be noted, however, in connection with the latter, that while they are of value when they can be employed, they are not indispensable. The work of the Division emphasizes the great usefulness of many kinds of evidence from many kinds of sources when these are appropriately handled.

In countries where there are "Iron Curtains" of varying degrees of opacity there will be serious difficulties, but even so there is much more information available than was at the disposal of the Division during the war. Vital details can be picked up in border areas by skilled workers who know what to look for and how to talk with those who have crossed the border. Such information cannot be accepted naïvely at its face value, but it takes on significance when cross-checked from multiple sources, analyzed for trends and interpreted in the light of basic principles. In addition, there are quantities of data available from printed sources, from movies and from the radio. Indeed, contrary to much popular opinion, so many are the forms in which fundamental human patterns are registered that it is virtually impossible for the power group of any nation to keep them hidden. Even those countries that have tried hardest to block communication emit in spite of themselves a flow of information that is vastly revealing when the right reagents are applied. There is far more information available than we now utilize.

It may be left as an open question where work of the sort being proposed can best fit in the Government, whether it should consist in one or several units, how it should be articulated with existing agencies and to whom it should be directly responsible. These are matters that could only be decided after intensive study by a commission. It is important to state, however, that although the main purpose is to establish a nonpartisan unit or units of applied social science for the use of policy makers, most of the results of the work must be widely published. This is vital for public understanding of and hence demand for sound policy, for protection against special-interest propaganda and to reduce the opportunity for misusing social science.

If we consider a single research unit, the general form might include a central, report-producing office in Washington with field units covering world areas selected for study. In the central office there should be a director with assistant directors under him, one for each of the world areas. Under the assistant directors there would be analysts and under each analyst one or more teams continuously engaged in processing materials coming in from the field. The analysts would be responsible for supervising the processing and for directing research on particular topics which would be determined by policy makers and the unit's directors in collaboration with the analysts. Research findings would emerge as memoranda prepared by the analysts and their teams and submitted to the directors. Finished reports issued by the unit would be based on the analysts' memoranda but would take many different forms. Some would consist of notes communicated by the director to individual policy makers, some would be reports for committees or agencies, and some would be articles for general publication. In order to make communication effective and to ensure that the different kinds of reports were meaningful to the audience for whom intended, there should be an editorial office headed by a professional editor immediately under the director.

Each of the field units would have a director and, in general, duplicate the structure of the central office. However, in place of processing incoming material, their work would consist in making firsthand observations and collecting data. They should also carry out research on particular topics related to their region and send the results as reports to the central office. Suggestions in regard to these special topics might arise in the field office or in the central office, but the decision in regard to actually undertaking the work should rest with the director in the central office.

Every year there should be rotation of a certain number of personnel among field units and between the field units and the central office. This shifting of positions would include the assistant directors who would change places with the directors of the field units. The director himself would spend half his time visiting the field teams. The purpose in these contacts and exchanges would be to promote integration of the work as a whole, and to make the members of the organization familiar with all parts. As a result those who sit in the central office analyzing data that someone else has collected would understand its potentialities and limitations. Conversely, those who are making firsthand observations would be aware of how their findings would be employed in analysis. There should be a constant effort to spread widely among all members a knowledge of the total picture and to progress through accumulating, shared experience.

It would be necessary to make arrangements for the in-service training of personnel. The supply of already prepared social scientists is exceedingly small and it is only by such a program that there is any possibility of securing a staff. Even so, it would be wise not to set up the project all at once but to establish it in a series of steps taking on one geographic area at a time with gradual expansion of field units, and corresponding divisions of the central office. It is probable that arrangements could be made with universities so that in-service training would include some academic instruction and the granting of diplomas or degrees.

It would be well if the research could have the guidance of an advisory board in which there were present people with a number of different kinds of background. There should be members distinguished for experience in international relations drawn from the executive and legislative branches of the Government, from business and labor, and from among journalists. At the same time there should also be included a number of outstanding social scientists. Such a group if kept small could materially aid in the formation of the research policy and in bringing the results to effective use.

II

A unit within the Government for continuously following changes in factors that influence international relations is a step in the right direction, but it is not enough. Indeed, it is not even half a loaf, but must be supplemented and counterbalanced by work under other auspices such as universities and learned societies.

There are a number of reasons for this. The flexibility and freedom that exist outside the Government make possible a more active development of basic research with emphasis on the discovery of knowledge and the improvement of concepts. This does not imply divorce from application, but rather the long-range view as compared to the more immediate. Research, as a form of exploring, involves spending time and effort in many projects that prove fruitless in order to reap the few that turn out exceptionally well. The whole of science, as a matter of fact, had its beginnings when some individuals pursued lines of inquiry which the majority of people thought futile. Therefore, while applied research that is directly in the Government must of necessity be

The Use of Applied Social Science

restrained in spending man power and money for doubtful ventures, it should be the business of enterprises under other auspices to take "calculated risks." These include, of course, projects financed by the Government, but not a part of an operating agency.

In addition to playing such a supplemental role, the work developed outside should cover many of the same problems that are being investigated by the unit in the Government and field work should be done in the same places. This is to provide safeguards through checking by independent observation and it will be readily understood that such duplication is fundamental in scientific procedures. However, there are additional reasons arising from the fact that any organization in the Government exists as part of a political institution. There are limitations and dangers inherent in this position even when from the start special safeguards are established to make the applied research nonpartisan and nonpolitical. There will be times when it will be difficult or impossible for the scientists in the Government to assert facts about which the public should know. It might be that such utterances, if from an official source, would embarrass the United States in its relations with other countries, or they might produce reactions at home damaging to national welfare through violent stirring of domestic politics. There will also be times when the Government scientists will be able to state conclusions without hindrance, but will have them ignored and called unsound because some other view is more popular or politically expedient. In all such situations, knowledge and the expression of that knowledge from professional sources outside the Government can play a most important role.

In addition to supporting and supplementing the findings of the Government scientist, work carried on outside the Government can be a significant influence in keeping him functioning as a scientist. There must always be a temptation to yield consciously or unconsciously to the strong biases that bear down on anyone

185

who occupies such a position and to make "discoveries" that have more to do with getting approval than with fact. The people working outside the Government will not, of course, be free of bias, but for the most part theirs will be of a different order. Since their status and economic base is outside the Government they can exert a necessary corrective influence on those whose ties are within the political institution.

Another important function of non-government research is the prevention of unwarranted secrecy. Groups with positions of power within government frequently try to keep items of information hidden from rival power groups and from the public. This is in the nature of politics but it can be dangerous for the national welfare, particularly in a democracy where there is dependence on an informed electorate. The requirements of "national security" is a handy excuse, one of the oldest and most standard of the tricks for building power, and it could well be used to conceal the findings of an international research unit in the Government. Research and reporting from outside the Government would make such abuse difficult or impossible.

A further help from independent work would be in training personnel in accordance with the large need and relatively small numbers at present available. Such teaching could include assistance with the in-service training suggested in the previous section and it could also include the production of competent individuals and teams ready to fit into programs.

Turning to considering the form of such work, it is not likely that a unit outside the Government would have the same degree of integration and standardization that one would expect to find within. Rather than an over-all scheme, it would be more practicable for different universities to concentrate on different areas of the world, distributed among them by mutual agreement. However, for each such area there could be a unit that would have the general form suggested for the Government, namely, a central office with radiating field teams, and there should be some

The Use of Applied Social Science

pooling of effort in all the research through establishing an organization composed of the participating institutions. The purpose in the organization would be to share experiences, concepts, methods, and discoveries and to cooperate in the publication and distribution of information for specialists, for college teaching, for adult education and for the general public.

The ground plan for such a world-wide network of university research is already laid in the "area studies" now going forward. Thus, Harvard and Columbia are concentrating on Russia, Yale on Southeast Asia, Princeton on the Near East, Harvard, Yale and California on China, Michigan on Japan, and so on for many others. According to John W. Gardner, who has made a study of all the area programs, these projects range freely across departmental lines:

Experts are brought in from whatever fields seem to promise a genuine contribution to understanding of the area. And this "understanding of an area" is conceived in somewhat different terms than heretofore. Preoccupation with the past and refusal to understand present realities had done much to stultify earlier work by scholars dealing with foreign areas. The modern study lays stress on the problems that face us today. This does not imply a rejection of the historical approach. We must study the past and study it well in order to understand the present, but we cannot afford to get lost in the past.

Another distinctive feature of the modern area program in the universities is the new emphasis on the social sciences. We now realize that if we are to arrive at any genuine appreciation of another society, we must study its economic structure, its industrial potential, natural resources, social organization, political myths, class structure and so on. We are just beginning to recognize that we must forge ahead into the relatively little explored social psychology of other peoples; we must understand their motives, their attitudes toward their own form of government and towards the outside world, their fears and their aspirations.

This emphasis upon the social sciences does not suggest diminished attention to traditional subjects such as language, literature, philosophy and religious thought of a society. On the contrary, these so-called "cultural" subjects — so long regarded by the supposedly hard-headed realists as "impractical" — have taken on a new and practical significance. No "hard-headed" assessment of economic and military resources can explain the behavior of the Japanese Kamikaze pilots or the fanatical Russian defense of Stalingrad. Such performances are rooted in the psychology of a people. The literature, art, religion and philosophy of a people will often succeed — where statistics fail — in offering deep and meaningful insights into such matters.

The new area study sets a higher standard (than before the war); it assumes that the student will acquire both speaking and reading knowledge of the relevant language. . . . The student going on to higher levels of expertness will undertake actual field work in his chosen area as part of his training.

Finally it is an accepted practice in the best modern area programs that the students shall receive not only general training with respect to the area, but specialized training in some one professional field.*

As Gardner observes, although these developments are encouraging, they still have a long way to go. From the point of view of the suggestions incorporated in this book, there is need for a much keener recognition that social change is a continuous process requiring study by continuous methods so that directions and trends can be perceived and that relationships of one to another uncovered. The emphasis is still too much on individual experts rather than developing the teams capable of doing the enormous, but possible, work necessary to reduce guessing about social and psychological forces.

In concluding these points on international studies in both the Government and universities, something must be said about the United Nations. Ideally, the most thorough and extensive

* "Are We Doing Our Homework in Foreign Affairs?" by John W. Gardner, *The Yale Review*, Spring 1948, Vol. XXXVII, No. 3, copyright Yale University Press.

research of the type proposed should be under the auspices of that body. Unfortunately, it is not likely that this can be accomplished very soon on any major scale, but there is a chance that units could be established in such branches as the World Health Organization, the Food and Agricultural Organization, The Educational, Scientific and Cultural Organization, the International Labor Organization, and render service of the utmost importance in developing their programs. A most significant start has been made in UNESCO in the current study of tensions.

III

Change suffuses all nature. Evolution, growth, metabolism, radioactivity, and the movements of heavenly bodies are forms of change. If social change is another manifestation of the same universal process, then all we know of nature tells that this is something we cannot hope to stop, though we may be able to guide.

Perhaps there is a useful analogy in the growth of the animal body. Development from a single-celled fertilized egg to an adult creature is a coordinated and integrated process, rarely perfect, but in general fairly successful in spite of inconceivable complexity. It happens at times, however, that some groups of cells in a body grow on their own, not in coordination with the rest. If this persists, the body is eventually destroyed through the interruption of its functions. Wild, unbalanced growth produces freaks, monsters, paralyses and cancers.

Some of the problems in the national body that are related to international issues and to which social science might offer help were outlined in Chapter VI, section IV. They included race relations, the position of minority groups in the larger society, the state of the family, the social development of children, industrial and labor relations, the functions of government, changes imminent with the availability of atomic energy and the problem of clashing ideologies. These and other matters linked with them are all aspects of the fact that society is in a state of change, a state that has been accelerating in recent times. Because different parts of the society are not changing at the same rate, nor even in the same direction, there are increasing possibilities for, and instances of, breakdown. The trends in society run like currents in a sea, many across and opposed to each other, whipping up rips and turbulence. The task for social science is to understand these currents, their causes, direction, range of variability and the opportunities for adjustment so that family, community, minorities, classes, industry, unions, government, religions and the systems of belief that accompany all these institutions move better in relation to one another and do not, through independent elaboration, threaten the existence of the whole.

One approach to the national counterparts of the international problems is an adaptation of the method that has been suggested for the study of other countries, namely, social science "weather stations" both in and out of the Government for continuous observation, analysis and reporting.

On the Government side of the picture, there should be research organizations attached to both the executive branch and to the legislative. In the executive branch the purpose would be to provide aid to agencies so that they can more effectively carry out their assigned duties. Some distinguished work of this nature has been done in the Department of Agriculture under both Carl Taylor and Rensis Likert with the aim of making the programs of the Department adjusted to the needs and characteristics of rural people. Mention may also be made of the efforts by the Office of Indian Affairs to understand the groups with which it deals. The latter work has been sporadic, while the former has conformed more to the ideal of continuous observation and analysis for the purpose of detecting trends and uncovering the related causal factors. These two examples do not exhaust the list, but much more than exists is needed before the Government's role in labor-management relations, fair employment practices, public health, social welfare, atomic energy and much else can fit the realities of what is happening.

In the legislature there might be a similar continuing research unit so that both new laws and the influence of Congressional committees on the executive branch could have a more substantial foundation. It would also have a role to play in the Representative's duty to report back to his constituents concerning the state of the nation and the needs of the times as he sees them. There is at present a Legislative Reference Branch in the Library of Congress that contains able men and does good work, but not of the type here advocated.

Work outside the Government is much more advanced and shows signs of still further development. A major deficiency was the fact that organizations which followed trends were lacking in research of any depth into the causes of those trends. There is good indication, however, that this situation is now being remedied.

As far as relations with government work is concerned, the major opportunities for universities are the same as those that have been described in discussing research in international relations — supplementing and cross-checking, providing both stimulation for and support of good work, training personnel and aiding in the wide dissemination of discoveries.

There is, however, one problem area that deserves special mention because of a particular and imperious need. This is the study of our own attitudes and capacities for action toward other nations, the changes occurring in these attitudes and the underlying causes. Even very casual observation strongly indicates that our international behavior has major roots not only in what other nations do, but also in events at home. Our feelings about Russia, for instance, are to an important extent determined by feelings about changes within our own nation regarding the control of property, capital, labor, the functions of government, civil rights and the preservation of privilege. Regardless of attempts at rational distinctions, fighting Russia in either a cold or a radioactive war is inextricably mixed with fighting Communism on the home front.

And Communism at home is itself by no means a clear-cut issue. It is, rather, entangled with a wide range of different struggles between competing social trends and between social change and resistance to change. The expression "Communists and fellow travelers" is becoming a symbol which to each individual stands for all who are to the left of the position which he happens to occupy. It is also a target that affords a means of expressing aggression that arises from many and varied sources of stress on the domestic scene. Numbers of these sources have nothing to do with Communism, but involve postwar maladjustments, housing shortages, inflation and other economic difficulties, tensions in labor relations and much else. Both the Communist and anti-Communist movements are rallying points for the dissatisfied. There are lusty satisfactions in having something to blame and something to hate and there is an almost blessed relief in freeing oneself from painful but indefinable anxieties by attributing all to one malevolent influence for which there stands a well-recognized symbol. But such temporary relief is exceedingly risky since it means a situation in which a chain of complex but discernible social and psychological relationships strongly predetermine our views and actions in regard to the principal nation with whom adjustment is necessary. There is no sovereign remedy for this, but an understanding of the chains of relationships can help us lessen the confusion, be on guard with our emotions, and be more level and even in our actions. More understanding may lead to finding certain positive actions, such as relieving stresses and making democracy work, that are more fruitful than the negative expression of hostility. There may be an increased chance, then, to break away from those blind reactions that relieve feelings but make the long-run situation still worse.

A related, but in some respects distinct set of internal influences that affect external relations has to do with an apparent increase in mutual suspicion within our society. One cannot stress too much the danger in this kind of social pathology, and history both ancient and recent makes plain its contagious and self-destructive quality and the appalling atrocities to which it leads. As far as relations with other countries is concerned, it paves the way for projection of internal hostility and suspicion onto an outside group. This makes for an international kind of madness which we have seen plainly enough in the Germans, the Japanese and the Russians. If we too lose our heads, what hope can there be?

Another consideration is the rise and spread of rumor and the machinery by which this is maintained. What are the circumstances, for instance, that motivate and permit public men to spread falsehood and sensation? Many individuals who today have been making dramatic accusations "uncovering" Communist plots are the same persons who, during the war, "discovered" trained Japanese infantry on Terminal Island in California, a Japanese admiral masquerading as a cook, caches of food hidden in the desert to assist Japanese parachute troops and other items that had no basis in fact. The influence of these men was all on the side of costly errors in the wartime handling of the Japanese Americans on the West Coast. These errors were a drag on the war effort, cruel to the people affected and damaging to American traditions and practices in justice and the rights of citizens. There can be little question now that the matter was much better handled in Hawaii where there were no mass evacuations despite the fact that the islands were more vulnerable than the coast. The same individuals who took a leading part in spreading the false rumors that kept emotions at a high pitch and helped produce the mistakes continue today in a far more dangerous situation making themselves heard widely and effectively, without notice being taken of the kite's tail of past error that is attached to them.

Yet the problem is not essentially the individuals who do these things, but rather the social and psychological situations that permit them to have such influence. Personalities that are readily preoccupied with plots and spy rings are plentiful at all times, but when the general health of society is good no more attention is paid to them than is appropriate.

In times of frustration, doubt and uncertainty, however, the sensational stories of spy rings begin to reflect a prevailing state of mind and to have strong emotional appeal. Such stories, often in exaggerated form, come not only to reflect the fears and suspicions that are widespread in society, but also to increase these emotions and the confusion of the real and the unreal. Hence, mutual confidence and national solidarity are progressively damaged and attitudes on international issues are more and more skewed.

Bearing on the spread of rumor and public excitement are distortions in the presentation of news. Although there are many types of bias in the reporting of foreign affairs that arise from special interests at home, three general tendencies are certainly outstanding: emphasis on the surprising, the colorful and the entertaining; the presentation of Americans in a favorable light; and the presentation of enemies, actual or potential, in an unfavorable light. The net result is a lack of reliable information as a foundation for sound opinion on international relations.

These distortions in news have numerous causes. It is not sufficient merely to blame newspaper editors and owners and accuse them of trying to manipulate public opinion, nor on the other hand should one stop with asserting that it is all due to the public's taste and that the papers and news magazines must give them what they want to read or go out of business. The people who own and publish papers are a sub-group within our society and like the rest of us they act in response to the social and psychological forces that play on them. But, like other sub-groups such as doctors, lawyers, businessmen and union members, they experience some influences and situations which are peculiar to themselves. Distortions of news are a part of the way the journalist-publishing sub-group functions in the larger society. As general troubles and dislocations increase, there is a tendency for the distortions in communication to increase also.

At present most people seem to be vaguely aware that much of what they read is unreliable and are ready to say that newspapers usually have some sort of axe to grind. However, people do not as a rule have any idea how to distinguish the more from the less reliable in what they read. The characteristic distortions could be defined and their causes and effects brought to more general notice as a first step toward improvement.

A final example of trends within the society that affect international affairs is one that has to do with the way people are selected for positions that will bring them in contact with Russians or in which they will make decisions that will influence our relations with Russia. In all foreign relations careful screening is necessary not only to prevent subversive persons getting positions of trust, but also to keep out both unwise enthusiasts and those who have strong prejudices against the other country. Within these limits, however, there is a natural tendency for those to gravitate to foreign service or dealings with foreigners who like such contacts and such people. When our relations are satisfactory with a nation, as they are at present with England, we send people who will get on well and help make a good situation better. On the other hand, when suspicions and hostile feelings are in the air, as they are with Russia, there is a trend toward "leaning over backward" in selecting persons who will not in any way favor the other party. This means that more and more individuals are chosen who are least likely to mitigate suspicion and develop understanding, and most likely to be prejudiced and uncompromising and to make a bad situation worse. A sort of automatic social siphon is established that draws to the surface, interacting with Russia, a large percentage of those who have a high potential for anti-Russian decisions. The requirements of the situation are, of course, to tread carefully a difficult, narrow and dangerous path. In such circumstances, the "leaning over backward" cannot be regarded as a safe procedure, since it is just as bad to fall in that direction as it is to fall on one's face.

Perhaps the worst feature of the "siphon" is the indications we have that exactly the same social mechanism is at work among the Russians with the result that there is a progressive piling up on both sides of materials for an explosion.

These notes have touched on only a few points wherein it appears that our international attitudes are under the influence of conditions in our own society. Our capacity to cope successfully with international matters is dependent on our ability to resolve these home-front problems, many of which have a spiral character like inflation — they are the product of social dislocation and in turn make the social dislocation worse. In order to deal with the problems, we must understand them, their rise and fall and their effects on each other, what situations produce them and how they can be modified. To make studies of the areas of the world is only part of the required task. Of coequal importance is knowledge of those aspects of ourselves that bear on each of the areas. Without this, even great advances in wisdom about others must be liable to waste and misuse due to ignorance of ourselves. If "know thyself" is a good rule for individual men, it is a good rule for nations also.

There is need for an institute to tackle this range of problems on a continuous basis. It should have the size and resources necessary for a thorough and comprehensive job and facilities for disseminating its findings to both citizens and policy makers. It should not be under the Government, but should be backed by a board made up of people whose devotion to public welfare is established and well recognized. It is certain that the backing could not be a passive affair but would at times tax to the utmost all the members of the board as well as the scientists in the institute. A resolute investigation, with strict adherence to veracity, of such living problems as have been touched on here would alarm at one time or another the proponents of virtually all the social, political and economic ideologies. It would be difficult and dangerous work, but if it could accomplish the task of providing both public and policy makers with information and illumination in regard to the mainsprings of our international attitudes, it is hard to imagine a greater service that could be rendered to the nation and to the world.

IV

The proposals made thus far consist in suggesting opportunities for developing applied research more or less after the pattern employed by the Division in detecting and analyzing trends in Japan. In making these points, a number of other opportunities and needs come to mind, some of them critical to the success of applied social science in any form. The remainder of this chapter, therefore, will be devoted to notes on these related matters.

The Government itself is one item. Since it is through government that some of the most crucial acts by a society are carried out, particularly those that have to do with international relations, it is obvious that effectiveness will be limited by the quality of this social machine. Knowledge about other countries will make little difference unless it can be efficiently expressed in action. The skillful policy maker or executive is sometimes so handicapped by the organizations through which he has to work as to make one think of a musician trying to play a piano with boxing gloves. Applied social science could be brought to bear on such problems as: clique and faction struggles that produce waste and inefficiency; failures in communication and coordination between different parts of the Government (especially between Washington and field offices); the deception of Congress by executive branches; brutal, irresponsible and demoralizing attacks on executive offices by members of Congress; the stacking of rewards and punishments in Government positions so that people are not motivated toward doing a good job but rather toward watching out for their own security (even at the expense of the supposed goals of the work); the lack of reward for creativeness and merit; the extreme lack of democratic philosophy in some bureaus where the chief feels that he must run the show himself and the people in the organization feel little sense of participation.

Some beginnings along these lines have been made. During the war the Army Service Forces maintained research on the morale of the troops and this ultimately included studies of army methods in leadership and training. More recently, the Human Resources Committee in the Research and Development Board of the National Military Establishment has been created, in a position favorable for advancing this kind of work.

In the civil branches of the Government, the scene is barren of any comparable activity. Some time ago a start was made in the Bureau of the Budget and also in the Council of Personnel Administration (now called the Federal Personnel Council) toward evaluating Government procedures and practices in terms of what is known about man and society and toward programs of teaching and training. Attention was given especially to the matter of developing well-rounded executive and supervisory personnel and to the better coordination of departments and bureaus. Despite continuing effort by individuals, these and other plans have mostly died from lack of support and from the dangers of trying something new, disturbing tradition and facing rather than hiding human problems. They could, however, be regenerated in a climate of Congressional, executive and public encouragement.

The Use of Applied Social Science

The question of public encouragement leads to the question of increasing everyone's familiarity with, and use of, social science and the functional view of human relations. There appear to be at least three principal fronts for such development: educational institutions, publications and community activities.

In the field of education, teaching should begin in one of the elementary grades and continue through high school. Postponement till college results in missing vast numbers of people altogether and in missing important, formative periods in the lives of everybody. Each child could be given a minimum of conceptual tools and skills to employ in dealing with what goes on around him in the family, in school, at work, and in the community. Mental and emotional hygiene could save him from many mistakes and permanent psychological scars and at the same time could give him some understanding of healthy and unhealthy social patterns and his own responsibilities in relation to them. The topics dealt with might include, for instance, such occurrences as making an individual or a group a scapegoat, a pattern that is common in any schoolyard as well as abroad in the nation. In simple and concrete terms different kinds of social groups and how they operate could be examined, such as gangs, athletic teams, scout troops, factories, political parties, cooperatives, etc. Different kinds of leadership and followership could be compared, with particular emphasis on the latter. In our society, the functions and responsibilities of followership are eclipsed by preparation for leadership. As a result, since we are most of us followers most of the time, we are likely to become frustrated and disappointed leaders rather than people with insight and capacity for the position we do occupy.

The materials used in training along the proposed lines could be drawn from life in and around the school, from the community, from the study of history, and from the plays and novels used in English and foreign-language classes, as well as in books prepared on social-science subjects. The techniques of presentation should not only include those that are conventional, but also various forms of learning by doing and of "role playing" — acting out critical situations and analyzing them in group discussion.

In colleges, liberal arts education can carry forward to more advanced levels the social-science studies begun in the lower schools. This should include a conscious effort to present and give experience in the functional type of thinking discussed in Chapter IX, section IV. Attention would again be given to preparing people to be intelligently critical followers, able to form and express their opinions on plans and programs that effect local, national and international affairs. There would also be further experience in using social science as a frame of reference in understanding the interdependencies of human groups, in perceiving long-range effects as well as immediate results, in detecting the signs and symptoms of social pathology, in viewing one's own behavior with insight, in distinguishing constructive and destructive types of leadership and similar matters.

In addition to general education, there should be courses and laboratory experiments designed expressly for those training in such special fields as law, politics, teaching, religion, journalism, and medicine. Men and women preparing themselves for positions of leadership in government, industry and labor should have a major portion of their total college work in social science, with at least half of this spent on an original problem that requires firsthand interviewing and observing together with systematic analysis of the results. Administrators and policy makers who emerged from such a background as this could be expected to have a "feel" for the empirical approach to human affairs, to be less given to elaborate rationalism and less prone to action without knowing the pertinent facts and concepts.

It goes without saying that the production of social scientists is one of the major tasks of universities. In the case of those preparing for applied work, there should be an opportunity for practical experience in administration and policy making, corresponding to the suggestion previously made for giving potential executives experience in social science. Such "interneships" could be arranged in a variety of different situations including government offices, industries and labor organizations. Even for those who expect to specialize in basic research there would still be advantages in having a period of practical experience, for, as has been stressed before, many of the key steps in basic research in human relations, like the key steps in medical research, can only be carried out in connection with an applied program.

The number one problem, however, in training the social scientist is facilities. More training centers are needed and those that exist should be able to handle more students. Increased numbers of scholarships and fellowships are also required so that opportunities may be given to the ablest individuals; and there is a need for more liaison with government, industry and labor in order to establish the programs of practical training.

Before leaving the subject of university teaching, mention should be made of extension courses. If these are developed for social science along the lines now well established in agricultural and industrial fields, an important section of the adult population can be reached.

In regard to publications, there is a place for a periodical that would present for the lay public, in an interesting, readable form, two types of articles: reports on social-science discoveries and analyses of world events as viewed through social-science concepts. The reports on social-science discoveries would include not only current work on national and international problems and on the development of new concepts, but would also include older discoveries, bringing them up to date and examining them in the light of modern circumstances. The analyses of world events would be clearly distinguished from reports on scientific findings and would stand out as interpretation and expression of opinion. They would, however, be quite different from any existing news analyses because of the concepts linked to them, and because they would not push any policy or program but would attempt instead, to state the probable consequences and implications of each. They would point up questions and emphasize influences that are commonly overlooked. Political planks, the speeches of Congressmen, reports and announcements of policy by the President and members of the Cabinet, statements by unions or the National Association of Manufacturers could be analyzed from a cause-and-effect point of view, with opinions given as to probable outcome if alternative courses are followed.* There would be a conscientious effort to put a striving to understand social process in the place of preference for any party, clique, faction or class.

To have any chance of being successful, the periodical would have to be produced jointly by professional journalists and social scientists. This would be a complicated and difficult adjustment on both sides, but certainly possible. It is likely that it would also be necessary for the publication to be financed in the beginning by a foundation, although the ultimate aim should be to make it self-supporting.

The third and last area to be mentioned here for the developing of public familiarity with social science is the community. Communities can develop projects for the active utilization of social science in their own affairs and thus give people practice in the functional view in daily life. They might tackle, from this base, such matters as local disputes, race relations, general apathy to problems of public interest, rumor, delinquency, and many more; or, turning to the positive side, the creating of better opportunities for all members.

Such an activity should have its base in the community, though outsiders with specialized training can be called in to help start, to give technical advice and to provide instruction in special pro-

---

* Some interesting comments and suggestions along this line may be found in *American Opinion on World Affairs*, by Leonard S. Cottrell, Jr., and Sylvia Eberhart, Princeton University Press, 1948.

cedures. There are many organizations in which the activity could form, and these vary as to desirability from community to community. Obvious possibilities are the service clubs, women's clubs, community councils, cooperatives, church groups and unions. However, it is essential that the initiating group not be irrevocably identified with one faction in the community, but rather be capable of growth into something that has representation and participation from all major elements.

The twofold benefit of this kind of community activity would be the contribution toward a solution of local problems and the development of people with more understanding and capacity to act in national and international affairs. Through working with local human problems there could be developed a familiarity with the principles of human relations in the larger society. The person who has acquired insight into the cause-and-effect relationships in his own community regarding race attitudes, rumor, apathy, social change and resistance to change will be far more ready to perceive national and international issues in functional terms and less likely to be satisfied with explanations that do not go beyond bad men and evil plots. He will have a far better chance than he can ever get from reading or lectures alone to see the interdependence of society and how movements in one part affect others.

In concluding this chapter, it may be recalled that reference has been made to social dislocations and maladjustments taking a form like the well-known spiral of inflation in which each step calls forth the next in ever-increasing deterioration. It is well to point out now that remedial steps and constructive events have in reverse order the same spiral quality. The proposals that have been made here cover much territory and many aspects, but for that very reason each has a potential toward reinforcing the others. The beginning must inevitably appear small, slow and insignificant in comparison with need and the brevity of time. However, if the steps are scattered widely enough and are numerous enough, there is reason to hope that spirals of progress can emerge so that from imperceptible stirrings at the beginning adjustments can come that have far-reaching effects upon the society of the world.

CHAPTER XII

SOCIAL SCIENCE AND VALUES

Lastly, I would address one general admonition to all: that they consider what are the true ends of knowledge, and that they seek it not either for pleasure of the mind, or for contention, or for superiority to others, or for profit, or fame, or power, or any of these inferior things; but for the benefit and use of life; and that they perfect it and govern it in charity. — FRANCIS BACON

I

WE COME NOW, at the end, to a consideration that troubles most thoughtful people when they contemplate applying science to man himself. What will such efforts do to human values? Is not the functional view essentially mechanistic and amoral? Is not social science in conflict with ethical and religious values, and with concepts of rightness, and does it not threaten their destruction?

This may be the case, and if so, we are lost indeed; for the findings of social science itself make plain that sweeping destruction in systems of belief of this sort is something which neither individuals nor societies can tolerate. There is the possibility, however, that the idea of battle lines, with science on one side and human values united together on the other, is false. It may be that in reality there is extensive conflict between many different kinds of values and that social science includes one kind that is in the jumble with the rest.

It is surely obvious that many of the ideas of right that people hold do contradict each other and play a part in numerous struggles. Consider the clashes between religions, between isolationism and internationalism, between individual freedom and the prerogatives of the state, between democracy and white supremacy, between patriotism and the concept of the world citizen, between liberalism and conservatism, between competition and cooperation, between "the integrity of the family" and careers for women, between the golden rule and common business practices, and so on through a long, long list.

One reason for these conflicts is the process of change and expansion in society. All the steps in knowledge since before the beginning of recorded history, all the inventions, all the new ways of making a living, all the philosophies and systems of thought, all the changes in human relations with progress from tribe to city state, city state to nation, and nation to United Nations, all these have brought with them new values at every step. The new values have always jostled their predecessors, displaced some, modified some and fitted pretty well with others.

With this perspective it is evident that social science does not "threaten basic human values;" it is merely one among many forces threatening some values and some dogmas through upsetting the assumptions that underlie them. It makes explicit and brings into the realm of critical discussion vague and implicit values current in the cultures of the world. Many values are strengthened. The Sermon on the Mount has for a long time been generally accepted in the Christian world as one of its main statements of ideals. Yet much of the Sermon has failed to materialize in customary action. The admonition to love your enemy, for example, is generally treated as a splendid idea but one that is not very practical. It seems a strain on human emotions that few people can meet, or even try to meet. The functional approach to human affairs, however, is in keeping with the idea that love, at least to the extent of seeking understanding and the elimination of vengeful motives, cannot be treated as a remote ideal, but is indispensable to the welfare of mankind.

As part of the accelerated changes and contradictory cross-currents in society, values today are probably more confused for more people than they have ever been in the history of the world. Consistency and stability can only be found in a few remote and simple cultures, and even these are disappearing year by year under the impact of increasing communications and greater and greater interdependency of all parts of the world. It is a wild tangle and there is need for some kind of order, some evolution of agreement, so that first things stand a chance of coming first if there is to be survival and general happiness. Social science has some role to play in this by unraveling causal and sequential relationships, detecting hidden incompatibilities, indicating the long-range as well as the short-range effects of practicing different kinds of values. However, the ordering of values is far too vast a matter for offhand discussion here. All that can be accomplished is to offer a few observations regarding that border line where social-science values touch on or interlock with others.

II

One often encounters the fear that social scientists will sell their skills to "conscienceless manipulators." While there is little possibility of overestimating the importance of this danger, it must be recognized that it is not a problem of social science alone, nor even of science alone. All great knowledge, all discovered powers, all human organizations, whether courts of justice, churches, or any other, can be misused. With each advance of civilization in the control of nature, and with each more efficient organization of society, there has come with the potential for new achievement a corresponding threat of disaster.

In this setting the social scientist has a responsibility for directing his work toward the welfare of mankind just as the physician has, but, like the physician, he shares this responsibility with others and cannot fulfill it unless the society of which he is a part understands and supports him in the effort. Responsibility for what the social scientist does also rests with those who employ him in government, industry, labor, universities, and foundations; and with the journalists, educators, and religious leaders who criticize and interpret his work; and with the public, whose opinion, right or wrong, has the greatest power.

Coupled with the fear of manipulation there is usually found the belief that social science, or at least the applied aspects of it, should be abandoned. This is an impossible solution. The clock cannot be turned back and social science cannot be withdrawn now from the web of life any more than knowledge of chemistry or the know-how of industry. Such efforts can, however, delay and deform the growth of knowledge in this field until disasters force the issue or eliminate the problem and us. The fact that there is no going back to innocence is wisdom our race learned long ago and cast in such stories as the expulsion from Eden. We have eaten the fruit of the tree of knowledge and must make the best of it. The hope now is in more knowledge, not less. Attempts at restriction only hinder responsible effort and leave the ground open for thick settlement by the undesirables. We are already socially and psychologically exploited for purposes that have nothing to do with the welfare of society. At every turn our physical and emotional needs, our spiritual urgings, our anxieties and our aspirations are baited by people who wish to condition us so that they can sell us something or otherwise use us for their own ends. In magazines, for example, attempts to play on our feelings for ulterior purposes are not limited to pages marked "advertisement," but occur in stories and illustrations where clothes, furniture and other articles are described in such a manner as to whet the appetite or make the reader feel he is socially inferior unless he acquires them. At least one national magazine has had the frankness to state publicly that its editors "know how to implant these mental pictures that so compellingly send women in more than 3,500,000 homes off on *buying* expeditions." The italics are theirs. The same techniques are used to sell ideologies and to intimidate opposition.

There can be no automatic devices at present to prevent manipulation, but two things can help: having as much social science as possible placed where the allegiance is to the whole of society and not to one element; and spreading everywhere knowledge regarding the principles of human behavior. The more people there are who have some insight into these matters, the more difficult it will be to succeed in tricks and the more demand there will be for wholesome use. It is for this reason that so much emphasis has been placed here on making the findings of social science widely known. This has been done with full realization of the fact that in the early stages of the struggle for recognition many first-rate projects will be exterminated because their findings, though true, are unwelcome. These projects will be made to suffer the common fate of the bearer of ill tidings. Nevertheless the only protection for society is common knowledge and this means forging ahead, not holding back; it means doing high quality work and doing it openly.

III

Of coequal importance with the problem of keeping social science from being used by special groups for purposes destructive to the general welfare of mankind is the problem of keeping social science operating as a science. Those who stress the moral responsibility of the scientist frequently urge him to be polemical and complain about his lack of moral indignation. Such people say in effect, "Come over on our side and help with your science in the good fight, but leave behind you the viewpoint upon which all science depends."

The maintenance of objectivity is a foundation without which other considerations can matter little. When a scientist ceases to be a scientist he ceases to produce in the field of his competence and is in this respect lost as a contributor to the solution of society's urgent problems. Worse than this, he may, due to retaining the trappings and prestige of science, become a false prophet and lead followers astray. Disaster arises not only from selfish design, but also from well-meaning error.

This returns to the points made earlier regarding the grave difficulties that always beset the human-relations scientist and the constant effort needed to control the pressure of feelings, his own and others. The scientist requires support and understanding from his fellow members of society in this matter just as much as in preventing the misuse of his skills and knowledge.

The dangers of destroying science must be matched with the dangers of misusing science and there is need for order in the relationship between non-scientific values and those inherent in science. Otherwise, emotional, moral, religious and aesthetic sources of human development can be harmed by pseudo-science, while science is destroyed by the introduction of assumptions that are not part of it.

A formula for such ordering is easily stated and may, indeed, be compressed into two sentences. *Within an area marked off for scientific investigation, the values of science reign supreme over each step in the process toward conclusions and in the conclusions themselves. Moral values when pertinent dominate scientific values at three contiguous points: the selection of the problem to be investigated, the limitation of the human and other materials that may be used, and the determination of what shall be done with the results.*

Although this principle is not difficult to present in the abstract, when it comes to specific application, the complexities and perplexities are enormous and varied. It is only through experience with particular cases that it can become, like common law, a living way of doing and deciding.

It is likewise through particular cases that the meaning of the principle can best be further presented and illustrated here. If

The Use of Applied Social Science

the notes that follow seem too narrative and personal, they may at least have the virtue of being actual, not hypothetical illustrations.

During two years at Cambridge University I had an opportunity to associate with leading scientists in the field of physiology. They had great energy, a capacity for exactness and a capacity for spreading their minds with the aid of mathematics and chemical formulae over incredibly detailed and complex ramifications of nature. On the other hand, they had vivid imagination, often reflected in original traits of personality. Adrian, who made outstanding discoveries in nerve function, would emerge from exhausting hours of exquisitely painstaking work to pedal his bicycle down King's Parade to the fencing club and there get refreshment through wearing out younger opponents. Matthews, his calm partner, liked to spend vacations in transcontinental auto races that might take him from John o' Groat's in Scotland to the heel of Italy. Barcroft, the blood physiologist, was a magician in the use of words, but he could rarely spell them and would stand nonplused before a blackboard when trying to write out a statement for his students, saying plaintively, "May I give you a rough phonetic sketch of the words I mean?"

From imagination and originality came the concepts and theories which enabled these men to break new ground. However, this was combined with the utmost stringency in devising checks to establish validity and a capacity for ruthless rejection when significant flaws were found. Their imaginations were strong, capable of leaps into the unknown, yet astoundingly disciplined and not allowed to escape from harness.

Although their science was sheltered from most of the pressures that beset social scientists, it was exposed to the constant danger of too much attachment to a theory. It takes fortitude to reject an idea that has filled your mind for months or years and which has come to be the star to which your wagon is hitched. One may readily begin reading the signs in its favor and omit thinking of the experiments which might disprove it. Precision instruments are no sure protection, for they are always in the hands of the human being who uses them. One afternoon a biochemist from Caius College sitting on a lab bench told me of how he had spent many months on an experiment which served to confirm the theory of a professor whom he respected. Years later, he said, it became evident that the theory was inapplicable. He repeated his experiments and got a different result, one which fitted the newer ideas.

"I thought I did those first experiments with objective accuracy," he said, "but I know now that I was unconsciously influenced by the professor's scientific stature. As a result, whenever I read the swinging pendulum in weighing a substance, or determined the end point of the color change in an indicator I introduced a slight bias in favor of my expectations. The many slight errors in the same direction mounted up. You can't be too careful."

Where, in contrast to "pure" science, "applied" science is concerned, the task of remaining true to induction based only on observation and experiment is still more difficult. This is so even when the scientific problems have boundaries that are infinitely more clear than is the case in human relations. Once when studying at the Academy of Natural Sciences in Philadelphia, I was a witness to a situation in which this was made very clear.

In certain parts of the country it was then the policy of the U. S. Biological Survey to seek the complete extermination of predatory animals said to be harmful to agriculture, an action which was fought with vigor by individuals and organizations interested in conservation. Both sides claimed science as their authority and endeavored to press scientists into service.

It was the consensus of scientific opinion that the practices of the Biological Survey were unsound and that, as a result of ignoring the realities of ecological balance in nature, both ranch land and the areas around were being harmed. Insect plagues, for instance, were thought to have been encouraged in some regions.

There were many scientists, however, who made their living as employees of the Government, either with the Survey or with some related department. While many of these refused to yield to a pressure that they should find "facts" to justify the current policy, some did give in with or without the self-deception that is so easy when one's own aspirations are involved, and they lapsed from the role of scientist. They forged the name of their profession on testimony to aid a special interest that was nourished on the political influence of farmers and ranchers who had sweeping prejudice against "varmints" and no understanding of natural balance.

The scientists who worked in universities and museums for the most part lent active support to the conservationists. They supplied information, served as educators and suggested workable plans which gave consideration to the ranchers as well as to the values of preserving wildlife.

There were some among the conservationists, however, who were not satisfied with this. They pressed the scientists for endorsements of dramatic and emotional exaggerations, for the suppression of facts regarding damage actually done by some kinds of animals, for having it "proved" that no kind of predator or rodent control was necessary, for presenting tentative hypotheses which happened to favor the conservation view as if they were established principles, and in general, for going beyond the limits allowed by scientific evidence and concepts.

Some of the scientists went along with these conservationists. This was easy to do (again with or without self-deception) under the influence of a strong belief in the rightness of the conservationists' aims. I was one of those so carried away, but I noted with some irritation that the men whom I respected most as scientists remained as meticulous about the truth in this matter as in any other and did not permit their sympathies to make a difference at any point where the scientific process itself was involved. On the other hand, those who succumbed to conservation bias became muddled, lost in a tangle in which scientific fact and what they wanted to think were indistinguishably mixed. Regardless of motive, they committed forgery just as certainly as did those employed by the Biological Survey, and like them lost much of their capacity to function and their power as scientists.

Science, it would seem, is a service that demands allegiance and imposes a discipline. It may be turned like a searchlight in response to moral, aesthetic and utilitarian values, but there can be no claiming by the scientist to see beyond the area illuminated, and within that area there must be no tampering. The penalty is failure of the light.

At the Johns Hopkins Medical School and Hospital I became acquainted for the first time with a situation in which there was daily interaction between moral values and the scientific process and in which the relationship between the two had come to work effectively. The leading clinical teachers made it clear that a primary value was the welfare of the patients, a master consideration guiding scientific inquiry, limiting the materials it might use and determining what should be done with the results.

Yet within this framework science operated and was protected from interference. What the research doctor or the diagnostician observed and his interpretation of these observations were not matters to be influenced by the patient's hopes and fears, by the hospital board of trustees, by the moral judgments of society, or by the physician's own desire for the patient. Experience made it evident that when personal or popular wishes influenced findings and judgment, medical skill deteriorated with results harmful to patients and stunting to the progress of knowledge. A man had or did not have syphilis according to what could be observed and tested, regardless of who he might be or his social position. The children of a slum area were found to have or not to have rickets according to examination and not according to anyone's desire to start or prevent a slum-clearance project.

Emotions were played down and the need to unravel the relationships of things to each other was stressed. Germs were not personalized or regarded as objects of fear and hate, but as elements in a process — a process which, if understood, might be altered. The retention of this attitude was far from simple, since the participants in the struggle between health and illness, between life and death, were real and suffering persons. However, it was my observation that those who did the most for the sick were not those who got most excited but those who best maintained the functional view.

"Don't think them heartless," says John Brown, M.D., in his classic *Rab*, ". . . in them pity as an *emotion*, ending in itself or at best in tears and a long-drawn breath, lessens, while pity as a *motive* is quickened, gains power and purpose."

In psychiatry the same relationship existed between moral and scientific values as existed in the other clinics, and there was a similar emphasis on understanding rather than reacting emotionally. However, where in medicine there had been some help in keeping non-scientific values out of the restricted field of scientific inquiry, because organs and bacteria are essentially impersonal, in psychiatry the factors significant in a patient's illness were the loves, hates, hopes and fears, the interpersonal relations, the conflicts, the ambivalences and the beliefs in values which make up in some degree the life of everybody. The physician at every turn had to deal in ideas and behavior which were prone to set going strong appeals or revulsions in his own feelings regarding what is desirable and what is intolerable.

Adolf Meyer, a Swiss and the son of a Protestant minister, made those who worked with him at the Phipps Clinic of Johns Hopkins feel his strong sense of respect for the patient as an individual. At the same time, he was meticulous in his scientific thinking and viewed the behavior and urges important in the illness as one would view the relevant forces in typhoid fever. The questions asked were: What works, what doesn't work so well and what doesn't work at all? What are the contributing factors? Why? What can be done about it? not, Who is right and who is wrong?

Such an approach to the problem of mental illness is very different from the one that was common in Western civilization and in other areas for many centuries. Those recognized as insane were regarded as possessed of a devil, with numerous additional religious and moral assumptions which resulted in rituals, beatings, and torturings. In the course of time, it became customary to have physicians in attendance at asylums to treat the physical ailments. As medicine developed, these doctors began to look on the behavior of their charges more and more from a scientific point of view and to drop from their thinking not only the idea of lurking devils, but also "wilfulness," "stubbornness," and "own fault."

The first medical conceptions ran to organic causes and investigation proved these true for many types of illness, as, for example, paresis. There still remained patients, however, especially among those not ill enough for hospitalization, in whom no organic disorder could be found, and this blank wall drew attention to their behavior as related to experiences of infancy, their current life situations, and the nature of their instinctual and emotional urges. The ideal was developed that the patient was not properly a focus for anger or fear, nor on the other hand one whose ideas should be uncritically espoused, but was both a person and a phenomenon to be understood.

The painting of Pinel striking the chains off the inmates of the Salpêtrière, copies of which so often hang in the offices of mental hospitals, symbolizes the introduction of humane treatment. It might also be said to symbolize a removal of the chains imposed by traditional assumptions and to mark the introduc-

The Use of Applied Social Science

tion of inquiry. The major advances in the treatment of nervous and mental disease from which millions have benefited have all been made since that time.

In our present-day thinking about the motives of human groups — labor relations, race relations, international relations — we are still, except for a narrow littoral, in the Dark Ages, seeing everywhere possession by devils. It is the human relations scientist's business to see as few devils as possible and in their place dynamically related forces to be understood. He has to mark off carefully the boundaries of his problem and within these boundaries strive to maintain the concepts, values and methods that are part of the scientific process. The social forces under consideration must not be treated with heat but with light, with the same interest that would be pertinent toward molecules and ions in physiology, the animals and plants in a problem of forest ecology, the hormones and organs in medicine, and the human complexes and conflicts that concern psychiatry. This does not involve self-excommunication from human feeling or carrying this attitude everywhere in life. Within the problem area, however, it does call for an open, inquiring, nonassertive kind of mind, working with assumptions and hypotheses of varying degrees of reliability from the very tentative to the fairly well established, but never with creeds.

This applies to one's own favored ideas as well as those which others may thrust upon him and urge him to adopt. He must be particularly wary of those nonscientific values with which he most sympathizes. All biases are poisonous to science, but the worst are those that appeal strongly to the scientist.

This course is not easy, but if there is another road in science it has not been found.

IV

Let us look back for a moment to the place at which we began, to man's first use of atomic energy, to the remains of Hiroshima.

Human Relations in a Changing World

All that culminated there and all that it portends for the future challenge human values and the moral nature of man comprehensively and with a finality that has not been faced before. There have been, in the past, times and places when particular human beings have achieved peaks of moral worth, but these have not been sufficient. It is a question now of achieving and sustaining a higher general level.

Social science, with its dangers and its possibilities, is a party to this challenge. It does not threaten basic human values if by these are meant belief in God, love of one's fellow men, desire for wisdom, and pursuit of truth, but it does threaten error, the cultivation of comfortable delusion, the use of moral values as props for selfish advantage. If the social sciences are to develop, they must have a social medium in which there is freedom to search for and share knowledge, widespread active concern for human welfare, absence of tyranny and a flow of force from the grass roots, a cooperative rather than a predatory competitive base, courage to face the new and the uncertain, and above all, a devotion to truth and to dealing honestly with oneself and with others. Such things do not undermine human ethics, but they are a test of the character of man, a test which he must meet or else submit to the many-colored, mushroom cloud, "like a globe of the world spinning."

EPILOGUE

POKING in the ruins of Hiroshima one day and thinking about the clock in the bank with its hands at 8:10, I came on the stone figure of a dog, one of that grinning type derived from China which commonly guards the entrances to temples. It was tilted on its pedestal, but undamaged, and the grin gleamed out as if it were hailing me. Its rakish air and its look of fiendish satisfaction with all that lay around drew me on to inspect it more closely.

It was then apparent that the look was not directed at me, but out somewhere beyond, in a way that brought home my little-ness and insignificance. It was, of course, only a piece of stone, and it displayed no particular artistic merit, yet in looking at it I felt that I was the clod, while it had a higher, sentient wisdom locked up within.

The look and the feeling it inspired were familiar, and I tried to remember where I had seen it before. The eyes were creased in a fashion that did not exactly connote mirth and the lips were drawn far back in a smile that seemed to blend bitterness, glee and compassion. The word "sardonic" came to mind, and this led to recognition and a realization of terrible appropriate-ness.

All who have had acquaintance with the dead know the curious smile that can creep over the face as *rigor mortis* sets in, a smile of special quality known in medical language as *risus sardonicus*. The dog had this look and it seemed to me probable that some ancient Oriental sculptor in seeking an expression for temple guardians that would drive off evil spirits had taken this death grin as his model, and thus it had come down through hundreds of years to this beast looking out on Hiroshima.

219

Epilogue

Many a soldier has seen this face looking up at him from the field of battle, before he himself wore it, and many a priest and doctor has found himself alone with it in a darkened room. As with the dog, at first the look seems to be directed at you, and then beyond you, as if there lay behind it knowledge of the huge joke of life which the rest of us feel vaguely but cannot comprehend. And there is that tinge of compassion that is as dreadful as it is unknowable.

As I continued to study this stone face it seemed to me that the grin was not directed at the waste and the destruction around, at the red and yellow and the smells, any more than it was directed at me. It was not so much a face looking at Hiroshima as it was the face of Hiroshima. The carved eyes gazed beyond the rubble, beyond the gardens of radishes and fields of winter wheat, beyond the toiling adults and the rippling children with their tangerines and shouts of "Hallo-goodaby!" surging up with new life like flowers and weeds spreading over devastation, beyond the mountains with red pines in the blue sky, beyond all these, over the whole broad shoulder of the world, to where in cities and towns clocks on wrists and public towers still ticked and moved. The face seemed to be smiling and waiting for the harvest of the wind that had been sown.

APPENDICES

APPENDIX A

SPONSORS AND MEMBERS OF THE
FOREIGN MORALE ANALYSIS DIVISION

THE following is a list of the persons associated with the project. Previous professional training or civilian occupation is given in parentheses followed by a descriptive title of work in the Division. Since there were some changes in personnel, the total number is greater than the actual size of the project at any one time.

Sponsoring Committee

Dr. George E. Taylor (Historian, Far East), Deputy Director for the Far East, Office of War Information.

Colonel E. W. Gibson (Lawyer, Republican Senator from Vermont), Supervisor of Research, Military Intelligence Service, War Department General Staff.

Dr. Harold M. Vinacke (Historian, Far East), Chief of the Japan Section, Office of War Information.

Colonel John Wesley Coulter (Human Geography), Chief of the Sociological Branch, Military Intelligence Service, War Department General Staff.

Personnel Contributed by the Office of War Information

Dr. Clyde Kluckhohn (Anthropology), Co-Chief of the Division.

Dr. Morris Edward Opler (Anthropology), Assistant Chief and later Chief of the Division.

Dr. Ruth Benedict (Anthropology), Senior Analyst.

Dr. John Embree (Anthropology), Senior Analyst.

Dr. Frederick Hulse (Anthropology), Senior Analyst.

Dr. Dorothea C. Leighton (Psychiatry and Anthropology), Senior Analyst.

Mr. William M. Doerflinger (Journalism), Editor.

Dr. Katherine Spencer (Anthropology), Analyst, Supervisor of Processing.

Mr. Royal Hassrick (Anthropology), Analyst and Assistant Supervisor of Processing.

Appendix A

Mr. Iwao Ishino (Community Analysis, Public Opinion Surveys, Japanese Culture), Analyst and Assistant Supervisor of Processing.

Dr. Herman Spitzer (Psychoanalysis), Analyst.

Dr. Elliot Fisher (Sociology), Analyst and Processor.

Mr. Yoshiharu Matsumoto (Community Analysis, Japanese Language and Culture), Analyst and Processor.

Mr. Tom T. Sasaki (Community Analysis, Japanese Culture), Analyst and Processor.

Mr. Toshio Yatsushiro (Community Analysis, Public Opinion Surveys, Japanese Culture), Analyst and Processor.

Mr. Robert S. Hashima (Japanese Language and Culture), Translator, Analyst and Processor.

Miss Rose Matsumoto (Japanese Language and Culture), Translator and Processor.

Miss Florence Mohri, Division Secretary and Stenographer.

Miss Frances Payne, Division Secretary and Stenographer.

Miss Atsuko Aoki, Translator, typist.

Miss Helen Holt, Clerk-Typist.

Mrs. Edna L. Quillin, Clerk.

Personnel Contributed by the Sociological Branch, Military Intelligence Service, War Department General Staff

Lt. Col. Felix E. Moore, Jr. (Sociology and Statistics), Chief, Japan Section, Sociological Branch.

Tech. Sgt. David F. Aberle (Anthropology), Propaganda Analyst.

Tech. Sgt. Y. B. Goto (Japanese Language and Culture), Translator-Analyst.

M/Sgt. Keith Kaneshiro (Japanese Language and Culture), Translator-Analyst.

Mrs. Agnes W. Brewster (Sociology), Propaganda Analyst.

Mrs. Mary E. Maltman (Sociology), Propaganda Analyst, part time in the Division.

Dr. George D. McJimsey (English Literature), Analyst and Processor.

Mr. Edward K. Merat (Political Science), Propaganda Analyst.

Miss Jerodene E. Tuck, Clerk-Typist, part time in the Division.

Miss Roberta Garner, Clerk-Typist, part time in the Division.

Personnel Contributed by the Navy

Commander Alexander H. Leighton, Medical Corps, USNR (Psychiatry and Anthropology), Chief of the Division.

Appendix A

Lt. Marion Levy, Jr., USNR (Sociology), Analyst and Processor.
Commander George Townsend Lodge, Medical Corps, USNR (Psychology), Training in preparation for assignment in Civil Affairs.

(The combined Army, Navy and Office of War Information personnel, working in collaboration, were ultimately named the Joint Morale Survey which was jointly directed for a brief period by Leighton and Moore. Since, however, most reports were issued as from the Foreign Morale Analysis Division, that title is employed in this book.)

Special Consultants

The Members of the Sponsoring Committee.
Dr. Owen Lattimore (Far East).
Dr. Charles Hepner (Japanese Language and Culture).
Mr. John M. Maki (Japanese Political Affairs).

Liaison

Dr. Florence Kluckhohn (Sociology), liaison with Office of Deputy Director for the Far East in the Office of War Information.

APPENDIX B

CURRENT PSYCHOLOGICAL AND SOCIAL TENSIONS IN JAPAN

June 1, 1945

SPECIAL REPORT V

OFFICE OF WAR INFORMATION

Bureau of Overseas Intelligence
Foreign Morale Analysis Division

TABLE OF CONTENTS

I. PRINCIPAL CONCLUSIONS

A. *Current Situation*

1. There is no evidence that any significant number of Japanese have lost confidence in the purpose of the war.

   Concerning Japan's capacity to win the war, however, there is grave doubt, and a considerable number already feel that it cannot be done.

2. As with the attitudes toward the righteousness of the war, so in the attitudes toward the Emperor and the Imperial Institution there is no indication of any weakening in popular faith.

   Regarding all other leaders and officials, from the Cabinet down to the neighborhood air-raid protection unit, there are both satisfaction and dissatisfaction, with the latter mounting.

3. The faith of the Japanese people in each other has been in some respects consolidated and strengthened due to their being under attack, but on the other hand it has been reduced by conflicting opinions regarding the way the war is being managed and what may be expected in the future.

4. The Japanese adjustments to the war have been extensive and have increased as the stresses have become greater.

   To a degree sufficient to be of major importance in psychological warfare, however, this is being counter-balanced by definite trends toward organization breakdown, confusion, decreasing effort, and resistance to the adjustments and compensations imposed by the needs of the war situation.

5. The general health of the Japanese people is suffering deterioration.

6. The emotional tendencies of the people, reflected in social changes, may be described as having five components:

   a. Some people are inspired to greater energy and determination which can move them either toward suicidal resistance, or to fighting for some sort of compromise that will seem honorable to them.

b. Some people are showing a variable type of activity in which they seek by "trial and error" and constantly shifting methods some escape from their stresses.

c. Some people have developed a high degree of anger and aggressiveness that is directed at others in Japan. They are blaming various leaders and groups of Japanese for the predicament the nation is in.

d. Some people are panicky and prone to hysterical outbursts and to flying from one extreme to another.

e. Some people have become apathetic, slowed down in their efforts, and imbued with defeatism.

It is difficult to say which trend is the most prevalent at present but there is some reason to infer that it is apathy.

B. *Future Developments*

The warning needs to be sounded that none of what has been said means that Japan is on the point of collapse or will be easy to invade. Most Japanese are conditioned from childhood to withstand hardships, are rigorously trained to endure physical discomforts, and are inculcated with a high esteem for such endurance and sacrifice. Similarly, the enormous strength of the Japanese mystical and religious systems of belief and their hold on the people must be considered in the balance. These beliefs have the Emperor as the focal point and as the symbol which binds the entire nation into one family where ideally each member has his place and where the highest duty of each member is to conform to the will of the whole, no matter what the cost.

Therefore, the weaknesses in morale due to psychological and social tensions now current in Japan are counter-balanced by sources of considerable strength.* Taking both elements into consideration, the following general tendencies may be expected:

1. There will long remain many energetic and determined Japanese in all walks of life, but particularly among the military, who will wage a desperate last-stand fight and will endeavor to force others to do likewise.

* The qualifications in these two paragraphs were not originally a part of the report but were introduced at the insistence of policy makers in the Japan Section of the O W I.

2. Extreme tendencies of the type just described will be countered by a determined effort on the part of other people to save Japan from devastation by ending the war.

3. There will be an increase in the amount of criticism and hostile feeling between various kinds of Japanese as the war situation grows progressively worse and they will blame each other more and more for the nation's predicament and their own sufferings.

4. As time goes on, there will be an increase in general fear, in emotional tension and in episodes of panic.

5. General apathy, resignation and slowing down of effort will increase among all classes of Japanese, but will be most characteristic of the lower economic and social groups in both city and country.

6. The downward trend in Japanese morale may take a long or a short time before it reaches a point that makes possible the termination of war. The military pressure brought to bear will be the principal controlling factor, but of major significance will be the degree to which most of the Japanese continue to believe that the Allies intend:

   a. To kill, torture or enslave the Japanese people.

   b. To destroy the Japanese way of life with its Emperor and related values.

C. Implications for Psychological Warfare

An outline of the implications of the conclusions for psychological warfare is given on page 258.

II. FOREWORD

This report contains much that is psychiatric interpretation.

When a psychiatrist — or any other kind of physician — approaches a patient to make a diagnosis, he has in mind a set of general concepts regarding the way human beings function, in good health or in poor health.

Appendix B

After making as objective an examination as possible he compares his specific findings with his general concepts and from this formulates his diagnosis, which is in essence an hypothesis concerning the patient's condition. Future events and further checking serve to confirm, modify or negate the preliminary conclusions.

In the present report the symptoms of the social body in the Japanese homeland are examined and some diagnostic conclusions are attempted. A statement is made concerning relevant general concepts of individual and social behavior and then the best established picture of the major stresses in Japan is reviewed. Combining these two and using them as a frame of reference, a diagnosis is made in the light of current intelligence data, and this is presented as a description of the reactions to stress at present going on in Japan. On the basis of this, future trends and implications for psychological warfare are discussed.

At the end an annex is attached which gives an account of the kind of data employed in constructing the interpretative picture.

III. STRESS

A. *Types of Stress*

The following specific types of stress, in proportion to their intensity and duration, are disturbing to all human beings:

1. Threats to life and health.

2. Discomforts from pain, heat, cold, dampness, fatigue and poor food.

3. Loss of means of subsistence, whether in the form of money, jobs, business or property.

4. Deprivation of sexual satisfaction.

5. Enforced idleness.

6. Restriction of movement.

7. Isolation.

8. Threats or harm to family members and close friends.

9. Rejection, dislike and ridicule from other people.

10. Unpredictable behavior by those in authority upon whom one's welfare depends.

Derived from these specific types of stress are a number of a more general sort:

1. Persistent frustration of goals, desires, needs, intentions and plans.

2. Circumstances that promote the dilemma of conflicting and mutually incompatible desires and intentions.

3. Circumstances creating confusion and uncertainty as to what is happening at present and what can be expected in the future.

B. *Stresses in Japan*

The following is a summary statement of certain over-all conditions in Japan. It is derived from Japanese home front and Home and Empire broadcasts, newspapers, captured documents, and prisoner of war interrogation reports, and is thought to be reliable. On this basis it may be presumed that the Japanese are suffering the majority of the types of stress just listed.

1. *Subsistence, Work and Shelter*

Food is everywhere deficient in both quantity and quality. Regular prices are rising in spite of measures to prevent inflation, while there is widespread black market activity.

Work is characterized by long hours, few days for rest, forced savings, and high taxes. All workers are under continuous pressure to produce more.

Migration to industrial centers has caused over-crowding and other housing problems in Japan just as it has in the rest of the world. Recently these difficulties have been intensified due to the bombings, which have not only destroyed buildings directly but have also affected the housing situation by making it necessary to tear down structures to make firebreaks to evacuate people from urban centers, and to decentralize industry.

Appendix B

The problems of subsistence and shelter are further complicated through grave difficulties in transportation by highway, railroad, and water.

Lack of fuel not only hampers transportation and industrial production, but it also reduces the amount of bathing (a matter of special importance to the Japanese).

The fuel shortage and the scarcity of clothing and materials for making wraps make living uncomfortable in winter.

2. *Health*

The general health of the Japanese people is deteriorating. There is malnutrition plus lack of medical personnel and facilities for taking care of the sick and the bombing victims. The government admitted during the Diet interpellations in February, 1945, that the physical condition of Japanese youths had declined.

The health situation gives suggestive evidence of the extent and degree of the detrimental living conditions.

3. *Social Dislocation*

As in other countries, the war has caused extensive social dislocation in Japan. Millions of men are in the army and millions of both men and women have moved from their homes into other parts of the country to participate in war production and similar essential jobs. There have also been migrations in the opposite direction of persons being evacuated from city to country.

The whole education system is disrupted. After a period in which there was drastic curtailment of colleges, middle schools, and even some technical schools, and after children were evacuated and then permitted to move back again, finally all schools in March, 1945, were made secondary to the mobilization of students for production needs.

These social dislocations are particularly disturbing in Japan for two reasons.

First, they have been very extensive.

Appendix B

Second, they are detrimental to Japanese family structure and the feelings and values that go with it. The absence from home of young men and women for long periods, deaths in battle, and a total population in the homeland in which women out-number men, all operate to hinder family and neighborhood unity and to prevent marriage and endanger the carrying forward of the family.

4. *Fear of Losing the War*

Very few people in Japan today regard victory as certain, and many are sure of being defeated. They know that the Japanese Army is losing ground; they know the Navy has not been able to keep supply lines open and to keep U. S. task forces away from Japan; they know their country is being severely bombed; they know they lack a sufficiently strong air force; and they feel that invasion of Japan is not only possible, but imminent. Related to all this is the conviction, going back at least several generations, that the West is superior to Japan in material strength and technical knowledge.

In addition to the above, the Japanese know that with Germany out of the war, U. S. and British power against Japan will be greatly increased, and that Russia is unfriendly.

In the event of defeat, most Japanese expect to be enslaved, starved and physically mutilated.

IV. REACTIONS TO STRESS

A. *Individual Reactions to Stress*

When individuals are exposed to any considerable combination of the types of stress that have been described, several reactions usually occur. Of the four primary emotions which all people feel, three — fear, anger and sadness — increase in both frequency and intensity while the fourth — gladness — decreases. As a result of this imbalance, individuals alter their behavior according to their basic personalities, the habits and customs of their culture and the opportunities of the immediate situation.

235

Appendix B

The resultant acts, however, are not of infinite variety, but tend to fall into a limited number of patterns which may be described. Some of the more important are as follows:

1. *Well Directed Action*

People may strive to come to grips with the sources of the stresses they feel in order to achieve release. As a result, they put forth greater effort, work longer hours, respond well to orders from those in authority, cooperate willingly with each other and are prepared to endure even worse hardship if it promises ultimate security.

2. *Variable Behavior*

Others feel that "something can be done; something must be done" but are skeptical of the existing plans for action. Hence, they embark upon or suggest a great variety of new projects. But their enthusiasms do not last very long. Such persons manifest the kind of variable behavior ("trial and error" responses) characteristic of animals caught in a trap or placed in a threatening and unfamiliar situation from which they cannot discover a route of escape.

3. *Aggression*

Aggression of a controlled sort is, of course, an ingredient in what has been described under *well directed action*. However, anger and the need to vent that anger immediately on some object can become so intense that it breaks out of control and leads to attacks, not on the enemy, but on substitutes and symbols that are much closer at hand. These substitutes are commonly people distinguished by clique, class level, minority status, race, or residence in a particular geographic area. Needless to say, such behavior may obscure real issues and increase, rather than decrease, the stress situation. In fact, because of the compelling nature of the need for aggressive expression it often leads, when once aroused, to extraordinary flights of inappropriate behavior. Hate can be more blind than love.

4. *Emotional Instability*

People who become emotionally unstable cover the range of emotional activity, now quivering with fear, now towering with rage, now grieved and dejected, and now buoyed up by fantastic hopes. As a result their behavior is inconsistent and shifting; they try many things and complete few.

5. *Apathy*

Numbers of individuals slow down in their talk and bodily actions. They retire into themselves and cut off, as much as possible, contact with those events in the world around them which arouse the unpleasant and unrelieved feelings of fear, anger and sadness. Sometimes this walling-off takes the form of a rather empty apathy, as if half asleep, with verbal expressions of fatalism and preoccupation with trivial but immediate details of life. Other persons develop a fantasy world in which bitter realities are displaced by wishful day-dreams.

In any large group of people, the distribution of the above five kinds of reaction among the members is not static. The same individual may show two or more of the reactions at different times or even at the same time. For the group as a whole, however, there will be, according to circumstances, a dominant trend from one type of reaction to another. Thus in a healthy society, stress within limits leads mainly to the kind of behavior that has been outlined under *well directed action*. On the other hand prolongation of the stress without relief sooner or later leads most of the people to apathy and perhaps ultimately to destructive types of aggression and emotional instability. This is not an absolute correlation but is the general story of how individuals behave under lasting and progressive hardship. Their individual morale is exhaustible and while some stress is a tonic, too much is poison.

People do not, of course, all change at once, since stress is unequally distributed and in addition they have individually many different thresholds of tolerance. At any given time some persons can be found who exemplify each of the five reactions. Yet in the long run there is likely to to be a general shift for most people in one of the directions indicated.

B. *Social Reaction to Stress*

Since we are ultimately concerned here with a society under the stress of war, it may be useful to regard this society as a huge machine attempting to manufacture a victory. This machine is made up of millions of individuals who interact with each other according to the only habits and values they know, and who form groups that constitute the major moving parts in the machine and are coordinated by a system of governors and controls that come from the top down and out to the farthest corners. The power of the governors, however, is limited by the capacities, attitudes and habits of the individuals who make up the moving parts.

The capacity of such a machine to manufacture victory will be influenced by two inter-related types of changes. The first consists in the military and political actions of other societies and the second consists in alterations in the parts of which the machine is composed. While both go on simultaneously, it is the latter which is the subject of attention here. It may be described as follows:

1. When the types of stress outlined under III-A above, become severe an overall result is a general deterioration in working capacity. People suffering from threats to life and health, and from emotional disturbance, cannot work as well as those whose basic living needs are being met. The general drop in working efficiency means a decrease in production and other activity necessary for the war effort, over and above what may be imposed by lack of raw materials and similar difficulties.

2. From those people who react to stress with well directed activity, there come attempts at compensatory adjustment aimed at keeping up production and fighting capacity in spite of the current weakening. One result is an effort to make up for lack of individual efficiency with greater numbers and longer hours. Thus people are drawn into unaccustomed work, and additional aid is secured from those with low working capacity such as the aged and the very young. There are technological improvements, and organizational adjustments are made by rearranging working groups and leaders, particularly at the lower levels in the power hierarchy. However, all such change is well coordinated and purposeful, with both flexibility in adjustment and conformity to the orders from higher authority.

3. From the people who show the variable "trial and error" type of behavior, also, there comes increased activity, but it is of a disorganizing and inefficient sort. New schemes are constantly being formulated for meeting the stresses, but they are then dropped before being properly established and are replaced by still newer plans and actions.

Appendix B

4. The people who become aggressive to the point of beginning to attack, by words or deeds, various groups and leaders, are a potential source for tremendous change in the organization of a society. As the number of such persons increases, the first effect is a widening and deepening of the lines of cleavage and conflict which normally exist between leaders and followers, among leaders, and between various inter-acting sub-groups in the society. This, of course, interferes with the capacity of the social machine to accommodate and adjust to the forces of stress. The power which the society has for aggressive expression, instead of being directed altogether outward at the common enemy, is thus in part turned inward on the society itself, to the detriment of production and fighting efficiency.

With further increase in the impulse to aggression as the stress remains unrelieved, explosions begin occurring which result in radical change in social organization. Some old groups disappear, while new and powerful ones arise and conflict with each other, often with extremes of violence. The social machine may come to spend much of its energy in tearing itself apart, because its different sub-groups develop into a number of autonomous machines which attack each other. In such a state of individual and social disorganization, habits, customs and traditional ways of behaving give way to far-reaching alterations. Numerous new patterns of leadership and new alignments in the society become represented by various slogans and formulas for remedying the situation, many of which are contradictory or mutually exclusive.

As the feeling of unity in the society as a whole fades, those people who are disposed to cooperation pin their loyalty to one or another sub-group and become divided from each other. Thus while the whole social machine grows weak, some of the sub-divisions (cliques, factions, social levels, families, and other groups) become more closely knit within themselves, and stronger.

However, if the force of stress continues unabated and if such groupings cannot meet the needs of the individual members, then these sub-groups go through the same cycle of disorganization as the larger society. Thus social chaos has many stages and degrees, and it is common to find one or more well integrated sub-groups in a society which is on the whole extensively disorganized.

239

Appendix B

5. To the above may be added the effects of emotional instability and general jitters. These lead to abrupt and repeated changes in the running of the social machine, which result in lack of coordination, misinformation, and rumors of disaster, betrayal, and atrocities. In consequence, reorganization and attempts at adjustment flounder. Additional reorganizations are piled on top of them only to misfire and be overlaid with still others. Unsuccessful attempts at compensation bring new stresses and are followed by compensations for the compensations, in accelerated confusion.

   It need hardly be pointed out that this trend in events increases rather than decreases most of the types of stress outlined under III-A, particularly the last three listed, and thus a vicious circle is formed.

6. The people who react to stress by cutting down on their activity and developing outward apathy retard the operation of the social machine and present a viscous resistance to the increased efforts, reorganizations and other compensatory actions that have just been described.

   The apathetic reaction — indifference and the desire to avoid initiative — is at all times present in a society and is of great importance in the maintenance of stability.

   During stress it continues to operate and thus, while it slows down or nullifies remedial changes, at the same time it equally inhibits all tendency to radical action, to widespread disorganization of the group relationships in the society or to alterations in the leadership patterns.

   As the trend becomes more widespread there is likely to be an increase in the seeking of solace in fantasy life. Religious bodies find their membership and influence increased, while new sects and cults appear, often primarily concerned with forecasting bright prospects in this or in a future life and with communication to and from the dead. Leaders who are able to use mystical appeals for whatever aims they may have, gain in popular support.

   In any society under stress, all six of the trends presented above will be found going on simultaneously. The critical question is which trend will achieve dominance. As has been noted previously, stress in moderate degree stimulates improved functioning of the

240

social machine, whereas excess and prolongation lead to deterioration which may be actively self-destructive as far as the total social body is concerned.

The ultimate result can take several forms. The society can finally adjust after a fashion at a low grade of organization and strength, or after having burned itself to ashes it can arise again like the phoenix, coalesced about some new philosophy and new system of leadership and sub-group relationships. In extreme cases it can become extinct altogether or in part as a result of the members' inability to maintain health and to feed and clothe themselves.

However, the great brake on the process of destruction is the social inertia arising from what has been decribed previously under apathy (III-B). If the social machine fails to achieve relief from stress in an acute stage of stepped-up efficiency and cooperative activity, there may be swings to fierce internal conflict, but chiefly it is prone to lapse into a state which resembles a chronic but never fatal illness. In this condition, while the main body of the society provides a slothful, stable matrix, members of the sub-groups may continue to battle with each other or live parasitically on the docile mass and even carry on outside wars, for the fact of being attacked by some other society strengthens and builds cohesion in the aggressive groups. Thus in spite of extensive social disorganization a society can have great tenacity and can last through defeats, economic depressions and famines and can survive its own inefficiency and wastefulness.

C. Reactions to Stress in Japan

If it is assumed that the range of reactions to stress just outlined apply to the Japanese, and that the types of stress now existing in Japan depicted under III-B are as stated, then it should be possible to combine theory and fact in such a manner as to see a little beyond the point at which "hard" evidence is available. Viewed in such a light, current intelligence on Japan warrants the following *inferences:*

1. General Reduction in Working Capacity

By and large, Japan's productive capacity is inadequate for meeting its current war needs. In differing degrees she is short of planes, ships, ammunition and other supplies, and of manpower. While much of this is due to sheer inability to match the strength of the enemy and to lack of raw materials, some portion is also due to the lowered working efficiency of the people themselves, resulting from physical debility and emotional disturbance.

2. *Readjustment and Compensation*

In Japanese culture there are deeply entrenched patterns of loyalty and conformity to group opinion which facilitate those readjustments in the society that spring from the kind of reaction to stress that has been described as *well directed*. Consequently, as stated previously, Japanese adjustments to the war have been extensive and have increased as the stresses have become greater.

Among the peasants there has been an intensification of farming, with women and younger children filling in for the men who have gone to war. The long-run effectiveness of this, however, may be doubted, since before the war the Japanese peasant family was already working close to the limit.

Factories have expanded and stepped up production. This has been greatly aided by feudal patterns of loyalty and protection existing between workers and owners. At the same time "domestic industry," in which family units in their homes formerly made such items as toys, has been converted to assembling motor parts and similar work.

For some types of labor, such as coal mining and stevedoring, large numbers of Koreans, perhaps two million, have been imported.

The business groups in Japan, as in all countries involved in the war, have been put under associations designed to control production and distribution. Most of the personnel in these associations have been recruited from the business men who previously controlled the industries. The result has been an adjustment of former organizations in line with government requirements. Small businesses, however, have in many cases been adversely affected, either abolished or incorporated into larger institutions.

Some of the greatest changes throughout the structure of the society have involved women, since they represented the nation's greatest reservoir for labor power. Women have stepped into much work formerly reserved for men in both country and city, and have increasingly assumed positions involving management and direction. Many jobs are now reserved by law exclusively for women. Even in family affairs, in the absence of men, women have assumed more responsibility. This development has involved conflict with custom and basic values in many parts of the society, and in consequence the trend has been delayed by various resistances, but that it has occurred demonstrates the capacity of the Japanese for adjustment.

Children and students have made extensive contributions to volunteer labor. The closing of school classes above the elementary grades has been resorted to, at least in part, in order to permit the fuller utilization of such workers. Older people who would normally be in retirement are actively working, and criminals also are being used.

A number of "Special Attack Corps" for labor have been formed, with members pledged to work at hard tasks for incredible hours, until they drop from exhaustion. Their chief function, however, is probably for morale building rather than actual contributions to production. Recently there has been a movement to enroll all Japanese in "Special Attack Corps" of various types.

3. *Variable Behavior*

In recent months there has been a steadily increasing volume of material from enemy sources reporting shifts in high official personnel; changes in administrative set-ups; reversals or re-phrasings of major policies; criticism of governmental action (or lack of action) by newspapers, members of the Diet, and individual citizens; proposals for a variety of contradictory courses of action; charges and counter-charges; and numberless inconsistencies. In part, this burst of activity undoubtedly represents a powerful and realistic response to the gravity of Japan's situation and the threat of imminent invasion — the readjustment and compensation which have just been discussed.

In the variety, vacillation, and mutual inconsistency of these "solutions," however, there is more than a little suggestion of the reaction of frenzied desperation to the actual insolubility posed by stubborn and irreducible facts.

Appendix B

In terms of individual response to stress some of these strivings represent:

a. Mutual self-deception on the part of the general public. The public veils the true situation from itself by strenuous activity (whether realistic or purposeful or not). A shadow world is developed in which constructive things appear to be happening, although in the actual world the Japanese are futilely beating their heads against the wall of reality.

b. A conscious diversion created by the leadership to deflect from themselves the aggression brought about by growing awareness among the Japanese people of the consequences of the disastrous policies which the leaders have carried out; that is, the leaders, by playing up home defense measures, are trying to convince the people that something can be done and that something is being done.

4. *Conflict Within the Society*

In addition to the well-known capacity of the Japanese for solidarity, their culture also gives them channels for expressing the inter-group aggressions which all people feel, and which become heightened at times of stress. From the country village to Tokyo there are forms of political and economic conflict at all levels which have in the past and can in the future run to such extremes as assassination of leaders, civil wars, and local mass revolts which follow a fairly consistent pattern of organization and leadership.

In a situation of emotional pressure, aggression in Japan has an opportunity to make destructive inroads on social organization. This is because the aggression arises in a context of mysticism, a tendency to extremes, an intolerance of uncertainty, a love of simple, obvious solutions and a high esteem for sudden, decisive action.

Ordinarily in Japan there is a balance of strong authoritarian controls counteracting covert or oblique tendencies to resist them. Both operate in a medium composed of a vast population where most of the people most of the time want to avoid trouble and are living a life in which there is a minimum of individual choice and a maximum of convention covering all human situations. When this balance is interfered with, the stage is set for clashes between hostile groups and for much confusion and bewilderment among the people, who then miss many of the customary guides upon which they rely heavily.

It is important to keep these points in mind in comparing the expected behavior of the Japanese civil population with that seen in military units where social homogeneity has been high and whose members are not only fired with national zeal, but also are hemmed in by a battle situation which in their opinion gives them no choice except to fight until dead.

Japan has not yet reached a stage of explosive internal conflict, but the pre-existing conflicts between some groups and sub-groups in the society are growing stronger.

a. City residents in Japan are far less homogeneous in their customs and values than are the people of the country, and have been more influenced by Western ideas and values. They are also suffering more from lack of food and, of course, from bombing. Always somewhat contemptuous of country people, they now show a stepped-up attitude of hostility toward the peasants, feeling that they are in part responsible for the lack of food through lying down on production and through hoarding. The tension is further heightened by the movement of many country people into urban production areas where they are ill-adjusted to the mode of life and annoy the city dwellers.

In the country, on the other hand, it is felt that the urban people are responsible for the heavy taxes, for the low prices paid for farm produce, and for the lack of much-needed manufactured articles such as clothes and fertilizer. It is thought that the soldiers who come from the big cities do not fight as well as those from the country and so let the others down.

There has also been an influx of former urban residents into country districts as a result of evacuation and industrial decentralization. Because of their poor adjustment to rural life and the strain they constitute on the housing and subsistence facilities, the city people are further increasing the hostility of the peasants.

b. To a lesser extent, there is mistrust felt by the residents of different cities for each other. Osaka has been singled out especially for adverse comment by people from other areas.

Appendix B

c. Wider and larger regional differences also play a part. It is well known that the inhabitants of Okinawa have been long regarded as not quite Japanese and hence to some degree inferior. To a lesser extent Hokkaido is considered as a place apart. Regions responsible for the production of commodities that are painfully scarce, such as coal, are probably targets for the resentments of other districts. Traditional clan loyalties and differences of view also play a part in regional cleavages.

d. The Koreans who have been imported for labor are feared and suspected of plotting against the Japanese. They are an obvious scapegoat of considerable importance. It may be recalled that in the earthquake and consequent fire in Tokyo in 1923 great numbers of Koreans were massacred. At present the Japanese Government is having difficulty trying to get work out of the Koreans, while at same time preventing them from doing harm or becoming the point of attack in a public disturbance.

e. Little is appearing on the surface about the Eta, Japan's low caste minority, but it is probable that they are liable to accusations of not doing their best in the war and in general are becoming a focus for blame in the many dissatisfactions people are feeling. The Eta, on their side, are probably harboring numerous deep resentments against the unofficial discrimination they suffer and for the accusations made against them.

f. The intellectuals — that is, people with higher education, and especially those who have traveled in Europe or America or have had other contacts with Westerners — are a source of concern to others and to themselves, and they occupy an uncomfortable position. They have long taken a gloomy view of Japan's hopes in the war, and have always hated the military system and its "thought control." They are not strong proponents of the emotional "fight to the end, even if with only a bamboo spear" type of nationalism. Although they are found among the members of the Government, politicians, the military and the business groups, they are not in harmony with many of the policies advocated by these groups and privately desire to see the war ended as soon as possible, even if it means giving up a certain amount of "face."

g. Students are to some degree disciples of the intellectuals. On the other hand, many are firebrands full of energy and passion and with little wisdom or experience, and so are easily swept away by military glamor, or were until recently.

A different type of student are those who are neither intellectuals nor yet budding suicide attack-corps members, but are youngsters under great pressure to work long hours in factories or fields. Numbers of them have not taken kindly to the program, but desire more glamorous occupations, and have had to be alternatively coaxed and threatened by the authorities.

h. Women are gradually becoming coordinated into groups, some of which may eventually be capable of unified action on a large scale. At present, however, the principal significance of women in the Japanese social machine is the extent to which they are members of a wide range of different groups and exert more or less indirect influence. As mothers and wives, or prospective mothers and wives, and as sisters, they are intensely concerned with the welfare of family members over and above the problem of self-preservation common to all people. As a consequence of this orientation and the intensity of feeling which accompanies it, women are as a whole, in spite of cultural trends to the contrary, less likely than the men of their social group to go along with plans for a dramatic fight to the end. There will be variations in this, of course, and some women will no doubt be examples of extreme fanaticism.

Once convinced that defeat is certain, the women are prone to take a very practical though conservative tack toward making the best of the situation and salvaging as much life and welfare for family members as possible. If terminating the war appears to offer them such opportunities, then national pride and the spirit of *Bushido* will not weigh so heavily with them. On the other hand, to the extent they are convinced that defeat means extermination of their families, to that extent they will exert supreme effort to carry on the war. It must also be noted that they are more ignorant than the men and therefore more retentive of traditional views and harder for us, the enemy, to reach and convince.

i. In the realms of politics, cleavages between different cliques and factions are becoming more evident. The evaluation of the plots indicated in these changes is in the province of the political scientist. However, from the point of view of interest in psychological and social tensions, the fact that political change is occurring as part of a total process in the society is very significant.

These political moves indicate not only scheming and counter-scheming by various cliques within and without the Government, but also indicate, as part of the cause, the dissolution of solidarity, the existence of hostility between factions, lack of clarity as to aims and methods and, above all, a roughened sea of rising public fear, hostility, and confusion. The maneuvers of the Government and the political parties are in part responses and in part measures aimed at control.

j. The Army has been losing prestige in the eyes of the general public as a result of its defeats, and has been reacting to this by trying to strengthen its hand wherever it can on the home front. At the same time, its old enemies, in the business interests, the civil Government and the Navy, are taking a stronger stand against it. Although opinion is not uniform within the Army, a major clique advocates a fight to the end, with the hope and perhaps expectation that they can inflict such losses on the Allies that a compromise peace will be achieved. They are trying, therefore, to extend their control, especially over industry and home defenses.

k. Business groups, on the other hand, are resisting Government control, and especially Army control, wherever they can. They have countered the Army's proposal of militarizing industry with a scheme for creating an "industrial army" which would have business men at the head of it. At the Diet interpellations in February, the Government showed weakness when questioned regarding the control of privately owned railroads and similar enterprises. It may be supposed, therefore, that the power of individual business interests is considerable, and it is not unlikely that some would at present like to see the war stopped in any manner that would promise them an opportunity to save some of their livelihood and investments and some hope of continuing in the future. It is probable that of all groups, they most clearly see the industrial power of the Allies and the hopelessness of uncompromising resistance.

Appendix B

l. The Navy is smarting under its loss of prestige, and even more under its loss of ships. Traditional hostility between it and the Army has been increased. It is trying in a rather frantic manner to secure public recognition, even claiming a fictitious victory at Formosa and playing up the fighting of its sailors on land in the Philippines. It may well be that the Navy would rather see the war stopped, than lose out further in playing its all in the defense of the homeland.

m. The regional administrative councils are in conflict with local Army and Navy commanders. The issues are air-raid defense measures, control of industries and the training of home defense guard. It is of interest that to date the home defense guard or militia is affiliated with the food production program and is not under the control of the Army, though it will pass into such control should invasion occur.

n. There exist in Japan a number of radical "secret societies" who have a definite interest in seeing the Allies win and who hope then to set up a liberal or a communistic government, taking advantage of the complete discredit of the existing rulers and their system, and of the suffering of the common people and their willingness to follow any one who will give them relief. At present these organizations are very much below the surface, but they listen to the Allied radio and get intelligence through other sources.

o. The Japanese Government and that large aggregate of individuals of all sorts and affiliations who may be termed "the public" are to some extent blaming each other for the war situation. The people say variously that the Government has bungled the conduct of the war, is ineffective, interferes where it has no business, does not take a strong enough stand in seeing that things get done, has too much red tape, does not trust the people, does not inform them adequately as to what is going on, does not tell them what to do, so that their desire to contribute is being wasted, has got the country into an economic muddle in which the food-supply situation is desperate, and does nothing to control black markets.

In some of these points the reader will note resemblances to our own public sentiments and may therefore be tempted to write them off as having little significance, on the assumption that since they are not serious with us they probably are not serious with the Japanese. Such a view loses sight of the fact that we are winning the war while the Japanese are losing it. Many of our present public sentiments, such as protests over rationing, would indeed be indications of bad morale if the Japanese were about to land on our coast. Furthermore, the available intelligence suggests that the extent and intensity of these public attitudes in Japan are such as to make them significant for our psychological warfare and for anticipating the trend of events in Japan.

5. *Instability*

Mercurial changes in the sentiments of the Japanese and in their social organization are already occurring. Most outstanding have been the panics in some of the cities during the bombing raids. Rumors ranging from those that are fantastic ideas of imminent collapse in the United States to false alarms of our troops already landing in Japan have spread in various regions from time to time. The past history of the Japanese shows that they have under some circumstances a tendency to hysterical group movements, and it is a matter that is giving the authorities much concern. The authorities themselves, however, are not immune, and there is a desperate note in much of their homefront propaganda, particularly in the last four months.

6. *Slowing Down and Apathy*

There is a trend toward decreasing effort and even resistance to adjustments and compensations. This is a type of behavior in response to stress that has a well recognized place in Japanese culture. It is just as much a part of the Japanese way of life as is the capacity to make supreme efforts. In a situation where there is an audience before whom to play and where there are dramatic opportunities which are soul-stirring to the Japanese, such as a suicide attack, they may be capable of astounding performance. If on the other hand it is a question of misery without glory in a hopeless situation, then the Japanese may think of the common slogan with which they endure the inevitable — "*Shikata ga nai*" — "There is nothing to be done about it."

Appendix B

In such an atmosphere there is a drift toward accomplishing personal and private aims rather than those which are national.

This reaction, always present to some extent, is now increasing and interfering with the various types of effort noted in the preceding section.

Many factory workers are not doing their best while on their jobs, and there is a significant amount of absenteeism.

In the country, there are farmers who are slacking off in their efforts, and some are resorting to the age-old Japanese peasant's defense against hard times and high taxes by growing little more than is required for their own subsistence needs.

There is considerable hoarding in both town and country and extensive black market activity. These are fostered largely by people with the apathetic trend, since they turn more to the consideration of their own immediate needs than to anything else.

Evacuation and air-raid precaution activities were slow and ineffective, in many areas at least, until the bombings became severe.

Drives to collect silver and other materials for the war effort have in some instances been far from satisfactory.

Mistrust of official statements and information has been widespread in Japan since long before the war and has existed side by side with active compliance to authorities. During the last year this mistrust has become greatly increased, heightened by the inconsistencies and false statements that have become apparent in the home front propaganda lines. Such suspicion and uncertainty are weakening the will to follow the Government leads and even leading to oblique and passive forms of resistance. They have not only helped build an audience for our broadcasts to Japan, but have also disposed that audience to credit some of what they hear. The Government has reacted to this and other circumstances by permitting more and more accurate statements to be made concerning the war situation.

Most noteworthy has been the Government's repeated and widespread campaigns against defeatism and lack of effort.

The seeking of solace in fantasy life and in mystical comforts is increasing, but so far has not greatly affected the society as a whole.

There is reliance on the belief that spiritual superiority will overcome material superiority and that if they "hold out to the end" and fight even with "bamboo spears" they will somehow win. The Emperor as a symbol of Japanese spiritual power and a magical father protecting his people is coming more to the fore. The general trend has been extensive enough to force the Government in some instances to launch counteracting propaganda which emphasized that it is work and machines which win in modern wars.

In this situation of growing apathy the Japanese tendency to go with the herd, which gives great strength under some circumstances, such as a suicide charge, may operate in the opposite direction. That is to say, as more and more people show slowing down of effort and activity, the greater becomes the force for the spread of this behavior to other people.

V. GENERAL SUMMARY

The overall picture for Japan may be summed up under the five major factors thought to underline morale, when morale is considered as the capacity of a group of people to pull together consistently and persistently in pursuit of a common purpose.

1. *Faith in the War*

There is no evidence that any significant number of Japanese have lost confidence in the purpose of the war. Most regard it as just or at least inevitable, though different kinds of people use different arguments in backing their convictions, and these range from altruism in Asia to simple self-defense.

Concerning Japan's capacity to win the war, however, there is grave doubt, and a considerable number already feel that it cannot be done. Some are hoping that if the war is made sufficiently costly to the Allies, a compromise can be achieved which will be satisfactory for Japan.

Appendix B

2. *Faith in the Leaders*

As with the attitudes toward the righteousness of the war, so in the attitudes toward the Emperor and the Imperial Institution there is no indication of any weakening in popular faith. In fact, there is an increased tendency to draw on the comfort of regarding the Emperor as a divine father able to protect his "100,000,000 children."

In regard to all the other leaders and officials, from the Cabinet down to the neighborhood air raid protection unit, there are both satisfaction and dissatisfaction, with the latter mounting. Mistrust of official statements and information has been common in Japan since long before the war, but during the last year this has become greatly increased.

3. *Faith in Each Other*

The faith of the Japanese people in each other has been in some respects consolidated and strengthened due to their being under attack, but on the other hand it has been reduced by conflicting opinions regarding the way the war is being managed and in regard to what may be expected in the future. Various economic, political, social and regional conflicts that existed before the war between different kinds of Japanese have become heightened.

4. *The Organizational Efficiency of Japanese Society*

The Japanese adjustments to the war have been extensive and have increased as the stresses have become greater.

This, however, is counter-balanced by definite trends toward organization breakdown, confusion, decreasing effort, and resistance to the adjustments and compensations imposed by the needs of the war situation. There is a drift toward the accomplishment of immediate private and personal aims rather than national objectives. In part, this confusion and disorganization stems from major changes brought by the war, such as the breaking up of families, the closing of schools, evacuations due to bombings, migrations of industrial workers, the absorption of a large part of the male population into the armed forces, the entrance of women into new occupations and the severe deterioration of the transportation and communication facilities. In addition to this, however, as the war has gone progressively against Japan, there has been a tendency to try more and more different organizational schemes in an effort to find some solution. This has appeared in the form of numerous reorganizations and shifts in leaders in many parts of the Government and is likely to continue in the future at an accelerated rate.

Thus, while the Japanese believe in the righteousness of their way of life and ideology, at the same time there is a widespread feeling that something must be done to improve the present state of affairs, and this leads to changes which in many instances increase disorganization and multiply confusions.

5. *Health and Emotions*

The general health of the Japanese people is suffering deterioration. There is malnutrition together with lack of medical personnel and facilities for taking care of the sick and the victims of bombing. Public health measures in the cities have suffered from lack of manpower and from the effects of bombings, and in the country large concentrations of evacuees are creating conditions detrimental to health.

The emotional tendencies of the people, reflected in social changes, may be described as having five components:

a. Some people are inspired to greater energy and determination which can move them either toward suicidal resistance, or to fighting for some sort of compromise that will seem honorable to them. Such people make positive contributions to all four of the previously mentioned morale factors — faith in the purpose of the war, faith in the leaders, faith in each other, and faith in the organizational efficiency of the Japanese wartime society.

b. Some people are showing a variable type of activity in which they seek by "trial and error" methods some escape from their stresses. They have a feeling that *something* must be done to improve the present situation, and this leads to rapid changes which in many instances only increase disorganization and confusion.

c. Some people have developed a high degree of anger and aggressiveness, directed at others in Japan. They are blaming various leaders and groups of Japanese for the nation's predicament. Although the solutions they propose vary greatly and the proponents are of many types, they are alike in having a high degree of animus which they want to vent on someone.

d. Some people are panicky and prone to hysterical outbursts and to flying from one extreme to another.

e. Some people have become apathetic, slowed down in their efforts and imbued with defeatism. Such persons are not very responsive to the leaders and contribute little to mutual faith in the struggle. To the organizational efficiency of the society they constitute a dead weight, and they largely make up the company of those who seek their immediate private ends before anything else.

These five general types of emotional reaction are not rigid classifications of individuals, for the same person can pass through various stages at different times or endure the conflict of feeling several simultaneously. On the whole, however, some of the members of almost every kind of Japanese group display each of the five emotional trends.

Which trend is the most prevalent at present it is difficult to say, but there is some reason to infer that it is apathy (e).

VI. DISCUSSION

It should be emphasized that none of what has been said means that Japan is on the point of collapse or will be easy to invade. Most Japanese are conditioned from childhood to withstand hardships, are rigorously trained to endure physical discomforts and are inculcated with a high esteem for such endurance and sacrifice. Similarly, the enormous strength of the Japanese mystical and religious systems of belief and their hold on the people must be considered in the balance. These beliefs have the Emperor as the focal point and as the symbol which binds the entire nation into one family where ideally each member has his place and where the highest duty of each member is to conform to the will of the whole, no matter what the cost.

Therefore, the weaknesses in morale due to psychological and social tensions now current in Japan are counter-balanced by sources of great strength.* The weaknesses are, however, none the less important for anticipating future developments and for psychological warfare.

* Idem.

Appendix B

A. *Future Developments*

Assuming that the conclusions reached concerning the present situation in Japan are correct, and that Allied military pressure will continue with increasing severity, a number of general trends may be predicted:

1. Japan's fighting efficiency and productive capacity will decrease progressively. There will be variations in different regions and there will be upward swings at times, but the overall trend will be downward, with increasing speed as time goes on.

2. There will long remain many energetic and determined Japanese, in all walks of life, but particularly among the military, who will wage a desperate last-stand fight and who will endeavor to force others to do likewise. Their numbers will decrease progressively, but because of their energy and aggressiveness they will be able to exert considerable influence and prevent outward moves toward capitulation on the part of many of those who inwardly desire it.

3. Extreme tendencies of the type just described will be countered by a determined effort on the part of others to save Japan from devastation. The people who take this line of action will be those who see more advantage in an integrated, even if defeated Japan, than in a country that has been physically crushed and socially disorganized. These people will be made up of political realists from the Court, from among the less extreme militarists (especially the Navy), from the bureaucrats and from the business and industrial interests. They will not for the most part be liberals; they will seize as much power inside Japan as they can grasp and will try to drive a hard bargain with the Allies. On the other hand, they will strive to control the last-ditch fanatics and will evolve formulae, in terms of recognized Japanese values, that will permit ending the war, and will do their best to achieve this aim.

4. The amount of criticism and hostile feeling between various kinds of Japanese will increase as the war situation grows progressively worse, and they will blame each other for the nation's predicament and their own sufferings. This feeling will run high between upper and lower classes, between military and civilians, and to a lesser extent between different regions. The latter type of animus will be encouraged by transportation and production difficulties which will result in certain regions having more of some vital commodities than others.

256

Appendix B

It is not likely that this aggression will break out in open and violent action on any large scale while the war is on, but it will greatly reduce production efficiency and other types of efficiency required in the war effort.

5. As time goes on, there will be an increase in general fear and emotional tension and in episodes of panic. These will be touched off at the time of bombings and the country will be full of rumors depicting famines, epidemics, inflation, new and terrible weapons launched by the Allies, and invasions. No class will be immune to these fears, but they will be commonest among the more ignorant.

It is probable that this feeling and behavior will never be as widespread as the more apathetic and resigned type of reaction, but its degree will be largely conditioned by the destruction brought by the war and the success of Japanese home front "Americans are beasts" propaganda. It is from persons who are possessed with these fears that some of the most desperate last-ditch fighting and suicidal charges may be expected, and this type of fear will continue to be a strong force in the hands of the more calculating military extremists.

6. General apathy, resignation and slowing down of effort will greatly increase among all classes of Japanese, but will be most characteristic of the lower economic and social groups in both city and country. Persons thus characterized by apathy will be relatively passive in the hands of either of the two more energetic types previously described, though somewhat more inclined to follow those who offer some form of escape from the war situation. If Japan is invaded by the Allies, these people will be docile and passive in their relations with Military Government.

7. As a result of the various factors which have been described, the general course of the war as regards enemy morale may be anticipated. If invasion takes place, it will meet with stiff resistance and there will probably be an acceleration of crash diving and similar suicide tactics. Military pressure is, of course, the principal controlling element in the progress of the war. However, assuming that the military pressure is sustained, the psychological and social tensions now handicapping the Japanese will continue to mount in severity until they actively cripple the Japanese war effort. This may take the form of extreme social chaos, but it is more likely that

257

in such a situation those leaders who wish to stop the war will be able to secure control, most probably through the Emperor.

Given equal amounts of military pressure, whether or not it costs many American lives and takes a long time before this point is reached depends on whether or not the majority of the Japanese remain convinced that the Allies intend:

a. To kill, torture or enslave the Japanese people.

b. To destroy the Japanese way of life, with its Emperor and related values.

B. *Psychological Warfare*

It may be said that this analysis strongly confirms many of the standing lines in psychological warfare. However, it does suggest some different emphases and it therefore seems appropriate to attempt to outline an overall plan.

1. *General Aims*

a. To shorten the war by undermining Japanese morale and by promoting the feeling that surrender is the best course.

b. To lay foundations for cooperation by the Japanese with Military Government and other agencies of the United States after the war.

(NOTE: Aim *a* must have precedence over aim *b*. However, in implementing aim *a*, no propaganda line may be taken which seriously threatens aim *b*.)

2. *Immediate Objectives*

a. To convince those Japanese who are alert, emotionally poised and capable of leadership and coordinated action that the war can and should be terminated. By this means part of their energy may be diverted from all-out fighting effort to the seeking of ways and means for ending the war.

b. To promote further a tendency toward rapid turnover and change now going on in many Japanese organizations and institutions devoted to defense, to industry and to various phases of government.

Appendix B

c. To promote further a trend toward hostility and aggression now existing between some groups of Japanese who are blaming each other for the adverse war situation. (See IV, C, 4, a-n.)

d. To promote further the hopelessness, apathy and weakening of resolution which already exist among many Japanese.

e. To weaken further the power of those Japanese who led the nation into war and/or who would carry on the fight to a last-ditch stand; and to promote the assumption of leadership by men who desire to stop the war, regardless of their political or social status.

(NOTE: Another objective might be the promotion of panic and emotional instability which have appeared among some Japanese. This, however, is an example of the kind of propaganda line which while it might help in aim *a*, would run counter to aim *b*. Furthermore, it could create fierce, if not well coordinated, resistance born of desperation. Consequently, panic-promoting propaganda as such is ruled out.)

3. *Themes*

a. Japan's war situation is hopeless and continuation of resistance is wasteful of Japanese lives and resources. The following lines should be stressed: The deteriorating military position of the Japanese armed forces; Japan's political and military isolation; the fate of Italy and Germany; increased destruction as a result of continued resistance; disastrous effects of continued resistance on family life, on education, on child welfare, on health, and on the finer things in Japanese culture.

(CAUTION: These lines must be presented without any false overtones of sentiment which suggest crocodile tears.)

b. Japan's leaders in the war are incompetent and to blame for the situation Japan is in. The following lines should be stressed: The militarists started the war; they have proved incompetent in foreign affairs and on the home and fighting fronts; they are responsible for national disaster; they have given Japan a bad name abroad, by the torture and abuse of people in occupied areas; they have abused the Japanese soldiers and deserted them in times of crisis; they have been ambitious and selfish, and have deceived the people who trusted them.

c. Japanese news and information are not reliable. The following lines should be stressed: The Japanese people have been given false information about the war, Japanese victories and the strength of the Allies; the Japanese leaders themselves have been severely handicapped by untrustworthy reports from subordinates and superiors. Japanese sources may be extensively quoted as a means of discrediting them; by contrast American news and information will be demonstrated to be accurate.

d. There is a way by which the Japanese can save themselves and their nation:

1.) President Truman's statement to the Japanese people is the foundation of this theme, which should be one of our most effective psychological warfare weapons because it offers an end to the war with hope for the Japanese people. While making it perfectly clear to the Japanese that we are going to eliminate the militarists because they went to war with us, we may point out how the militarists have harmed the Japanese and we may make it clear that we have no intention of punishing the Japanese people once the militarists are overthrown. In this manner, the militarists may be effectively used as a scapegoat, with the double result of weakening their hold and leading other people to feel that there is something to hope for in surrender.

(We must be careful, however, not to spoil our credibility by implying that we are coming into Japan to clear out the militarists for the good of the Japanese people, and we should make no direct statements committing America to a promise of a better life for Japan. The latter idea should emerge in our output as something which the Japanese hope for themselves.)

2.) Each section of the Truman statement which defines the meaning of unconditional surrender should be fully developed, especially the constructive sections.

Appendix B

3.) It should be repeatedly shown that there are many Japanese prisoners of war in American hands, and that they are being well treated in accordance with international agreements.

4.) It should be equally stressed that many Japanese civilians are now living and working under American military authorities and are cooperating with the Americans.

e. The Anglo-American point of view and ideals should be thoroughly presented. The aim here is not to reform the Japanese while the war is in progress, nor to suggest that the Japanese are going to be forced to conform in every detail to English or American ways of life after the war, but rather to make it clear to the Japanese that the Allies do operate on the basis of firmly established values and principles. These naturally will be reflected in the attitudes which the Japanese should expect from their conquerors.

4. *Cautions and Negatives*

a. Avoid any material (such as drawings of Japanese being burned to death in American air attacks or direct threats such as, "We are going to bomb your homes and kill your families until you surrender") which could be used to encourage anti-American attitudes.

b. Statements of fact and clear concise interpretations and explanations of them, rather than argument, will be our most effective propaganda. For the masses of people the appeal must be to feeling and sentiment rather than logic and reason.

c. In discussing surrender, always have in mind that Japanese pride and "face" are serious obstacles, and that stopping the war must be presented in honorable terms. In this connection, it will be useful to point out historical instances in which Japanese have surrendered with honor, as in the case of Hideyoshi.

d. Never produce a leaflet or script in which pressure is put on the Japanese without at the same time indicating that there is a way out for them.

e. In all commentary on Japan's present situation and future fate, avoid speaking in terms of Japan's wickedness and our moral indignation. While not deviating from our position that there is a difference between right and wrong and that we firmly believe that our cause is right, state our attitude as one of believing that acts have consequences, that Japan "took the wrong course," and that until she accepts unconditional surrender and starts anew she will be unable to escape the tragic consequences of her course of action.

5. *General Comment*

a. If the objectives and themes of psychological warfare against Japan are organized in the manner outlined, then it will be possible through analysis of the proper material to follow in an approximate manner certain alterations in the Japanese home front target that are significant for control and change in our propaganda. These may be itemized as follows:

1.) Increases in apathy and weakening of resolution in the war effort.

2.) Accelerations in the process of rapid change in Japanese organizations and institutions.

3.) The growth of aggression and hostility among different groups of Japanese.

4.) General trends in leadership changes, whether toward militarism or toward peace.

5.) The rise of panic and emotional instability.

6.) The appearance of overt demands for peace.

7.) Indications of the degree to which American propaganda is reaching the Japanese.

8.) Reactions to American propaganda.

b. It will be noted that direct attacks on Japanese ideology have not been included in the outline, except those related to militarists. It is thought that the general program and the impact of the war will undermine much of the ideology but that direct reference would only serve to harden resistance to change. The values which people hold deeply and the beliefs which orient their lives are the least profitable objects of attack, especially by an enemy.

Appendix B

c. Since many Japanese believe that the war is lost, and that they will sooner or later be in our power, the things we say have a force in Japan they did not enjoy previously. This will be increased as more and more groups, from industrialists to labor associations, become divided among themselves as to whether or not the war should be pushed to a fight to the finish. It is therefore opportune for us to begin putting the responsibility on the Japanese people for stopping the war.

From this we need not anticipate immediate results, but it will be helpful to "get the people thinking about it" — as the Japanese often phrase the purpose of a propaganda line — and it will have some effect, possibly cumulative, in the splits and divisions within the society that have been outlined.

As part of this plan, it is important not to slam the door in the face of any leader put forward as a liberal and collaborationist because we may have good reasons to consider him merely a front for an aggressive group. Abruptly to reject such persons is to suit the purposes of those Japanese propagandists who try to keep the people fighting by telling them that the Allies will not listen to reason. A better policy for us would be to recognize that the Japanese had made a move in the right direction, but then insist that it had not gone far enough.

d. A number of broadcasting programs should be prepared which are aimed at some of the special sub-groups in Japanese society outlined in IV-C, such as women, intellectuals, business men, religious denominations, etc. Such groups should not be addressed by name and thereby brought to the special attention of other Japanese and forced to demonstrate that they are not influenced. Nevertheless, the program should be designed to make their principal appeal to certain types of persons.

For almost all purposes, nothing is more important than getting more Japanese who are in our hands speaking and writing to those in Japan. "Free committees" made up of prisoners of war and captured civilians should be developed to the full. Their numbers are constantly added to as we occupy more and more Japanese territory. In addition, groups of alien Japanese in the United States should be encouraged to broadcast and write articles for transmission to Japan.

263

Appendix B

It is through the activity of such people, more than in any other way, that we can expect to match our military force with a force of ideas and suggestions which can shorten the war, cut our losses, and lay constructive foundations for the post-war period.

e. There is one implication in the analysis of Japanese psychological and social tensions which has not been brought into the plan suggested for psychological warfare. The omission is due to the fact that this implication suggests a course of action which conflicts with present United States policy and so could not be put into operation. However, it should be mentioned, since policy may change and since this problem has bearing on the price we shall have to pay for winning the war.

It has been pointed out that virtually all evidence to date from all areas, particularly the combat zones, indicates great strength and tenacity on the part of the Japanese beliefs, especially those symbolized by the Emperor. Support is therefore given to those Americans who feel that the duration of the war could be greatly reduced if we combined our attack on the Emperor's militarist advisors with a statement that we are not going to destroy the Imperial system nor regard the Emperor as a war criminal.

VII. ANNEX

As stated in the Foreword, this report consists in inferences drawn from intelligence data and evaluated in the light of certain general concepts regarding human behavior. The intelligence data is voluminous and has come from studies of 2451 prisoner of war interrogation reports, 1200 captured documents, monitorings of Japanese broadcasts, and over 200 translations from Japanese periodicals and newspapers.

Reliability and significance has been considered from three points of view:

I. *Frequency of reference.* The material is not of a sort which permits statistical treatment, but it is possible to note in a general way that certain items and themes are mentioned repeatedly while others occur more rarely.

II. *Multiple sources.* In addition to general frequency of reference there is also the fact that the same item may appear in data derived from

Appendix B

widely different sources, as for instance, home-front radio, prisoner of war interrogations, newspapers, and reports from neutral observers. The multiple sources are considered to be an approximate cross-check which increases the reliability of any item or theme.

III. *Individual value of items.* The quality and significance of each item varies according to its context in a single source, and this must be estimated as well as possible on a commonsense basis. Thus statements made in a radio broadcast beamed at North America would be considered to have low reliability, while a captured document classified Secret and issued over the name of a top Japanese official would be considered high.

It need hardly be said that in sifting the material as much attention has been paid to securing evidence concerning factors that contribute to high morale as to material suggesting various weaknesses.

A measure of general checking has been achieved by having 10 analysts who have special and detailed knowledge of various segments of the total available intelligence data examine the report, while two analysts have independently searched a large cross-section of the intelligence data in order to validate, refute or modify the principal conclusions in the report.

The bulk of the intelligence data and the limitations imposed by time and space preclude any attempt to compile a complete annex or to give documentation and explanation for every point that has been made in the body of the report. Another limiting factor is the security restriction which prevents some of the best material from being quoted even in this confidential report.

Within these limitations, samples of the various types of material that have been utilized have been compiled and are given below. Ideally, these should be arranged to follow the principal headings of the report, but this is difficult since one item frequently contains material and implications that have bearing on several topics. Thus statements concerning food, working conditions and reactions of hope or apathy may all appear in the one quotation. For this reason the samples have been arranged according to type of source, and so far as possible in chronological order, but without regard to topic. It will be noted that more explicit dates, places of publication, etc., are given for some samples than for others. This arises from differences in the amount of detail supplied in the sources from which quotations are taken.

Appendix B

PRISONERS OF WAR

(The quotations are from interrogation reports)

A PW, formerly head of the Education Department in a shipyard, who was in Japan in December, 1943, and was captured in July, 1944:

". . . The majority of the workers knew the reasons for the war, but some of them were negligent in their jobs. The group of absentees amounted to 3,000 daily. The penalty for absenteeism exceeding one week amounted to from six months to three years of hard labor (depending on previous offenses)."

A Korean PW captured on Saipan in July, 1944:

". . . Over 3,000 Koreans were on Saipan, of whom 600 were killed after the American landing, being accused of being American spies. . . ."

A civilian official captured on Saipan in July, 1944:

"PW believes that a little over half of Japan's population has been in full support of the war. They believe the war had to come and America and Britain (had to) be crushed because of their obstructing Japan's expansionist program. The remainder of the people have been divided between downright opposition and general luke-warmness. However, these groups have been silent and appear on the surface to be prosecuting the war as enthusiastically as the former section. Their thoughts are against the war.

"Because of the definite assurance by the leaders, the people entered the war with confidence. Now this confidence has been shattered, and PW believes that as bombings increase and perhaps an American invasion takes place, the people will arise and demand an end to the war."

A PW captured in July, 1944:

"The first result of bombing would be to heighten civilian morale and cause them to increase their efforts. However, continued bombing in urban areas and in concentrated factory zones could seriously damage and hamper Japanese production, and would disrupt and undermine the *Tonari-Gumi* (neighborhood group) system."

266

Appendix B

A PW captured on Saipan in July, 1944:

". . . Other shortages included charcoal, sugar and clothing. For some months there was no charcoal in his village, and when it arrived, his family received only one small bale, 3' by 1½', per month. The . . . fibre clothes do not wear well, and villagers constantly complained about this fact."

A 40-year-old PW, member of a Naval Construction Unit on Saipan, who left Fukushima-Ken in January, 1944, and was captured in July, 1944:

"Villagers generally felt that the war was useless and that they wished it would soon be over. They were tired of rationing — e. g., one small cake of laundry soap and one cake of toilet soap per family per month. Woolen and cotton cloth rationed to persons in certain trades also produced unnecessary hardships."

A PW who left Japan in May, 1944, and was captured on Saipan in July, 1944:

". . . There is no underground movement comparable to (those in) other countries. . . . Communist element among college men, but 10 years ago most of them were imprisoned; but it still exists, although quiet at present."

A PW who left Japan in June, 1944, was captured on Saipan in July, 1944, and was interrogated in October, 1944:

"Health conditions among civilians were very bad and . . . many more young people succumb from disease now than before the war. . . ."

A PW captured in July, 1944, (statement made in December, 1944):

". . . increase in circulation of yen, 20 billion to 70 billion. Increase in food prices, 50% to 100% on rare items. Sixty percent tax in 'high-class' restaurants, 20% in medium-class and none in lower-class."

A civilian technical adviser who left Japan in February, 1944, and was captured in New Guinea in July, 1944:

"Prior to January, 1944, Japs felt that they would win the war, but reports of the increasing number killed and wounded tended to dampen their enthusiasm and patriotic spirits. Despite their increasing doubts, they displayed their patriotism by voluntarily giving up their metal utensils, purchasing war bonds, etc., on a competitive basis between districts. If the war became unfavorable they intended to fight to the end."

Appendix B

A PW who left Japan in September, 1944, and was captured at sea near the Philippines:

". . . Acute shortage of food was one of Japan's greatest problems. . . . Large-scale sinkings of merchantmen by Allied SS and Airplanes aggravated food and supply situation."

A PW who left Japan in June, 1943, and was captured in the Philippines in August, 1944:

". . . Thirty millions (of Japanese farmers) are tired of this war. Farmers sell rice to the Association. (The farmer) receives small payment; rest (is) deposited for him. No control over this money. Farmers are angered over the fact they work so hard and have no money to spend. Interest in war is lukewarm. . . ."

A PW who left Japan in October, 1943, and was captured on Leyte in September, 1944:

"Upper and middle classes were against the war, but not openly, as it was too dangerous. . . . Many big business men connected with the Army were short-sightedly anxious for the war to continue. Those not connected in any way wanted it to end as soon as possible. . . . Underground anti-war societies were more numerous, active and powerful. PW believed Prince Chichibu to be the guiding light and influence of these societies. Although he had never been seen in public since his quarrel with the Emperor, PW heard he was active in his work to alienate the Emperor from the Army clique."

A 2nd Class Petty Officer who left Japan in October, 1944:

". . . growing disaffection of the country people far away from the metropolitan areas, and overwhelming desire of those people for the end of the war. . . . He said that even in Tokyo there were a great many who covertly admitted that the people were disillusioned beyond believing any official utterances. . . ."

A Radio Operator in a bomber crew, captured in China in October, 1944:

"While in Kyushu, PW felt that the civilian population was extremely apprehensive of bombings by B-29's, but for the most part took the view that the only course left was to take whatever measures of precaution could be taken and to let the inevitable take its course. What this inevitable might be no one could know, and it was the better part of wisdom to leave discussion of such matters to those in charge."

A PW who left Japan in October, 1943, (statement made in March, 1945):

"Police investigation and questioning necessary for permission (for railroad travel).... Only second or third-class travel permitted."

PERIODICALS AND CAPTURED DOCUMENTS

An MP Service Regulation issued 10 August 1941:

"There are many reasons for disturbing the peace. The main causes are the insecurity of living conditions of the people because of depression in foreign trade, economic disturbances, change in thought, and the irrationality of the people due to air attacks, sabotage, or fire. The conditions cause dissatisfaction and uncertainty, which then develop into restlessness, confusion, riot and rebellion."

A round table discussion, "Don't Lose the War of Nerves," in the magazine BOKU, August, 1943:

"Shigeomi Nomura, publicist and member of a Cabinet Committee, states: 'The fact is, the important question is how people will react in case of an air raid. It may happen that as a result of a raid their will to fight will be lost and defeatism and war weariness (will) spread."

From the magazine BOKU; Lt. Colonel Otsubo of the General Staff states:

"Small towns show high morale and patriotism not sufficiently evident in the urban areas."

A novelist in the magazine HINODE for September, 1943, writes:

"The poor people are pulling their weight and doing all the cooperating in this savings scheme, while there are many unsatisfactory points about the attitudes of the wealthy."

An editorial published in the October, 1943 issue of GANDAI describes:

Farmers and laborers as 'faithful' but complains against the failure of intellectuals to support the war effort.

Appendix B

Letter printed in the Moji Mainichi Shimbun, 7 November 1943:

". . . There is a good deal of talk on the encouragement of marriages, and we are by no means opposed to this; but the marriage problems which are raised at the marriage information bureaus are the problems of expense and too lofty ideals, while the real difficulty is more serious than that — it is the problem of housing. . . . The parrot-like reply of the authorities year after year is, 'Measures are now under consideration.' "

Article in the SHIMPO for 23 December 1943:

"The entire inhabitants of a village sacrificed themselves to the point of leading a life of starvation in order to supply their rice to the nation, and this attracted the attention of the Agriculture Minister, Yamazaki, who gave them hearty praise, saying: 'As long as there exists such a village in our nation, we are sure of victory.' "

The newspaper Tokyo Mainichi Shimbun, 27 January 1944, reports that during a session of a Diet committee on the increase of taxes, Misugi Tanaka, Representative from Hiroshima, questioned Finance Minister Kaya as to what plans the Government had for maintaining a minimum wartime standard of living in Japan. According to the newspaper, Tanaka said in part: ". . . even in Japan there is scope for cutting down on clothing and housing facilities, and also on luxury foods. I believe, however, that there is a limit to this. In regard to this limit, I would like to know what plans the Government has."

"The thing which really matters," Kaya is quoted as replying, in part, "is to keep up our health, techniques and education for the next generation. The rest can be cut down."

The Japanese magazine of economics, DIAMONDO, 21 March 1944:

". . . .checking absenteeism of workers, Mr. Watanabe, Sakae, learns that from 10% to 15% of the workers in plants around Tokyo are absent without excuse."

Letter to a soldier dated 23 March 1944, from Tokyo (Captured in Aitape, New Guinea) in April, 1944:

"Whatever we buy, we have to pay tax for same. For example, we have to pay tax for even rice bowls and chopsticks used during meals. It is a matter of fact that all luxuries are being taxed, but when we have to pay tax for something which we need for our living, this is serious. . . ."

Letter to a soldier from his wife, dated 28 March 1944 (captured in Hollandia):

"A pair of shoes costs 200 yen, and included is an additional contribution of *sake*. Clothing material for uniforms has the initial cost of 150 yen and one *to* (3.97 gal.) of rice. This cost is only for locating the source of the material. In every transaction, rice, sugar, or *sake* is demanded by the merchant."

Article in a newspaper, March, 1944:

". . . a new sort of black market has been discovered in Japan. Groups of a dozen or more men in a factory co-operate in stealing materials to sell at tremendous profits to other factories, or even to the factory from which they were stolen. Not only do these dealings upset production, but through their influence on prices, they also promote inflation. Further, when offenders are caught, their trials and the production of witnesses in court consume many valuable man hours. . . . Trials of such offenders is now to take precedence over those for murder, robbery and arson."

The newspaper, Tokyo Asahi Shimbun, 1 April 1944, sheds further light on the internal transport situation by the revelation that people have been camping for the night at Tokyo stations, bringing with them blankets and even charcoal stoves, waiting to buy tickets to travel.

Letter to a soldier from his wife in Okayama-Ken (captured in April 1944):

"The prices of commodities are gradually rising. For instance, one *sho* (3.18 pint) of wine costs 5 yen and one packet of Asahi cigarettes costs 75 sen. However, prices of commodities for daily use which are sold under fixed prices remain unchanged."

Letter to a soldier captured in Hollandia in May, 1944:

"It is difficult to live in Tokyo, too, especially for women whose husbands are absent. A person who wishes to purchase vegetables would have to wait for about two hours, and when she obtains them, she finds that she has to pay also for extra, unwanted things. I really feel like crying. It is easy to spend three or four yen a day, and one spends at least one yen a day.

Appendix B

Even if I wanted to buy clothing for the children, I can't very well pay fifteen to twenty yen. I am hoping that you will send me lots of things from there. I cannot send anything, for there is nothing to send."

The magazine HINODE, May, 1944:

A laborer at an industrial camp says that holidays are given when the electricity is cut off — these days are used for sleep. However, the sleep does no good, because the men are limp the next morning. "That is because we are worn out, but while we are working we don't feel it."

The newspaper Tokyo Asahi Shimbun, 4 June 1944, stated that farmers could not work hard with the ration of 2 *go* and 3 *shaku* per day that they were receiving.

An editorial in the newspaper Osaka Asahi Shimbun, 15 June 1944, expresses worry as to whether Japanese students, most of whom, especially college students, have been drawn into military service or factories, will retain their academic interests. "It is regrettable," the newspaper states, "to note that students have lost their zeal for learning, especially when modern warfare requires not only actual physical fighting strength, but also mental power. . . ."

Letter from a student published in Tokyo Mainichi Shimbun, 19 July 1944:

"Students want to be organized as emergency soldiers."

Letter in the same edition of Tokyo Mainichi Shimbun:

"I am a student majoring in science. Thinking about the critical war situation, my heart is filled with desire to follow the Literature major students who have left school in order to save our country. . . . Education exists as long as a nation exists. What good is education if a nation is destroyed?"

Letter from a war worker, in Tokyo Mainichi Shimbun, 21 July 1944:

"I am working at a certain war plant. On my day off I went to Ginza Matsuya to see the remains of the B-29 Bomber. On my way I was stopped by a policeman who was stationed at a certain corner, and from the beginning he questioned my identity and movement in a threatening manner. I was confused because I didn't know what it was all about.

Appendix B

"I asked the reason for his questioning me. He said that the police authorities were asked to report and punish any war worker who is off duty without reason because there are many among the war workers who are neglecting their duty. I was disappointed to hear such a thing. From the standpoint of solidarity responsibilities, I am sorry to hear that there are such people among our war workers. I presume that there is no one who does not realize how great and critical our national situation is. If there are any fellow workers who are loitering at a time when we should devote ourselves to our utmost to our duty of mass production, in collaboration with the Imperial soldiers who are fighting hard at the front lines . . . I plead, against their lack of conscience, that they rise and fight with us."

An editorial, "The Voice of the Nation," in the same issue, (which announced the resignation of the Tojo Cabinet):

"Unless the hearts of the people are revived (*i.e.*, unless the people are awakened from languor) we can never expect to turn the present (war) situation into a favorable one. Hindrances such as the problems which have arisen about mass production and national living, are due wholly to the peoples' sluggish hearts. The only way to bring light in this terrifying situation is to have absolute confidence in the national leaders and to face the national crisis. In general, what sort of a movement was the nation expecting? They have been seeking a Government with dignity and justice. At present, when the country's destiny is at stake, our only desire is to have our aim designated clearly and to the point. Again, in case it is discovered that there are those among the people who betray the country's highest interests, such misconduct must be punished severely, and we expect the nation's new Cabinet to do so."

Another article in the same edition:

"Confronting the critical situation, the (Tojo) Ministry has endeavored to reinforce the Cabinet set-up by awakening the people's hearts and uniting the nation as one so as to speed up the annihilation of the enemy, but has not succeeded in that respect. Therefore, Premier Tojo has decided to hand in the total resignation of his Cabinet, because he realizes the importance of awakening the people's hearts and uniting the nation.

Tokyo Asahi Shimbun, 4 and 15 August, 1944, comments on the high rate of fatigue among both old and young workers. A report from the doctor of a sanitorium on the increase of symptoms of T.B. as a result of the lack of proteins, is published.

Appendix B

Tokyo Asahi Shimbun, 7 November 1944:

"Following the air-raid alarms on 1 November, confusion and rumors were widespread. . . . Worst were the . . . rumors which terrified everybody."

Tokyo Asahi Shimbun, 11 November 1944:

"Factory owners and employees are accused of failing to grasp the importance and significance of production for a decisive battle. . . . They are charged with eating the worker's special ration at their homes or at their mistresses' home.

"Chagrin is expressed over the fact that the organization of girl volunteers is not going on so smoothly. The Government's order calling for conscription and for volunteers is not being obeyed. The number responding to the first call didn't meet half the quota."

An unidentified Japanese newspaper, quoted in December, 1944, considered the Government's evacuation policy to be half-hearted. Evacuated school children eligible for entrance to middle schools, the paper stated, are given the choice of going to schools in evacuation centers or returning to schools in the cities, and the majority are likely to return to their parents.

A Tokyo newspaper in December, 1944:

"In connection with more frequent raids on the capital, the tendency of spreading rumors is increasing. People who spread rumors are actually more dangerous than incendiaries."

An unidentified Tokyo newspaper, late 1944:

". . . while the number of women in industry is gradually increasing, the majority of them are not accustomed to such work. They have a much higher absentee rate than men and in most factories no consideration is given to the maintenance of women workers' health."

A recent article in a Japanese economic journal:

". . . An attempt is, therefore, being made to keep farms going without use of any hired laborers, by adjusting methods of cultivation and introducing mechanization and collective work. The help given by students and children at harvesting is only a temporary substitute. In particular, the country women must be relieved, as with work both in the house and in the fields they are now reaching the limits of their physical capacity. Housework must be rationalized and communal kitchens introduced."

REPORTS FROM PEOPLE WHO HAVE RECENTLY LEFT JAPAN

A Former Treasury Attache who returned on the Gripsholm, August, 1942:

". . . Whether or not the quantity of food available in Japan in 1941 was sufficient to maintain a reasonable standard of health, is debatable. . . . For the country as a whole, the food supply, regardless of income, was insufficient."

A woman who left Japan in September, 1943:

"With the shortage of labor and fertilizer, and with the Government-controlled prices, the farmer's discontent is growing daily. His discontent, however, is not against anyone in particular in the Government or against the war, but just against his lot. . . . The fisherman, like the farmer, is dissatisfied, as there is so much work involved for so little profit for the main catch."

"Medicine of any kind is rarely found, and bandages must be washed and used over and over again. Hospitals are filled to overflowing, but women are urged to have more and more babies and surprisingly, they do, even after many miscarriages and with general ill-health. . . . One can readily see that, with the insufficient diet and all the very trying exercise and hard work, people do not have any resistance to disease. Many have chilblains, pneumonia, T.B., beri-beri and plain ill-health."

A group of travelers arriving in occupied territories from Japan reported that "the Japanese people are experiencing much hardship and that morale is low. There is an extreme shortage of food."

An uncensored letter received from Japan in January, 1945:

"I was unable to obtain a blanket in Tokyo and am therefore forced to use a curtain for covering. . . . The Japanese Government has ordered that wooden houses in Tokyo be torn down."

An Allied source stated in March, 1945:

"The shortage of cloth is very severe and practically everyone is wearing the clothing he had before the war."

Appendix B

A Japanese who had recently arrived in China from Tokyo wrote in March, 1945:

"The Japanese Government has stipulated that each city dweller shall get 65 ounces of vegetables per day, and that 50% of this shall be provided by the 'supply circle' near the cities. In actual fact, however, the ordinary Japanese gets only 15-20 ounces of vegetables per day."

A Korean Independence Army leader:

". . . Thousands of Koreans have been shipped to Japan to work in industries there. . . ."

RADIO

Source not specified but presumably radio; 5 December 1944:

"Recent speakers on the effect of mobilizing school children complain that:

(1) Children are being urged to neglect their education entirely, in the interest of war production.
(2) Ill feeling is caused between regular factory workers and part-time student employees.
(3) It is difficult to examine children applying to pass on to secondary schools, as the work they have done varies greatly in standard.
(4) The movement of children backwards and forwards between the cities and evacuation areas has caused difficulties in the keeping of school records."

Koiso in Home Broadcast, 27 December 1944:

"The war situation has become more critical. Although the spirit of the special attack units is fully manifested by the officers and men of the Imperial Forces on the fighting fronts, it is very regrettable that the spirit of the special attack units, which should be manifested also on the home front in response to the fighting front, is not yet fully expressed."

Tokyo in Japanese to Southeast Asia, 6 January 1945:

"Urging that increase in aircraft production is the only manner in which the spirit of loyalty of the Divine Eagles of the Special Attack Units can be matched, the first of the Special Attack Units of the Aircraft Production

Front completed its organization, even while the enemy B-29 attacks are close at hand."

Medium-Wave Broadcast, 8 January 1945:

". . . If this special charcoal train service system works out satisfactorily, hereafter charcoal will be sent on exclusive charcoal trains, and the people of Iwate Prefecture are very enthusiastic in replenishing the shortage of fuel in Tokyo. . . ."

Home and Empire Broadcast, 9 January 1945:

"Preparations are under way for the establishment of a Prefectural Women's Medical College in Akita Prefecture, in order to protect the health of the people of the Prefecture. . . ."

Jyukei Shimada in a talk, "Slackness in War Effort Criticized," to Home and Empire, 23 January 1945:

"The Kamikaze Spirit is present all about. Despite the fact that we think there should not be a single idle person at this time of extremely violent, decisive wartime, when we are engaged in a vital struggle which decides whether Japan will win or lose, . . . (and) when the 100 million people are required to make a total stir to action in order to destroy the enemies, the U. S. and Britain, there are many who are violating the total national mobilization program and cause headaches for the authorities. And because of this those who should be receiving special training are not. . . .

"Those industrial trainees have family backgrounds and (there are) other reasons which call for our sympathy. Nevertheless, the fact that there are many people who hold the wrong attitude . . . proves that each one of us is not fully sincere. We still have a slackness somewhere in us. . . . Let us eat tasty foods, even though we must get them through a black market channel."

Home and Empire Broadcast, 24 January 1945, on Diet Interpellations:

". . . Next, Mr. Koyama took the floor: 'The important industrial enterprises should be quickly taken under the wings of the Government and supervised. . . .'

"Koiso: 'It is not so simple as that bringing a project under the supervision of the Government would bring the required results. Rather than (this) . . .

it is necessary to take the path of bold cooperation in regard to the matter of labor power.' "

Domei in Romaji to Greater East Asia, 24 January 1945 (concerning the dissolution of the IRAPS):

"There are examples where the one-party system has been effective, but for various reasons, the one-party theory in our country has led to pitfalls. By this force of circumstance the right of the majority to a voice should be recognized, and it should be permitted for various political parties to compete with each other as long as such action will contribute to the winning of the war."

Sato, Keichi, in Home and Empire Broadcast, 12 February 1945:

"There is absolutely no room for individual concerns and the people must work together for united effort. Are we going to sulk just because his (the enemy's) advance has steadily brought the front lines closer to the homeland? . . . This is not a time to lament; it is a time to act."

Home and Empire Broadcast, 13 February 1945:

"As an answer to the demand of the intensive war situation, the Justice Ministry, upon deliberation with the Navy Ministry, mobilized four large prisons for the whole nation. . . .

"This corps has been resolutely building (word missing) freighter and (word missing) type tanker. . . ."

Domei in Romaji to Greater East Asia, 19 February 1945, attributes the following to ASAHI SHIMBUN:

"To punish student workers who absent themselves from work without leave, although they are not ill, and run around seeking their own pleasure, the Tokyo City authorities have decided, as a disciplinary measure, to cut down the rice ration of anyone who is absent for more than 15 days without sufficient reasons.

"If we could be rid of such student workers and factory workers who absent themselves from work without sufficient reason and whose attitude toward the war effort is not proper, we would be greatly benefited."

Appendix B

Medium-wave Broadcast, 28 February 1945:

"Hitherto, the punishment of those who have indulged in illegal transactions has tended to be (too lenient). In this (word missing) of (hidden) and retained materials, however, the police control will be further tightened and made flawless, and will put pressure upon the vicious (offenders), without mercy. . . .

"Violators will be dealt severe punishment so that the hidden and retained materials may be sent to the decisive war production places as fast as possible and in as large quantities as possible."

Home and Empire Broadcast, 2 March 1945:

"The first reaction heard at the various factories reportedly went something like this: 'Let's go,' 'Increased production by all means.' 'Without increased production, why Government management?' 'I'm grateful,' 'This is the way it ought to be — but our responsibilities are so much greater.'

"Workers, in general, all hailed the new set-up as making them really feel like 'soldiers fighting at the front.' They expressed their hopes that Government management would not be 'in theory only.' Several complained about laxity in factory discipline and welcomed this step as a forerunner to the adopting of 'military discipline' in the factories."

Editorial attributed to YOMIURI HOCHI, in Romaji to Greater East Asia, 4 March 1945:

"The reason we say this is that in the first place, there has been a tendency to form several political parties instead of a single, united political group. This has been caused by the resignation of numerous persons from the IRAPS. In the second place, there has been a tendency for various groups and departments to act in their own interests. But it must be recognized here that the force which at one time appeared as though it might supersede the IRAA and the IRAPS has been completely stopped."

Home and Empire Broadcast, 5 March 1945:

"Tokyo students (who) are already lending valuable aid to the nation's war effort in the air corps factories were given another special task from today as special members of the city's fire fighting brigade.

279

Appendix B

"In view of the increasing tempo of the enemy's indiscriminate aerial attack, special student fire brigades have been formed and will be dispatched in three shifts to respective fire stations throughout the nation's capital, beginning today."

Quotation attributed to YOMIURI HOCHI, in Home Broadcast, 6 March 1945:

"Of course, no matter how much power the enemy might exert and express upon us, with all military weapons and by words, the unity which exists between the people and the military cannot be shaken in the least. No matter what the situation, the very worst that is imaginable will not sway the state of affairs which now exists between the people and the military. . . ."

Home Service Broadcast, 7 March 1945:

"During the enemy raid some days ago, some people did not do things they should have done, but bitterly indulged in wild talking (*literally,* 'wagging wild tongues' — Ed.). In spite of the fact that the war situation may necessitate making our national territory a battlefield, they still continue in their own way, forgetful of the (plight) of the nation."

Home Broadcast, 10 March 1945:

". . . The air defense system in Chugoku District is awful. Preparations for air defense are inadequate and public negligence is extremely surprising. . . . Many think the Chugoku District is safe from air raids, but this is unwarranted complacency." *

Domei in Romaji to Greater East Asia, 10 March 1945:

"Tokyo — The Marine Transportation General Bureau has recently decided to carry out the unification of marine transportation, and at the same time to revise the official charterage on ships. Marine transportation companies are, however, cool towards the proposed revision of the charterage rates, as they believe that it is already too late for that. . . . They feel strongly towards the Government's failure in not taking proper measures long ago. . . ."

* It is of interest to note now that Hiroshima City is in Chugoku.

Appendix B

Koiso in a Home and Empire Broadcast, on 10 March 1945:

"Upon looking at numerous victims who rise out of these ruins of fire by gritting their teeth and by taking this misfortune as a mere misfortune, and who are preparing themselves for tomorrow's battles as they sob, and upon hearing parents calling their children and children calling their parents, I felt that I found the real figure of the Japanese, and I felt an immeasurably deep reassurance."

Medium-Wave Broadcast, 14 March 1945:

"The children in the fifth grade or above of the Kawaguchi National School in Nozoki Village . . . have been receiving training in bayonet charges every night since December of last year. These children have been very enthusiastic in this training, saying they are going out to the decisive battle front by polishing their fighting spirit for the destruction of the U.S. and Britain....

"It was recently decided that children in the grades below the fifth will also be given training. All of them are now continuing their enthusiastic and gallant practice in the school auditorium during the night and on the snow-covered school ground during the day."

Medium-Wave Broadcast, 15 March 1945:

"Finally, as regards fire fighting (word missing), we want you to take more and more precautions. Recently there has been an increase of places here and there where fire-fighting (word missing) is not sufficient. There have been reported reports of this."

Medium-Wave Broadcast, 15 March 1945:

"The calmness with which the victims of the enemy raid conducted themselves made me realize that, after all, human beings are capable of meeting any disaster as long as they have food and clothing.

". . . Even in our small bath we could hear the cheerful voices of neighboring wives and the wails of babies. It seemed that in this atmosphere one could realize the strength of the Japanese people.

"No doubt there will be many homeless Japanese in the future, but Japan will become more and more determined as the enemy's bombings increase and as the people are bombed out of their homes."

Appendix B

Broadcast, 15 March 1945:

". . . Each district will form its own Special Attack Corps and plan its activities. . . . Every district, working as one body, will realize the formation of a Special Attack Unit and strive for a National Special Attack Corps. It will be noted that already the other districts have followed suit and that the preliminary preparations by the Tohoku, Hokuriku, Chugoku, Shikoku, and Kyushu districts have been accomplished."

Home Broadcast, 16 March 1945:

"Yesterday, March 16, the Information Board announced that our Premier was especially ordered by H.I.M. the Emperor to participate in the Imperial Headquarters conferences in view of the pressing war situation at this time. . . . The present step is, indeed, a great factor in bringing about the further unity of the Government administration and war strategists from both a personnel and structural point of view."

TASS in English Morse on 16 March 1945:

"Correspondent Samoiloff sends the following dispatch from Tokyo to TASS in Moscow. 'As a result of the night air raid on March 10, thousands of refugees are crowding around railway stations, trying to leave the capital. Everywhere there are various kinds of vehicles, from lorries to rickshas, loaded with the belongings of people evacuating the city. Hospitals are overcrowded with sufferers injured during the raid and have stopped their ordinary work.

(Quoting ASAHI SHIMBUN)

" 'What means were taken for the transportation of air raid sufferers?' *Answer:* 'Special trains were run on the 11th and 12th for the transport of raid sufferers, without tickets. However there is a limit to the transportation power, so sufferers must wait two or four days more. The transportation for raid sufferers and food will be secured, but for the time being no preference can be given for the transportation of those who are dispersing from the capital.' "

Domei in Romaji, 19 March 1945:

"All students will be mobilized to participate in essential work directly related to war operations, such as food and munitions production, air

Appendix B

defense, and important research work. . . . In order to carry out the afore-mentioned objectives, school studies for students excepting those in the primary grades will be suspended for a period from April 1, 1945 to March 31, 1946. . . ."

750 Kc. Station Monitored on 20 March 1945:

"Drastic measures should be taken by the authorities against the large profiteers aiming at profits only. However, those who are forced, in order to earn their living, to deal in this illegal business, should be given consideration relating to their time and needs. As a beginning, these should be converted gradually on the basis of a sound rationing system, while lenient punishment should be administered. . . ."

Major-General Chuon Sakurai in Yomiuri-Hochi, as quoted on Home and Empire Broadcast, 21 March 1945:

". . . . Should there be anyone idly indulging in a pessimistic view because of the possibility of enemy pressure being brought to bear against our homeland in the future, how can we express our apology to the heroes of Iwo Jima."

Agriculture and Commerce Minister Shimada in Medium-Wave Broadcast, 25 March 1945:

"With regard to self-sufficiency in food, it is as often declared that the basic ration of the main food item of 2 *go*, 3 *shaku*, is not enough, but on this occasion I reiterate that I have the absolute confidence and determination to maintain this ration."

Domei in Romaji, 29 March 1945:

". . . Some people are in a terrible fix. They do not have any place to go or any relatives to rely on. Some people are saying, 'If only the authorities would indicate where we should evacuate. . . . The authorities are encouraging these people to walk if need be to nearby prefectures. Even this is not unreasonable, when you consider it from their position. . . . At any rate, after the evacuation is over, the city will be able to get rid of all the buildings interfering with air defenses, and the arming of the city will be strengthened much more."

Appendix B

Editorial Attributed to Tokyo Asahi Shimbun in Home and Empire Broadcast, 1 April 1945:

". . . Should we lose this island group (Okinawas) by one chance in a million, we will face the predicament of being almost completely cut off from our southern shores. . . ."

Home and Empire Broadcast on 3 April 1945:

". . . We should not be impatient, but it is for us to wait patiently. Impatience will bring defeat. . . . There may be some people who will ask, 'What is the Navy doing?' I say that I would like for you to place your confidence in the bosom of the Navy Minister and wait for the true time for the decisive battle."

Medium-Wave Broadcast, 5 April 1945:

". . . Unfortunately it is true that recently 57 students precipitately left their factory work. On the basis of data from all quarters, this occurrence is caused by (1) failure of the students' endurance, (2) inability of the factories to realize the limitations of the students, whom they treat as if they were workers of the general type. . . . This should not have happened under any circumstances at a time like the present, when the need for increased production is most urgent. . . ."

Domei in Romaji to Greater East Asia, 5 April 1945:

". . . The most difficult problem during this period of work is the lack of sleeping quarters and food; but whenever there are no proper sleeping quarters, these workers merely lie down in a nearby grassy field for their rest, and as for their food, they eat a meal of one *go* of rice four times a day, and manage to appease their fierce hunger. . . ."

Medium-Wave Broadcast, 6 April 1945:

"Despite this, should there be any who consider our accurate announcements somewhat similar to the demagogic announcements of the enemy, this, indeed, is very regrettable. Persons with such an idea often unwittingly spread rumors and unreliable information, and they tend to be influenced by a slight incident. We believe, therefore, such persons must be strictly kept under control.

Appendix B

"With the intent of stirring confusion on the home front of Japan, the enemy has set up a broadcasting station on Saipan, and they are desperately sending Japanese language programs, in an attempt to address the general public of Japan.

"To cope with this, the affiliated authorities have adopted carefully prepared counter-measures, and they are doing everything that they can. However, should such demagogic propaganda come into the general public's homes, the best thing for them to do is not to listen to it, with a clear understanding that it is enemy strategic propaganda. However, should there be anyone who listens to such a broadcast, contrary to our expectations, he must naturally be subjected to our questioning. So, we wish everyone to be very cautious."

Home and Empire Service, 7 April 1945, carried a talk by Genzo Naomi on "The Mental Attitude of the Japanese," saying that the "unfavorable progress of the war had absolutely nothing directly to do with the recent political changes," (fall of the Koiso Cabinet) but after reviewing the military situation and the "achievements" of the Koiso Cabinet, he says that the changes came about "as a result of one important consideration, and that for the sake of the country, so that even more powerful parties could take over the helm to fight this war to the bitter end."

Genzo Naomi on Home and Empire Service, 17 April 1945:

"It is regrettably true that the latest war situation is anything but good. But then, suddenly, so very suddenly, the Koiso-Yonai Cabinet resigned *en masse.* One can easily surmise that the Japanese people, notwithstanding the fact they reside in the Japanese homeland, as well as those residing in the outer territories (*Gaichi* — Ed.) were given a great shock. This shock may have lasted only for a moment, though you may have been acquainted with the circumstances (*Jijyoo ga wakatta ni itashimashite mo.* — Ed.).

Japanese Home and Empire Service, 8 April 1945:

From a talk, "The Greater East Asia War Started in Manchukuo and Will End in Manchukuo," by Hisatoshi Oya, East Asia Section of the *Mainichi Shimbun:*

"The battle in the Pacific has now entered a very serious stage where no optimism is warranted. Despite all the gallant battles being put up at the front lines, and despite the heroic efforts being made at the home front, we recently lost Iwo Jima and now the enemy has come to lay his foot on Okinawa Honto — so very close to our homeland."

A letter from a villager of a Kumamoto district broadcast over 750 kcs. on 13 April 1945:

". . . Therefore the gendarmerie commandant issued the following warning to the populace: 'The war becomes increasingly tense, and the time has come when we citizens must hold firm to our belief and keep our heads. Nevertheless, some of the people, sensing insecurity in the war, have become listless. . . .'"

Home Broadcast, 14 April 1945:

". . . Beginning today, and for some time to come, train tickets will not be sold to anyone other than military and Government personnel and those with urgent business, for arriving at or passing through the following stations. . . ."

Home and Empire Broadcast, 15 April 1945:

". . . Admiral Toyoda, Commander in Chief, of the Combined Fleet, emphatically declared that the rise or fall of Imperial Japan is truly dependent upon the battle around the Okinawas."

Statement by Director Endo of the Aircraft Ordnance General Bureau of the Munitions Ministry, as quoted in Romaji to Greater East Asia on 18 April 1945:

". . . We must never allow our supply of air weapons to cease for a moment. If the attacks of our Special Attack Corps, whose pilots are sacrificing their lives, suffer a setback because of a lack of air weapons and if we should lose this opportunity for a victory, a thousand generations will be left a legacy of remorse. . . . The responsibility of taking this heaven-sent opportunity and of crushing the enemy rest upon the shoulders of both our fighting forces and the production lines on the homefront."

Asahi Shimbun editorial as broadcast in Romaji to Greater East Asia, 19 April 1945:

". . . If we fail to supply enough aircraft at this crucial moment, the opportune moment which will pave our way to victory will slip us by. . . . In

Appendix B

spite of the fact that the enemy has been subjected to tremendous losses, he is in such a state that he cannot disentangle himself from the battlefield."

Home and Empire Broadcast, 20 April 1945:

"If we run short of aircraft now, then the divine opportunity will never arrive again. . . . We must break up all bottlenecks and determine to send planes to the front lines to destroy the enemy. . . ."

Broadcast from Kumamoto (750 kcs.), 26 April 1945:

"By various treacherous methods and by destruction of our productive output (the enemy) is pressing against us. First the enemy's broadcasts, and secondly the enemy's pamphlets . . . are the means of this propaganda. But what does this deceitful propaganda really intend? In the first place, to put a wedge between the civilians and our military leaders in order to destroy their mutual trust . . . to undermine the good feeling existing between the people and our financial and political leaders, in order to destroy their mutual trust. . . to undermine the good relations existing between our Navy and our Army in order to undermine their mutual trust . . . to undermine the good relations existing between the enlisted men and officers of our Army, in order to destroy their mutual trust . . . to create bad feelings toward our Government on the part of the people. . . ."

TASS, 26 April 1945, reported:

"The population of the Japanese capital spreads all kinds of rumors about the war.'The entire population,' the newspaper [Tokyo(Mainichi)Shimbun] states, 'must be warned that it should not listen to or give faith to such rumors. According to the data of the Tokyo Police, an average of 40 to 50 cases of dissemination of groundless rumors are recorded monthly. All persons disseminating such rumors will be sentenced to no less than 7 years of imprisonment.' "

Short-Wave Romaji to Greater East Asia, 23 April 1945:

". . . In some quarters, there are some people who imply . . . (that) a certain rivalry exists among the lower ranks of the Army and Navy, or with civilians who come in contact with them. For this very reason, opinions were exchanged by the leaders in an atmosphere of earnestness and harmony. Views were exchanged on ways substantially to strengthen the Army's and Navy's combined efforts in line with the critical war situation and to break down such fabrications, thus strongly manifesting the united fighting power."

Broadcast from Osaka (870 Kcs.) 2 May 1945:

"The question of increase in the production of foodstuffs is of the utmost importance, and since the Government is much concerned with this problem, all of us should lend all our spirit and energy to this cause. . . . Producers of sweet potatoes . . . effect free trade of their produce in different localities that have no limitations. But the question of whether or not such practices as this will have an ill effect in this production scheme deserves our consideration and study. Although we have not stated that such business will be restricted, it does appear to effect increase in production harmfully."

Home and Empire Broadcast, 2 May 1945:

". . . A point of caution pertaining to food. . . . Special care must be given to prevent the growth of molds and to keep it clean. . . . The next thing requiring attention is the eruptive typhus which is carried by lice. . . . Thus, adequate measures must be taken for the prevention of lice, and especially at such a place as the public bath. . . ."

Domei in Romaji to Greater East Asia, 4 May 1945:

". . . In order to make up for the wartime shortage in medical doctors, the National Clinical Regulation was passed as an emergency measure. This act provides that, for the time being, the graduates of private dental colleges, approved by the Education Minister, and who have had more than a year's practice or training, will be qualified to take the examination for medical practice. . . ."

Letters to the editor of the "ASAHI" as given by Domei in Romaji to Greater East Asia, 11 May 1945:

". . . A Tokyo contributor writes that if the authorities cannot be trusted, the people will be looking out for themselves, seeking safety even if they have to push others aside. . . ."

". . . A contributor from Yamagata says: 'My first request of the new Cabinet is for it to restore the people's faith in the Government."

". . . The *Asahi* received more than 100 articles expressing a pessimistic stand regarding evacuation and decentralization."

Appendix B

". . . One writer has criticized the complicated procedure regarding evacuation, not to mention strained transportation problems and corrupt practices. The writer has revealed that some are intimidating people and that 'money talks.' "

Kanetomi, Managing Editor of Japan Press Society, in Home and Empire Broadcast, 10 May 1945:

"The people of Japan must refrain from offering further comments on the surrender of Germany. . . ."

Home and Empire Broadcast, 13 May 1945:

"Why, then, is the war situation still unfavorable in spite of these facts? The cause lies in the fact that our seemingly all-out national might is actually not only far from being all-out, but cannot even be considered fair."

Domei in Romaji, to Greater East Asia, 24 May 1945:

". . . Moreover, the war situation which we face today demands a consistently unified strategy, summoning the excellent fighting morale of the officers and men, and the best that modern science has to offer. There must not be such an outlook toward war as fighting the enemy with bamboo spears. Indeed, we must possess an unshakeable determination to decide the outcome, with air-craft serving as the core. . . ."

Domei in Romaji to Greater East Asia, 1 June 1945:

". . . The transportation of coal, which is a basic raw material in the war effort, is showing a decided change for the worse, and there is a demand for the immediate establishment and enforcement of a policy to assure transportation strength. . . . The transportation of coal in Kyushu recently has suffered, as the cut in the allotment of essential fuel for motorized sail-boats and a shortage of coal for ships prevented the execution of any systematic transportation. . . . Depredations of the enemy into the Inland Sea and northern Kyushu have disrupted our navigation services. . . . This has resulted in a 40% or more drop in transportation of coal to the Kansai area compared with tonnage carried in the same period the year before last."

APPENDIX C

NOTES ON THE U. S. STRATEGIC BOMBING SURVEY
AND ITS RELATIONSHIP TO THE DIVISION

THE U. S. STRATEGIC BOMBING SURVEY endeavored to cover all the main aspects of the effects of strategic bombing — military, political, economic, etc. — and among them morale. The total complement provided for 300 civilians, 350 officers and 500 enlisted men. The Survey began operating from headquarters in Tokyo early in September, 1945, with sub-headquarters in Nagoya, Osaka, Hiroshima and Nagasaki, and with mobile teams in other parts of Japan, the islands of the Pacific and the Asiatic mainland. Seven hundred Japanese military, government and industrial officials were interviewed and a great many documents were recovered and translated.

In order to understand the effect of bombing on the Japanese, it was necessary to make extensive studies of the total situation, including numerous factors that were not directly connected with bombing. According to the Survey's report, much of the Japanese wartime military planning and execution was reconstructed, and "reasonably accurate" statistics were secured on Japan's economy and war production, plant by plant and industry by industry. In addition, studies were made of how Japan came to enter the war, the internal discussions and negotiations leading to surrender, the effectiveness of the civilian defense organization and the effects of the atomic bombs.

The unit within the survey created for the study of morale operated over the islands of Honshu and Kyushu with ten field teams. The total personnel numbered about 140 individuals. A cross-section sample of some 3,150 Japanese civilians were interviewed in accordance with the Likert technique, a large number of official and nonofficial informed persons were interrogated, and a mass of secret and public Japanese documents were collected. In addition, pertinent data from all the other divisions of the Survey were available to those working on morale.*

* Further details regarding data and methods may be found in the official report, *The Effects of Strategic Bombing on Japanese Morale: U.S. Strategic Bombing Survey,* June 1947, Washington, D.C., Government Printing Office.

Appendix C

The Survey's work on Japanese wartime civilian morale is, of course, not the last word on the subject. In spite of the size of the report, much more data was gathered than has as yet been thoroughly analyzed. More than this, there are probably important sources which will become evident in the course of time that the Survey did not touch. It must be admitted also that not every one of the conclusions of the morale unit can be considered well founded. Items that have appeared to me doubtful have been excluded from Chapter VI in making comparisons with the Division's findings. This has meant the sacrifice of some data which would otherwise have been corroborative.

However, in spite of faults, the Survey's study is by far the most thorough and comprehensive investigation that has been carried out. In regard to the main points there can be no reasonable doubt, for, to use its own words, they are indicated by the "overwhelming mass of evidence."

Some of these main points confirm the main findings of the OWI Division, as can be seen from the excerpts that have been presented. A comparison of the report by the Survey with Appendix B will reveal additional items of agreement. Although in a number of other points the Division's conclusions must still remain a matter of doubt it is possible to say that, just as with military morale, no major finding made during the war has been demonstrated to be an error.

The question may be raised as to whether the presence of Division personnel in the Bombing Survey introduced an unconscious bias in favor of the Division's findings. Some facts may help the reader form an opinion about this for himself.

Out of approximately ninety individuals who worked as interviewers for the Survey in Japan, four had formerly been in the Foreign Morale Analysis Division. Of the eighteen people who were chiefly responsible for the analysis and writing of the Survey's report, five had formerly been in the Division. Of the thirteen research leaders who participated in planning the questions or supervised field work or both, two (including myself) had been associated with the Division.

My own role consisted in participation with the other twelve research leaders in planning the questions and in leading a field team half time, the other half being spent in interviewing individuals thought to be particularly fruitful sources of information. Out of the 3,150 individuals interviewed in the cross-section sample, approximately 300 were handled by a team supervised by me. I had no share in the analysis or in the preparation of the report.

APPENDIX D

THE DEVELOPMENT OF THE RESEARCH METHODS
OF THE FOREIGN MORALE ANALYSIS DIVISION

November 30, 1945

REPORT NO. 29*

INTERIM INTERNATIONAL INFORMATION SERVICE

(O W I)

Foreign Morale Analysis Division

* This report was written by Katherine Spencer, the Division's supervisor of processing.

TABLE OF CONTENTS

I. INTRODUCTION

A. *PURPOSE AND TASK OF THE RESEARCH UNIT*

During the war an acute need was felt in many quarters for a better understanding of Japanese social and psychological characteristics as they related to military morale on the battlefront and to civilian morale in Japan. It was recognized that knowledge of Japanese thought and behavior was essential for dealing with the Japanese both as an enemy during the war and as a defeated nation in the postwar international world. The need for better understanding was felt particularly by those agencies charged with conducting psychological warfare against Japan. The Foreign Morale Analysis Division (FMAD) of the Office of War Information was organized to see how these problems could be illuminated by the application of social science methods and procedures to a particular body of wartime source materials made available by Allied military and civilian agencies.

The research was centered on two fields of interest — first, military morale at the battlefront and, second, civilian morale and internal social conditions on the homefront. The analysis of military morale was first concerned with clarifying the character and mainsprings of the Japanese soldier's morale, with determining whether the traditionally accepted picture of uniformly high and impregnable morale was a true one, and if not, with discovering its vulnerable points and the conditions under which it had wavered or was likely to weaken or break. The research unit explored the question, for example, of whether Japanese soldiers inevitably lived up to their ideal of suicidal, last-ditch resistance, of how their patriotic and religious indoctrination had been achieved and maintained, of the circumstances under which resistance weakened and surrenders took place.

The study of civilian morale and internal social conditions in Japan was likewise carried forward with the purpose of discovering any variations in civilian morale and support of the war effort and of estimating vulnerable points. FMAD was prepared to investigate critically the assumption of a populace uniformly and effectively mobilized in support of the war. It was interested in determining the effects of increased

Appendix D

food shortages and physical hardships, of air raids, evacuation, and the disruption of normal life. It wanted to know how these hardships affected the capacity for war production and how they might influence the will to resist in the event of Allied invasion of the homeland. It gathered data on tensions existing between classes or factions within Japan — industrial workers, farmers, women, students, intellectuals — and asked whether any of these groups showed signs of uncooperativeness or dissatisfaction with the war. Current information about such internal social conditions and attitudes of the people was felt to be of immediate importance during the war and of long-range significance for the occupation and administration of a defeated Japan.

These military and civilian fields of interest were not so sharply divided as might at first appear. The average Japanese soldier came from, and could be expected to return to the civilian population. His military and patriotic indoctrination was part of the larger Japanese ideology. Even the professional soldier represented an element in the greater Japanese community. From both fields it was hoped to obtain information that would throw light on Japanese cultural patterns of thought and behavior that appeared so baffling and incomprehensible to the Western mind.

Military and civilian intelligence reports were the source material upon which the research was based. These documents were brought together from all battlefronts and from a variety of civilian agencies. At it was received, the information of social and psychological importance was mingled with other kinds of operational or strategic data concerning order of battle, military installations, and economic or political affairs. The initial task of the research unit was to devise methods and procedures for handling this great volume and variety of source material and for systematically culling out, recording and cataloging the data pertinent to its special interests. This recording, extracting and analysis had to be managed under wartime pressures at a time when it was necessary not only to keep abreast of the continuous flow of incoming documents but to have the results of analysis immediately available. Also the recording had to be carried on in a way which would give time perspective and show current developments against the background of previous conditions. The review of documents and systematic recording of data were of such dimensions that they required a team of analysts. Uniform procedures for recording and extracting had to be worked out so that processing of a given document could be done by any one of the team of analysts with comparable results.

Appendix D

On the basis of the system which was developed, the research unit was prepared to supply information about Japanese morale and internal social conditions to military and civilian war agencies whenever it was requested or when it was thought that it would be helpful. In practice the specific activities and aims of the research unit became channelized along certain lines. As an OWI unit one of its primary aims was to provide information of use in the central planning of Allied psychological warfare policies and programs. Its analyses of military morale were based on comparative source materials from all battlefronts and were thus strategic in character and supplementary to tactical analyses of similar but more localized material made by operational units in the field.* Thus it was possible to supply an over-all picture which often gave perspective and comparisons to those in particular theaters. The use of the information was not limited to OWI units but extended also to the military and to such civilian agencies as OSS and the State Department. Aside from this specialized aim of the research in psychological warfare, the unit proposed as far as possible to supply other intelligence of a strategic nature, particularly for the War Department, as it was requested or as the research itself revealed significant leads. Although these two information and intelligence functions were primary, the FMAD also participated in training programs for overseas Civil Affairs and intelligence (OSS) personnel. Despite the wartime pressure to provide information of immediate utility, throughout the research the importance of the findings for occupation and reconstruction policies was taken into consideration.

The social scientists who conceived and directed the research project brought to it the point of view and accepted methods of the social sciences in general and of sociology, psychology, social anthropology, and psychiatry, in particular. They were impressed with the usefulness and necessity of applied social science and the utilization of scientific methods in the clarification of the social and human problems of our own civilization. A basic premise of the research was that social phenomena are susceptible of scientific analysis through systematic observation and classification and the consequent formulation of inductive generalizations. The body of general social science propositions about the nature of society and the behavior of its members formed part of the background of the research. Commonly accepted techniques of definition, classification, and measurement of social phenomena were

* Such tactical units did not, however, employ social science methods and concepts.

used as far as was permitted by the limitations of the data and by the compromises and adjustments made necessary by their quality. The acceptance of the possibility of generalization about social phenomena from specific instances opened up a further field, that of prediction. It was a major concern and expectation of the research unit to be able to foretell the effect of changing factors in the morale picture and to estimate trends in time.

Among the fundamental propositions of social science, two were considered of basic importance to the research. The first was the assumption that certain uniformities exist in the behavior of individuals and in the operation of social groups due to common human and social factors. Equally important, on the other hand, was the recognition that between different social and national groups there exist certain contrasts in belief and behavior which are culturally conditioned and which can be understood only in terms of the cultural context of the groups in question. The importance of this comparative point of view cannot be overestimated for the study of morale and social conditions in a culture so different from our own.

How the various aims and demands were met by the research unit is described in the remainder of this report.

B. *ORGANIZATION*

The FMAD operated as an OWI unit under a cooperative arrangement with MIS (Military Intelligence Service) of the War Department. From both agencies in varying degrees it drew personnel and equipment, and through both it had access to the military and civilian intelligence documents that were used as source material. As an analysis and information unit it served both OWI and MIS by means of reports and representation at conferences.

The research unit was established under OWI in the spring of 1944 and began working with the nuclear personnel of a chief and three analysts. From the beginning this staff worked in space provided by the War Department and with access to MIS intelligence sources. In these first months, attention was centered primarily on problems of military morale. During the fall of 1944, the staff was gradually enlarged to an overall personnel of seventeen with part housed in the War Department and the other part in OWI offices. With increased personnel and facilities it was possible to turn attention to social conditions and morale on the Japanese homefront while further developing and refining the study of military morale.

By the beginning of 1945, the OWI personnel consisted of the division chief and co-chief, ten analysts, two translators, and three secretaries. From time to time additional temporary personnel was made available from OWI for special tasks.† The permanent staff represented a wide range of experience and training in the social sciences and psychiatry. The division chief had directed a social research project in a Japanese Relocation Center, following the evacuation of West Coast Japanese and Americans of Japanese ancestry, and had brought with him from the project four analysts and a secretary, all of Japanese ancestry. Ten members of the total OWI staff of seventeen (plus two who were later contributed by the Army) were persons of Japanese ancestry with linguistic or other special qualifications for working with Japanese materials. Another of the senior analysts had also had experience as head of social research in a Japanese Relocation Center. In all, a large proportion of the staff had had first hand knowledge of Japanese culture either through personal or research experience or through both. In addition to these special qualifications the remainder of the top personnel had had training and wide research experience in sociology, social anthropology, and psychology.

As an OWI operation the research unit was known as the Foreign Morale Analysis Division. It had two sections — the group housed in the War Department engaged in analysis of intelligence material made available through military sources, and the staff in the OWI office working on translation and analysis of other material available through non-military sources. In the War Department office, emphasis was on analysis of military morale, but data on homefront conditions were also assembled. The work of the staff in the OWI office was concerned with translation of current materials from the Japanese, independent background research on Japanese cultural and psychological characteristics, and the coordination of activities of the research unit with OWI psychological warfare policies and operations. Needless to say, there was free interchange of materials between both of these sections; joint meetings were held; and the data accumulated by one were accessible to the other.

† The author of this report has included Navy members with the O W I group. This is done because they were assigned by the Navy to O W I.

Appendix D

As a War Department operation the research unit worked in cooperation with the Sociological Branch of MIS, had access to MIS intelligence materials, was assigned space and personnel by it, and prepared reports for it on request. The cooperative arrangement with MIS went through several stages. Under the final arrangement, completed in the spring of 1945, the cooperative research unit was known as the Joint Morale Survey. The JMS was comprised of the FMAD staff and the following personnel assigned by MIS: a joint chief of the unit correlative with the OWI division chief, three civilian and three military research analysts, plus occasional other professional workers and clerical assistants. The JMS was divided into two sections — the morale research unit and a propaganda section concerned primarily with analysis of Japanese radio propaganda. The latter section was mainly an Army operation distinct from the morale research unit except for the loan of one OWI analyst to it and the utilization of its radio material by the research unit.

ORGANIZATION CHART FMAD-JMS

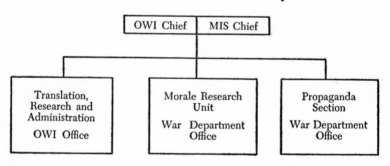

The results of the research were presented to policy-making and operational units in OWI and to the War Department essentially through two media — by formal reports and memoranda, and in formal and informal conferences. The series of reports issued by the research unit, on subjects ranging from over-all studies of military morale and effects of Allied propaganda to reports on special topics, were circulated to policy-making units in OWI and the War Department. These formal reports reached a relatively wide audience of military and civilian agencies, and proved to be particularly useful to certain offices in OSS, the State Department, the Navy, and a British liaison unit concerned with morale problems. In addition to the regularly circulated series of reports, special memoranda were prepared in response to specific requests from MIS or when it was felt necessary. Although the subjects of the reports were in general geared to the known interests of OWI and MIS, suggestions and impetus for following certain lines of investigation also came from the research unit and from leads provided independently by the data.

Probably quite as effective as a means of presenting the point of view and results of the research to persons in key positions were the formal and informal conferences carried on with members of OWI, MIS and other agencies. Representatives of FMAD participated regularly in policy-making meetings of the Far Eastern Division of OWI. Early in the summer of 1945 the co-chief of FMAD left to become director of an OWI over-all planning and coordinating unit for psychological warfare to Japan and provided a strategic link between the research and planning programs. Communication with War Department policy-making officials was likewise maintained through participation in conferences, principally on the part of the Army chief of the unit.

Conferences and particularly informal contacts, not only in OWI and the War Department but also with key persons in other agencies, were of great importance in establishing the research point of view, in communicating the results and in indicating the usefulness of social science research methods in this context.

II. SOURCES

The source material upon which the research was based covered a wide range of intelligence documents, both civilian and military. Military intelligence materials included documents obtained through collection, translation, and interrogation agencies of the Allies, principally American, British, Australian, and Chinese. The military intelligence documents were, of course, the principal source materials for analysis of Japanese military morale, but they also provided data not elsewhere available on internal

Appendix D

social conditions and civilian morale in the Japanese homeland. Of the military documents, the most useful were prisoner of war interrogation reports, and the methods devised for their systematic analysis will be discussed later in detail. In addition to POW interrogations a variety of other types of strictly military intelligence sources, such as captured diaries and enemy military publications and orders, also provided rich data for the study of morale.

Intelligence materials from non-military sources and containing data on homefront conditions and morale were made available through MIS and civilian war agencies, principally the following: OWI outposts, for translation and summaries of Japanese publications (OWI outposts also furnished special POW interrogations on psychological warfare subjects); OSS, for background material and special translations and interrogations; IDC (Inter-Departmental Committee for the Acquisition of Foreign Publications), for translations and summaries of newspapers and periodical articles; and FCC, for translations of Japanese radio broadcasts. Except for certain types of materials, such as Japanese newspaper and radio broadcasts, the sources of data on internal social conditions were less uniform and less susceptible to measurement and systematic analysis than those for military morale. However, the greater variety and wider range of topics in this civilian data opened up unexpected and interesting possibilities. These intelligence documents, both military and civilian, were received currently insofar as translation and transmission facilities permitted. In general, the military documents were forwarded to Washington headquarters from the field with higher priority and became available for analysis more quickly than did civilian documents. As a result, it was possible to keep the analysis of military morale more up to date than that of the civilian data.

One disadvantage in the use of all of these materials for FMAD's research purposes was the inability of the research unit to participate in the gathering of the data and its lack of control over the sources. The materials had originally been collected for a variety of purposes—military, technical, economic, political. In many cases the original observations and collection of data were not made for sociological, psychological, or morale purposes. Except to a very limited extent in some POW interrogations, the research unit was not able to determine nor influence the range and quality of field observations nor the methods of collection of morale data. It used the materials gathered by others, often with different ends in view, as they were presented to the unit. Despite this lack of control over its origin and collection, much of the material proved to be useful and rewarding for the research purposes.

Appendix D

In the following description of specific types of documents utilized, more attention will be given to military than to civilian sources, since their nature and the possibilities for their use are presumably less well known.

A. MILITARY SOURCES

1. POW Interrogations

Interrogation reports were the richest sources of information on Japanese military morale and the most susceptible to systematic analysis. In volume they formed about half of the intelligence documents that came to the unit. POW interrogations, although conducted primarily for military information of operational value, contained other kinds of data useful for morale analysis. Almost all interrogations, except some on specialized subjects, enumerated at least a minimum of personal background items about the prisoner, such as his age, rank, home residence, education and occupation. Statistics on such background items were essential in describing the "total population" of Japanese POWs. The principal data on morale resulted from direct questioning on such subjects as the state of discipline and military spirit in the POW's unit, attitudes toward last-ditch resistance and suicide, or the effects of Allied propaganda. Much could be inferred about the morale pictures from less direct questions on such topics as circumstances of capture, health and food conditions in the unit, supplies and reinforcements, training and patriotic indoctrination. In several series of interrogation reports the POWs were routinely questioned about homefront conditions.

The extreme readiness of Japanese POWs to talk under interrogation and their willingness to cooperate with their captors have been matters for surprise on the part of Allied observers. Such apparent reversal of loyalty becomes more understandable in the light of Japanese psychology and particularly in the light of the Japanese military attitude toward the taking of prisoners. Japanese military ideology did not acknowledge the possibility that a Japanese soldier would surrender, had not in the early part of the war provided security training for this eventuality, and had denied to a soldier once taken prisoner the possibility of his return to Japanese society. Thus cut off from his life as a Japanese, the POW saw himself as starting a new life, and his behavior under interrogation made sense in terms of this new adjustment. The extraordinary cooperation of the Japanese POWs made available a quantity and kind of information that would not have been possible otherwise.

Several different kinds of interrogation reports were used. Their form and content differed according to the place and circumstances of interrogation, that is, whether it was conducted in front line units immediately after capture or later at rear echelons. Reports differed also in respect to the kind of information sought, whether primarily operational for use in the immediate situation or, on the other hand, for long range military, economic, or morale purposes. Three fairly distinct types of reports were used: 1) brief frontline interrogations concentrating on tactical information but containing identifying background data about the POW and, usually, brief notes on morale and the effect of Allied propaganda; 2) more detailed interrogations at rear echelons on both technical and morale subjects; 3) specialized interrogations made in rear areas or at special interrogation centers, often including extended questioning on military morale or homefront conditions. Sometimes in the latter type, essays on subjects pertaining to Japanese ideology and morale and to prospective occupation problems were solicited from POWs or even volunteered by them.

2. *Captured Military Documents*

Of the large volume of Japanese documents captured in military operations several types contained data particularly useful for the research unit. Perhaps the most revealing information about the attitudes of Japanese soldiers under battle conditions came from captured diaries and personal notebooks. The Japanese soldier was apparently accustomed to record his intimate thoughts and feelings in a personal journal to a much greater extent than is usual among Western soldiers. Although sometimes these diaries had a flavor of being written for an audience and reflected ideal soldierly attitudes, they also revealed quite clearly the strains and discontents of the soldier's life. The lengthier diaries often showed a change of attitude as the soldier proceeded from rear areas or successful campaigns to defensive fighting with its cumulative hardships and strain, and diaries from the early part of the war reflected a different mood from those covering later periods. Occasionally, comparable information came from captured letters and personal correspondence.

Appendix D

Captured official documents provided data on indoctrination, training, and official efforts for maintenance of discipline and morale. Information of this kind came from combat operational orders, official communications between rear and frontline headquarters, and training manuals and instructions. Such documents revealed weak spots that were the subject of official concern at various levels of command and the measures by which it was sought to strengthen them.

Translations of captured documents were published by Allied Translation Centers in the various war theaters. Full translations were made of important documents, but in most cases only pertinent extracts or summaries were published. The volume of Japanese documents was greater than the translation centers could handle, and only those judged to be of particular importance for military or other reasons were published. Presumably a great deal of morale material, especially personal data that was of no operational importance, was lost because of this. In some cases, when the catalogue listing of untranslated documents indicated one of particular interest, the original document could be obtained. In general, however, this remained an untapped source because of unavoidable delay in obtaining such originals and the limited facilities of FMAD's own translation unit.

3. *Miscellaneous Military Intelligence Documents*

In addition to these first-hand Japanese sources, military intelligence channels gave access to secondary accounts by non-Japanese individuals and agencies. These included reports by Allied experts on certain aspects of Japanese morale or by non-Japanese who for some reason, such as long residence in Japan, were qualified to give special kinds of information. For knowledge of the military background and progress of campaigns the periodic intelligence reports of Allied units were available.

B. CIVILIAN SOURCES

1. *Japanese Civilian Publications*

These were mainly newspapers and periodicals. Abstracts and translations of articles were received principally from the Inter-Departmental Committee, but also from OWI outposts and other military or civilian field agencies. In addition to translations, the original copies of newspapers and periodicals, or microfilms of them, were in many cases available to the FMAD's own translation unit. The supply of untranslated Japanese materials of this kind, however, was much larger than the resources for handling it. Miscellaneous Japanese civilian publications, mostly of government origin, were also used. It was not possible to keep this material as up to date as the military analysis because of delay in translation or in the transmission of documents.

All of these publications in a sense represented the official Japanese point of view regarding the war effort and homefront conditions. More personal material from "inside Japan" which diverged from this official view was obviously difficult to obtain. Nevertheless, it was possible to use the official material, with due regard to its propaganda bias. It provided a more or less dependable record of internal events and official pronouncements. It also gave a basis for estimating current Japanese attitudes and stresses. By watching the kind and frequency of criticisms of certain social groups — for example, farmers, students, intellectuals, or women — it was possible to judge what problems and what elements of the population were causing most official concern.

2. Radio Monitoring

This last qualification regarding the propaganda bias of Japanese publications holds even more strongly for radio material. But, again, with due regard to this bias, the radio was found invaluable for keeping track of current internal events and the official propaganda line directed by the Japanese toward their own people and toward Greater East Asia. Translations of the daily monitoring of Japanese broadcasts to the homeland, to GEA, and to the Allies were provided by FCC, and were supplemented by monitoring reports from other Allied agencies in the Pacific. The monitored material quoted extensively from current Japanese periodicals. These daily radio reports had the obvious advantage of being more up to date than any other source.

3. Other Publications

Throughout the research, historical and background sources were used in connection with the current intelligence materials. These were writings both by Japanese and by Western observers or "experts" about

Appendix D

Japan. A special FMAD study by Dr. Ruth Benedict* on Japanese behavior and psychology made use of such historical and literary sources, particularly by Japanese writers, as well as first-hand information obtained from intensive interviewing of Japanese who had been reared or had lived in Japan.

III. METHODS AND PROCEDURES

A. *RESEARCH NOTES*

Before discussing in detail the methods and procedures used in one special aspect of the research, the POW interrogations, some of the general office operations and procedures as they were applied to all data used in the research will be described. In brief, the essential procedures consisted of taking notes and extracts of information relevant to the social and psychological interests of the research and classifying and filing these notes under topical headings so that they would be readily and quickly available for analysis and report writing.

1. *Topical Outlines*

The topical outlines grew out of a combination of empirical and theoretical considerations. It was assumed that certain aspects of social organization would have importance for the research. Topics of this order had to do, for instance, with evidences of internal social divisions along class or factional lines, information about ideology and methods of patriotic indoctrination, information about political or military leadership and attitudes toward it, information about child rearing and education. Such topics, or their parallels, are familiar landmarks in any social analysis. The topical outline was organized against such a background of established theoretical interests. In addition, however, the choice of many of the specific topics was conditioned by the kind of data available in the documents. Subdivisions of larger topics were often made on this basis. The homefront sources were found to contain, for instance, a great deal of information about civilian reactions to bombings, about attitudes toward Allied propaganda and Allied military

---

* FMAD Report No. 25, *Japanese Behavior Patterns*, 15 September 1945. Enlarged and expanded, this has since appeared as *The Chrysanthemum and the Sword* (Boston: Houghton Mifflin), 1946.

successes, and about various aspects of the civilian war effort. Military sources yielded sufficient data on certain crucial subjects, such as attitudes toward suicide, maintenance of discipline, or emotional attitudes toward the enemy, to warrant separate topical headings in the outline. Two separate topical outlines were devised in this manner, one for military or "fighting forces" material, the other for civilian or "homefront" material.* These topical outlines were used by the analysts as guides to the kind of material to be extracted or on which notes should be taken; they were also used in the organization and filing of the completed research notes.

2. *Processing*

Certain fundamental procedures were used in the processing of documents received by the research unit. These procedures were applied to all incoming material, although certain types of documents, namely POW interrogations, were in addition subjected to a more elaborate scheme of analysis. Incoming military documents were routed to the research unit before being sent to the MIS library. Documents received from other agencies could in some cases be retained in the files; in other cases they had to be processed and returned. All incoming documents were scanned, and if they contained relevant information, notes were taken, whether or not the document was to remain in the office files. Notes were made in the form of summaries or brief indication of content when the document was lengthy or would be easily accessible in the files or from the library. Direct quotations and more or less extended extracts were made from documents when the material was of crucial importance or when the original document would be difficult to regain. The large volume of incoming MIS documents and the time limit that they could be held for processing (72 hours in the case of important documents) put constant pressure upon the research unit to devise ways and means to expedite their handling. It also meant that compromises had to be made in the completeness with which notes could be taken.

A uniform system of note-taking was devised. All notes, whether summaries or extracts, were made on 5" x 8" sheets, easily manageable in the research files, and were made with sufficient carbon copies to allow

* The *Fighting Forces* and *Homefront* Outlines are given in Appendix I.

Appendix D

the note to be filed under each of the topical headings to which it applied. Some series of brief OWI documents were received in multiple copies that could be cut up or filed in toto under the appropriate headings. The necessary bibliographical information was recorded on the note together with sufficient additional identification to indicate the context or source of the data. In the case of captured documents such identification would include a description of the document, the number of pages it contained, where and when it had been captured, etc. Bibliographical references to all documents processed were also kept on index cards, together with reference to where a complete copy of the notes had been filed, and thus provided a catalogue of all documents processed and a mechanical means for locating the notes taken from any given document.*

3. Research Note Files

The research notes were organized under the headings of the topical outlines in the *Fighting Forces* and *Homefront* Files. Any one note usually was pertinent to several topics in the outline. The mechanical means of marking and filing notes had gone through several revisions in the course of operations. The final and most satisfactory arrangement was to type across the top of the note at the time it was made all of the topics under which it was to be filed, at the same time ensuring that sufficient carbons of the note were made (or cross-references if this were impractical) to be filed under each topic. Each copy was designated for filing by underlining the appropriate topic. Notes were dated according to the time reference of the material contained in them, and in most cases they were filed chronologically under each heading.

In addition to the Fighting Forces and Homefront note files built up in this way, it was felt necessary to maintain a master *Area File*.† One copy of all notes pertaining to a given area, exclusive of Japan proper, was filed chronologically under an appropriate area heading. Thus, at any time a survey of all notes taken on the Philippines or Burma, for example, regardless of the topics dealt with, could be readily made. The Homefront File itself constituted the area file for Japan proper, and

* For detailed description of note-taking procedures, see Appendix II, *Handbook for Processing.*
† See list of Area Headings in *Handbook for Processing*, Appendix II.

within it notes were filed chronologically under each topic heading. The chronological arrangement of notes in the Area and Homefront Files gave a rough time perspective even at this stage of the analysis and facilitated handling the data for estimating time trends.

Other files were maintained for special kinds of material. The files for notes from POW interrogations will be described later together with the special methods for processing POW material. The amount of material from newspapers and periodicals was sufficient to warrant another master file, known as the *Current Opinion File*. One copy of all notes from newspapers and periodicals (or cross-references) were filed here chronologically by publication name. The Current Opinion File thus brought together in convenient form all notes on newspapers and periodicals that had been translated or processed by the research unit. Similarly a separate *Radio File* was kept for notes from FCC and other monitoring. The headings for the Radio File were a duplication of those of the Homefront File, but it was found advisable to keep notes from this special source separate from all other homefront notes.

The research files constituted the materials from which analyses could be made. At any one time they represented all of the materials processed to date. The notes in many cases contained the data in a form in which it could be used directly in preparing reports; in other cases they provided a means of reassembling the original sources. Once used, it was merely a mechanical operation to return the notes to their proper places in the files ready for future reference and reuse.*

---

* A note is required here regarding one aspect of the work organization not touched upon by the authoress of this report.

Research and report writing on particular topics was achieved through what the members of the Division came to call "task forces." After a subject had been selected, or after a request had come in from a policy maker, one of the senior analysts would become head of the work related to the project. He would draw together such staff as he needed from among the processors and the other analysts, but, since the processors had to keep up with their daily routine of handling incoming intelligence material, the "task force" usually operated as such only during half of each day. When the first draft of a report was finished, it would be examined by all the professional members of the Division and then discussed at a meeting. Following this it would be reworked by the "task force," with additional research if need be, and then submitted to the chief of the Division or the co-chief. As a rule the chief would pass it informally to a number of appropriate policy makers for their suggestions and then return it with their and his own comments for a final going over by the "task force." After this the report was given

Appendix D

POW INTERROGATIONS

1. *Definitions and Concepts*

The Definition of Morale

Early in the course of research a basic definition of morale was formulated. While this conception of morale was used as a background and point of orientation in all of the research, it was only in the analysis of military morale from POW interrogations that it was possible to apply it systematically to a comparatively uniform body of data. The definition of morale was stated in most general terms as: The capacity of a group of people to pull together consistently and persistently in pursuit of a common purpose. Five general factors were conceived as contributing to the group capacity for sustained action, as follows: Faith in the Common Purpose, Faith in Leadership, Faith in Other Members of the Group, Organizational Efficiency of the Group, Health and Emotional Balance of Group Members. Choice of these five "morale factors" was based on general social and psychological theory of what elements are assumed to contribute to the state of morale of any group.

In order to reduce these basic factors to more concrete terms, a series of subdivisions was set up to be used as classificatory units in handling the material in POW interrogations. The choice of sub-factors was made partly from theoretical considerations, but also on the basis of the particular group under consideration and the kind of material available. The specific elements to be considered in the case of military morale under combat conditions were, for obvious reasons, different from those that enter into a non-military situation. This necessitated, for example, the phrasing of Faith in the Common Purpose in terms of military vic-

---

to the Division editor who prepared it for publication, checking when necessary with the head of the "task force." When all the research and report writing was completed, the "task force" disbanded. Its members, however, would before long be reassorted and reassembled in a new project of a similar character. Sometimes two or more such groups were in existence simultaneously.

This kind of organization was employed instead of a permanent division between processing and topical research for two reasons. First, it saved the processors from the deadly monotony of an entirely routine task and from the falling off in work quality that often comes as a result of boredom in such circumstances. Second, it kept the processors familiar with how the material they collected daily was actually used and hence it sharpened their judgment and interest in selecting items and placing them in the best categories. — A. H. L.

Appendix D

tory or the phrasing of Organizational Efficiency in terms of adequacy of reinforcements, coordination and weapons. The choice of subdivisions was also conditioned by the kind of information found in the POW interrogations. POWs were questioned more or less directly on some specific subjects, such as their faith in Japanese war aims, hope of victory, or their anticipation concerning what the future might hold for them personally. Information about Organizational Efficiency and the Emotional Balance of Group Members was often revealed as a by-product, in the course of questioning primarily directed toward more strictly military matters. For instance, in describing the events leading up to his capture, the POW would often express in his own terms the state of unit disorganization, disruption of communications, lack of adequate weapons or reinforcements, or health and food conditions. According to these considerations, in the early part of the research the following sub-divisions were made under each of the basic morale factors:

Faith in the Common Purpose — *i. e.*, faith in the purpose of the war, in Japanese victory, in Japan's "mission" in Asia.

Faith in Leadership — *i. e.*, faith in the Emperor, in political leaders, in military leaders, in official Japanese news and information.

Faith in Other Members of the Group — *i. e.*, faith in immediate associates, in the military services as a whole or their major branches, in the people at home.

Organizational Efficiency of the Group — *i. e.*, adequacy of supplies and pay, of communications, reinforcements, coordination, quantity and quality of weapons, and of Japanese military training and efficiency.

Health and Emotional Balance — *i. e.*, POW's health prior to capture, deaths among associates, adequacy of food, feeling of good or bad treatment in service, feeling about conditions at home, confidence in the future, other emotions conducive to good or poor morale.

Theoretical Problems

Some of the theoretical and practical problems encountered in the use of the morale factors and the consequent revisions necessitated will be

Appendix D

discussed later. For the present it is enough to indicate some over-all considerations that were kept in mind in handling the morale factors. It was not considered that positive or negative evidence regarding any one factor could be used directly in judging the level of morale in a given situation. But the factors taken in combination were so considered. This matter has been discussed in previous reports, and one of these summaries is again presented here:

> "We cannot judge Japanese morale directly from any of the data available to this division. We can only deal in comments that manifest attitudes or portray situations which are usually associated with high morale or with low morale or with greater or lesser fighting efficiency. Since we cannot observe morale as such, we must operate with factors which, *in combination,* affect morale or bear on the morale picture. For the most part we are not concerned with single factors but with a set of variables that, taken as a group, are known from much experience to be useful as indicators of morale or of fighting efficiency. Any one indicator may be misleading or of doubtful value when taken by itself, but *the combination* is assumed to be meaningful in the study of morale."

A second important consideration was the fact that the data yielded by interrogation reports were of several different levels. Easiest to deal with were the personal *background* items about the POW, such as his age, rank, education, residence, occupation, etc. Of a different order were his expression of *attitudes* bearing on morale. These were more or less direct statements of faith or lack of faith in items falling under the first three basic morale factors, such as faith in victory, in Japanese war aims, in the Emperor, etc. A third kind of data presented greater difficulty for the analysis. This was the POW's description of *situations* that presumably would affect morale, such as hardships and deprivations undergone. The descriptions might or might not also include expressions of the POW's attitudes toward the situation or indication of its effect on his or the group's morale. This kind of data has been termed situational, or situational-attitude factors. Most of the situational data falls under the last two of the basic morale factors — Organizational Efficiency, and Health and Emotional Balance — and includes, for example, statements about health or the adequacy of food, supplies, and weapons.

Appendix D

Practical Problems

The research problem was to devise procedures whereby the data in interrogations could be recorded and handled both quantitatively and qualitatively. The procedures used were a combination of "code" recording, in which statements or evidence appearing in interrogations were classified under morale or background categories, plus the verbatim or summary recording of the statements on the basis of which the classification or "coding" had been made. On the quantitative side it was desirable to know how often, or in what combinations, various of the items or factors — background, attitudinal, and situational — recurred. Thus, from a simple tabulation of the number of occurrences of all factors, positive or negative, for groups of POWs captured at different times or places, a basis could be derived for estimating and comparing the overall state of morale of these groups. Within a given group of POWs the occurrence of a given factor, positive expressions regarding faith in war aims, for example, could be correlated with such background items as age, rank or education. On the qualitative side, it was necessary to know the content of the statements on the basis of which the statistical count had been made and the kinds of expression that had been classified under each category.

Two systems for quantitative recording were devised in the course of the research. Both were based on the same concept of morale, although the use of "morale factors" was greatly modified in the second system, and both used a procedure of "coding" whereby the information was reduced to manageable units for tabulation and "statistical" treatment. The first system, known for convenience as the *IR Card,* Interrogation Report Card), grew out of the early handling of interrogations and was used substantially in its original form during the first eight months of the research. By that time the experience gained and the increase in number and diversity of incoming interrogations indicated a revision of this procedure. The new system, known as the *POW Code,* was set up in a manner to allow use of statistical machine tabulation.

The POW Code was an extension and refinement of the IR Card system and was intended to remedy some of the theoretical and practical drawbacks that had become obvious in its use.

Appendix D

2. IR Card

Processing an Interrogation Report

The use of the IR Card can perhaps best be explained by describing the procedure used in processing an interrogation report. The essential materials which the analyst has before him are the interrogation report, the IR Card form with its standard category symbols, and the Handbook-Key describing the kind of information to be classified under the standard category symbols of the IR Card.*

The usual interrogation report begins with enumeration of certain background items about the POW — his rank, unit, date and place of capture, age, education, occupation, etc. These are entered by checking the proper symbol on the card, or where necessary by writing in date, age, etc. Next the interrogation normally gives a brief history of the POW's military experience from his induction, departure from Japan or arrival overseas to the time of his capture. From this account such items as the POW's length of service and participation in previous campaigns may be entered on the card by symbol.

So far the transcribing of information has been largely factual and its reduction to symbols a comparatively simple mechanical process. The remainder of the interrogation contains information that is not so directly reducible to symbols, i. e., attitude and situation-attitude data. Usually the report describes in some detail the immediate events leading up to the POW's capture and the circumstances of his capture. This may include his own account of conditions in his unit — the state of disorganization, food and health conditions, inadequacies of men and material, etc. In a full report in addition to interrogation on strictly military matters, the prisoner may be directly questioned on morale subjects such as the following: his contact with and reaction to various forms of Allied propaganda, the state of morale in his unit, his attitude toward suicide, his feelings about being a POW and his future prospects, his attitudes toward various aspects of leadership, toward the possibility of Japanese victory, and his opinions about the righteousness of Japanese war aims.

This kind of material was reduced to symbols by providing a series of categories and sub-categories for data relevant to the morale factors

* The IR Card and the main topics of the IR Handbook-Key are reproduced in Appendix III.

315

Appendix D

(see *IR Handbook-Key*, Appendix III). Sub-categories were set up empirically from the kind of information found to recur in the POW statements. For example, the range of possible circumstances of capture was originally set up as follows: *

R. Circumstances of Capture
1. Surrendered with minimal or no resistance.
2. Ill, wounded, unconscious, or asleep; or weak and exhausted.
3. Overcome while resisting, taking risks rather than be captured.
4. Picked up at sea.
X. Others.

Each of these became a sub-category for this topic and, according to the evidence in the report, the POW was classified under the appropriate symbol.

The method of handling subdivision of the basic morale factors (U to Y in the *IR Handbook-Key*, see Appendix III) was slightly more complicated. Here, in addition to the usual range of sub-categories, provision was made for distinguishing between positive and negative expressions for any one of these. For example, the subdivisions for attitudes toward Leadership were as follows:

V. Faith in Leadership (A. Positive; B. Negative)
1. Faith in the Emperor.
2. Faith in political leaders.
3. Faith in the military high command.
4. Faith in immediately military superiors.
5. Faith in the reliability of Japanese news.
X. Others.

For each of those numbered sub-categories it was necessary to designate whether the expression of attitude was positive or negative by using the additional symbols A and B respectively.

All of the categories were "open-ended" in the sense that in each case information not provided for by the series of symbols could be checked under an additional symbol "X" or "others." The fact that a given

---

* This list was added to later. As far as the system permitted, there was continuous revision of the categories and sub-categories, of the *IR Card Handbook* to cover new kinds of data.

interrogation contained no information whatsoever on a particular subject was revealed by the lack of any symbol marking under that category.

Qualitative Recording

This was done simply by copying onto the back of the card quotes or summaries of POW statements when these varied from or added something to the symbol notation checked on the face of the card. All cases where the "X" or "others" category was checked necessitated some such explanatory comment. Complete notes were taken separately from reports that contained particularly full comments on morale or data not covered by the IR Card categories. For more intensive qualitative studies the symbol markings on the face of the card and the brief notes on the back provided a means of locating and reassembling a series of interrogation reports with information on specific topics.

Some Limitations of the IR Card

The foregoing description outlines the way in which the data from interrogation reports were reduced to a symbol notation that allowed tabulation and quantitative manipulation. The IR Card system had certain theoretical and practical drawbacks that became more evident in the course of the research. As the number of interrogations piled up, it became increasingly cumbersome to make statistical counts and correlations by hand tabulation. It was recognized that the categories needed sharpening and refinement. Comments of different qualitative weight had inevitably been subsumed under the same category and the necessity for further qualitative distinctions had become obvious. The problem of handling some mixed situation-attitude factors had not been satisfactorily solved by the attempt to cast them in the twofold positive-negative framework that served more satisfactorily for simpler attitude expressions. To obviate some of these difficulties a new and more elaborate system of coding and recording data was instituted.

3. POW Code

The coding of interrogations under the new system was begun in April of 1945 and continued to the conclusion of the war. During this time the volume of incoming interrogations was considerably greater, due both to the increasing number of POWs captured and to opening of new military channels for receipt of interrogations. The kind of data in the reports continued to be substantially the same. In addition to the regular interrogations of the previous period, two new series of reports were now being received. One of these was a series of brief interrogations conducted at advance echelons (principally from the SWPA* and Okinawa) immediately after capture. Although brief, these reports had the great advantage of being current, since they were received within a week or two of the POW's capture. In many cases additional interrogations of the same POW at rear echelons were received subsequently. Another special series of reports on POWs who had been questioned fairly extensively on morale and Japanese homefront conditions provided a new and valuable source during this period.

Code Categories

The form of revision of the symbol notation under the POW Code was set by the requirements of the Hollerith card system for machine tabulation. Essentially this required a series of categories (termed "columns" on the Hollerith card, limited to a possible total of 80) referring to major topics found in the POW interrogations. Each of these was divided into sub-categories (termed "punches," limited to 12 for each column) covering the range of possible variations of the data applying to this topic. In general the main categories or topics were analogous to those of the old IR Card but with many additions (76 columns as opposed to 25 major headings on the IR Card).† The additions were in the direction of expansion of the former categories and generally took the form of raising a topic that had been at the sub-category level under the old system to that of a column heading. The main categories, or columns, again included the three fairly distinct kinds of data already indicated — background items, attitudes, and mixed situation-attitude elements.

The kind of expansion and refinement made under the POW Code may be indicated by some comparative illustrations. The IR Card had originally provided a range of five possibilities for classifying evidence about the circumstances of capture of the POW (as enumerated in

* Southwest Pacific Area.
† See Appendix IV for list of *Column Headings of POW Code.*

Appendix D

the previous section). In the POW Code this topic was broken down into two columns, "Circumstances of Capture," and "Physical Condition at Time of Capture." Under each of these columns was a series of 10-12 sub-categories or punches of the following order: *

CIRCUMSTANCES OF CAPTURE

1. Voluntary surrender alone
2. Voluntary surrender with others
3. Formal surrender as part of military unit
4. Minimum or no resistance
5. Attempts to escape when captured
6. Resisted capture
7. Picked up at sea
8. Captured through surprise attack where no possibility of resistance
9. Captured by or with aid of natives
0. Not specified
11. Resistance or escape out of question because of physical condition
12. Not clear

PHYSICAL CONDITION AT TIME OF CAPTURE

1. Ill, wounded, or exhausted — incapacitated
2. Ill, wounded, or exhausted — partially incapacitated
3. Ill, wounded, or exhausted — not incapacitated
4. Ill, wounded, or exhausted — degree of incapacity not clear
5. No evidence that POW ill or wounded
6. POW in reasonably good physical condition
7. Not clear
8. Evidence that POW could move around, but no more specific information
9. (Punch not used)
0. Not specified
11. Report shows evidence that POW's statement re his condition at capture should not be taken at face value
12. (Punch not used)

Those categories of the old IR Card that had been phrased in terms of "faith" or "lack of faith" were no longer handled according to this twofold classification. Under the former system it had been possible to check only whether there was positive or negative evidence of faith in certain factors bearing on morale, regardless of the quality or shading in the POW's expression of his "faith." For example under the general topic of Faith in Group Members the only choice had been between positive or negative expressions of faith concerning immediate associates, the armed services in general, people at home, etc. The POW

---

* The wording of these has been somewhat modified and abbreviated here, although the sense remains the same.

Appendix D

Code elevated each of these sub-categories to the status of a column heading under which it was possible to choose among possibilities that did show those finer qualitative distinctions. For example, the column for Faith in the Homefront contained the following sub-categories:

FAITH IN THE HOMEFRONT

1. Positive — whole-hearted backing up of soldiers.
2. Positive — but with qualifications, such as moderate support, could be better.
3. Negative in general, e. g., people at home shirking their duty, etc.
4. Negative in some one or two particulars only, e. g., profiteering by war workers, etc.
5. Multivalent.
6. "Never thought about it much before capture."
7. Not clear.
8. Attitude of people at home has changed from good to bad, or vice versa.
9. People at home have low morale.
10. Not specified.
11. Majority of people at home think the war is lost.

In general the POW Code made provision not only for classifying various shadings of positive and negative expressions but also, as in the column cited above, for taking care of mixed or "multivalent" attitudes as shown by statements within the same report that were inconsistent or contradictory, and of "not clear" statements that could be classified under a specific punch only by forcing a somewhat arbitrary interpretation. With the increased range of choice afforded, it was not always necessary to keep the main categories "open-ended" by providing an additional punch for "others," since in many cases the specific punches presumably exhausted all possibilities.

Qualitative Recording by Notetaking

A more detailed system was worked out for recording of qualitative data in connection with the POW Code. In general, verbatim notes or extracts were taken on all interrogation material bearing on morale that had been classified under the code categories. In other words, notes were taken to justify all punches marked under the attitude or situation-attitude columns (as distinguished from the background columns). As with all research notes, these were made on 5″ x 8″ sheets for filing under the appropriate headings. In the case of notes from POW interrogations, these headings for filing were the column and punch headings of the POW Code. Since the statements extracted usually applied to more than one column and punch, notes were made in sufficient carbons for filing under all appropriate headings. Thus, it was possible to locate immediately, for example, all description of circumstances of capture made by all POWs processed to a given date and within this to isolate the statements of those who had surrendered voluntarily or of those who had attempted to escape or resist capture. These notes showed the kind of POW statement that had been classified under any given category or sub-category, and, as they grew, provided in a sense an empirical definition of the category. In addition to the notes filed under column and punch headings, one complete copy of all notes taken from the interrogation of a given POW was filed by area and date of capture, thus giving an area survey of the POW material. This body of qualitative material was built up as the processing of interrogations progressed and could be used for study and analysis even before a sufficiently large sample of POWs had been coded and made available for statistical treatment.

From the foregoing description, it is obvious that the POW Code provided for classifying and reducing to symbol notation a much greater amount of detail than had been possible by the IR Card. It allowed the handling of finer distinctions and shades of expression. Machine sorting under the POW Code would permit much speedier tabulation and facilitate the making of correlations that would otherwise be out of the question. We may now turn to a consideration of some of the practical aspects of handling the POW data in such a refined system and to a discussion of the broader problems inherent in categorization and quantitative treatment of the POW material in general.

4. Discussion of Methods

Reliability of POW Statements

The extraordinary cooperativeness of Japanese POWs under interrogation has already been noted. This fact greatly facilitated the study of

Appendix D

military morale from the point of view and with the techniques employed by the research unit. Despite their willingness to talk, it was necessary to take into account certain problems of validity and interpretation in using the information recorded in interrogation reports.

The factual data given by POWs was considered generally reliable, including both personal background items and military intelligence when the POW was able to or did give such information. Most reports contained the interrogator's estimate of the reliability of the data. The dependability of military information supplied by POWs, such as identification of units and description of installations, was subject to check in subsequent operations, and the evidence in the reports indicated a remarkably high degree of reliability. The impression given by seeing a large volume of POW interrogations was that only very infrequently was there intentional falsification by the POW and that when it occurred it could be spotted by the interrogator's evaluation, by internal inconsistencies, or by comparison with later interrogations.

The validity of statements about attitudes or descriptions of situations experienced by the POW was of a slightly different order. With complete sincerity on the part of the POW such statements might be incomplete or misleading and liable to different interpretation. One danger here lay in evaluating statements that might be colored by attitudes developed in the post-capture period. The Japanese POW, cut off sharply from his society by the very fact of having become a POW, appeared in many cases to experience a shift of loyalty to his captors. The passage of time, altered circumstances and the POW's post-capture experience might considerably change his former attitudes about defeat, patriotic ideology, leadership, etc. The research unit was aware of these complications. Insofar as possible, reactions and attitudes of the pre-capture period were distinguished from post-capture attitudes and only the former used in the morale analysis. However, attitudes developed in the post-capture period were also of interest for their bearing on future military occupation and reconstruction.

Quality of Interrogations

The quality of interrogations for morale purposes varied greatly. This was true both of the type of questions asked and, presumably, of the methods of questioning used, the time taken for interrogation, and the kind of rapport established. The attention paid to morale data varied according to the purpose of the interrogation, whether at front or rear echelon, according to policies of the theatre commands, and other factors. In general it was not possible to know whether absence of morale information was because the POW was not questioned on these subjects or because he did not respond when questioned. In one group of early interrogations it was specifically stated that the POWs had been questioned on morale subjects but that the material had been withheld since it was not felt worth including in the reports. In this case the supplementary material was obtained by special request, but the incident illustrated an all too prevalent attitude toward the value of morale data. It was necessary to keep all of these facts in mind in the quantitative analysis to guard against having the statistics reflect merely the thoroughness of interrogation. Although the research unit did not in general have control over its sources and the methods or completeness of interrogation, it did directly influence the operations of one OWI interrogation team by actively participating in the construction of questionnaires and formulation of interview policies. Toward the end of the war improvement was also apparent in the quality and extensiveness of Army morale interrogation.

Sampling

Another aspect of the POW material over which the research unit did not have control was the sampling process. Certain series of interrogation reports were available to the unit, but it was not known what proportion this represented of the total interrogations made. Furthermore, there was no way of knowing what proportion of the total prisoners taken were questioned, nor, if selection was made, what types of POWs were chosen. In general, because of the connection with MIS, interrogations made by the Army were more readily available than those from Navy sources. By comparison with figures of total POWs taken in the various campaign areas it was clear that the number of reports available for coding by no means represented the totals of POWs captured.

The number of POWs processed (by IR Card and POW Code) had reached about 2500 by the end of the war. Up to March 1945 all individual interrogation reports available to the division, including reports on Japanese Army, Navy and civilian POWs, were processed by the IR Card system. Beginning with the use of the POW Code a procedure of sampling was worked out. All Navy POWs were coded since the number captured was so small. Civilians were not coded although they were processed and notes taken on pertinent data. The reports on Army POWs, which constituted the largest group available, were sampled on a random basis, *i. e.*, by coding all POWs who had been assigned odd serial numbers in the field. Since more than one serial number was often assigned to the same POW as he progressed to rear areas, it was found necessary to maintain an elaborate card index by POW name and number to prevent duplication. Later during the analysis and shortly before surrender, it was found necessary to limit still further the proportion of incoming reports to be coded due to limited personnel and facilities. At this time the proportion from certain by-passed areas was cut down, but POWs were still selected on a random numerical basis. At the same time the total number from certain crucial areas (such as Okinawa) were coded. Thus, while the representativeness of the sample of POW reports reaching the research unit was not known, the unit's choice of reports for coding, when such choice was necessary, was made partly on a random basis and partly according to type of report desired.

Problems of Categorization

The refinement of categories made in the POW Code was an attempt to overcome certain difficulties that had been encountered in classifying and categorizing the kind of material met in POW interrogations. The original IR Card leaned heavily upon a twofold positive-negative classification scheme. In this system statements or evidence of widely differing intensity were lumped under one positive or negative heading, thus losing the variations and weight of the original expressions. For example, under the dichotomous classification a statement that the people at home were generally discouraged at the course of the war and had low morale would receive the same negative symbol notation as a mere specific criticism that under wartime conditions a certain group was able to profiteer at the expense of others. Multiplication and subdivision of the categories in the POW Code attempted to make just such qualitative distinctions. The new punches classified separately these two degrees of dissatisfaction about homefront support.

Appendix D

But the possible range of POW expression, and the even wider range of possible interpretation of the significance behind the expression, could by no means be exhaustively covered within the practical limits of the new code. Although more refined; the sub-categories could still not be exact in many cases. The attempt to be more specific ran into the opposite danger of developing into an infinite itemization of categories, none of which contained sufficient cases to be usable statistically. In practice the extension of sub-categories was limited by the number of punches allowed on the Hollerith cards (12 for each column). Some changes in content of the punches were necessary as the work progressed in order to cover data that had not been anticipated. The final definition of the content of any sub-category could always be checked empirically by reference to the notes taken to justify punches made under it.

POW data in the form of mixed *situation-attitude* statements, as contrasted with expressions of *attitudes,* presented certain difficulties for categorization and analysis. It was felt that under the IR Card system the distinction between these two kinds of material had not been clearly drawn. Nor had the necessity of handling them differently in the analysis been realized. In some cases they had not been classified under the twofold positive-negative scheme, as in the range of choices under Circumstances of Capture. In other cases, principally in sub-categories of the last two of the basic morale factors — Organizational Efficiency of the Group, and Health and Emotional Balance — some of the situation-attitude expressions had been forced into this twofold positive-negative scheme. Statements about adequacy or inadequacy of supplies, weapons, or food were rated as positive or negative and thereupon treated directly as contributing to high or low morale respectively. The legitimacy of this treatment was questioned, since the relationship of such situational factors to morale is more complicated than in the case of attitudes. It is true that high morale may, and certainly in the case of the Japanese often did, surmount material inadequacies and the immediate hardships of the combat situation. The effect of such hardships on morale differs when considered in the short or the long run. The form of the POW Code did not limit classification of this kind of material to the positive-negative scheme. As in the case of attitudes it provided for more subdivisions and gradations, although in the analysis the problem still remained of interpreting the relation of these situational factors to the general morale picture.

Appendix D

Problems of "Statistical" Treatment

Some of the problems of statistical method and presentation that were encountered in the POW analysis warrant explanation here. The foregoing discussion has indicated the quality of the data. In general, it may be said that the data, in the form in which they were available, were more amenable to a "clinical" than to a "statistical" treatment. A review of the research unit's attitude on this point, as discussed in a previous report, is repeated here:

> ". . . Both the quantity and quality of the materials necessitate an approach which is more clinical than it is that of the statistical laboratory. Quantitative trends and breakdowns are presented because it is believed that this is one useful means of communicating the facts upon which reports are based. But there is no implication that every chart or table shows relationships which a statistician would accept as unequivocally significant. At the same time it should be remembered that statisticians agree that a consistent trend where small numbers and small differences are involved can be as meaningful as a statistically significant difference between a single pair of adequate samples. Our whole method is that of proceeding on the basis of successive approximations. As more data accumulate and as experience provides greater skill in analyzing them, each succeeding approximation approaches closer to full trustworthiness."

The quantitative treatment was felt to be illuminating and necessary, but it was not considered essential to conform to all requirements of a rigorous statistical method.

One of the most important uses of the results of coding was not statistical at all in the strictest sense. While the coding was in progress and before a large enough body of material had been accumulated for statistical analysis, the notes taken and filed under any of the coding categories provided an exhaustive qualitative and a rough quantitative survey of the particular subject. Thus, for example, all statements regarding suicide — the POWs' own attempts or thoughts about it, instances of suicide in their units, descriptions of "banzai" charges or suicide missions—were readily and conveniently accessible at any time. The material in this form was maintained up to date with the current processing of interrogations, while the detailed quantitative study had to wait upon the completion of a larger group of interrogations, over 500, before machine sorting and analysis could be undertaken.

Appendix D

IV. SUMMARY AND FUTURE POSSIBILITIES

The traditionally high morale attributed to the Japanese and the spectacular early successes of the Japanese Army, made it imperative for the United Nations to bring together all information possible about Japanese social and psychological characteristics and about ways in which psychological warfare might be successfully carried on against this enemy. As a result of this interest and need, the Foreign Morale Analysis Division of the Office of War Information was established with a staff consisting of social scientists and analysts with wide social science interests.

Soon a cordial reciprocal relationship was developed with the Military Intelligence Service of the War Department. Space and facilities in the Pentagon Building were made available for members of the FMAD staff, and War Department documents, especially Prisoner of War Interrogation Reports and captured papers such as diaries, were routed to the unit for analysis. A particularly friendly and useful liaison was established with the Sociological Branch of the MIS, under whose aegis the FMAD operated as far as War Department matters were concerned. Helpful exchanges with personnal of the Political Branch of MIS were also frequent. Out of the cooperative arrangement with the Sociological Branch grew finally the Joint Morale Survey, a project to which both the FMAD and the Sociological Branch contributed staff members who worked together on assignments of particular interest to the Army and to OWI. This experiment in collaboration became one of the outstanding examples of successful joint effort by different government agencies during the war.

In the largest sense, the principal task of the FMAD was to define the social-psychological concept of morale with enough precision and accuracy so that its main outlines might be followed, its fluctuations measured, and the effects upon it of our military action and psychological warfare estimated. This was essential, of course, in order to anticipate the degree of enemy resistance that could be expected and to plan future operations both of a military and propagandistic nature.

With these ends in mind, an analysis of data for the factors involved in morale was undertaken. A system was devised for quickly and uniformly processing the large amount of material which came to the unit. This was accomplished in such a manner that items pertaining to morale were so recorded and filed that their correlations with each other and with background elements could be readily studied and changes over time indicated. The problems presented led to the employment of various techniques, such as coding of data for machine tabulation or utilization of content analysis.

The findings of the unit have been described in 45 formal reports and a large number of substantial memoranda. But perhaps the most important contribution has been the demonstration that matters of human motivation and behavior affecting our national safety and our relations with other nations, can be rigorously studied by social scientists using established methods of their fields, and that such organized and disciplined inquiry can provide a basis for interpretation, prediction, action and policy. The history and development of the FMAD squarely raises the question of whether this type of activity should not be perpetuated and even expanded under government auspices in the post-war world.

APPENDIX I. TOPICAL OUTLINES

GENERAL INSTRUCTIONS ACCOMPANYING OUTLINES

The headings in these outlines are the topics under which notes and extracts on Fighting Forces and Homefront data are to be taken and filed. Capital letters (e.g., PROPAGANDA, SOCIAL STRUCTURE) indicate main headings under which notes will be organized in the files. Ordinary letters italicized (e.g., Allied Propaganda, Classes) indicate specific sub-headings under which notes will be filed. Topics written within parentheses following a specific sub-heading are merely guides as to the material to be covered by the sub-heading, warnings to be sure to include such material.

It should be remembered that the primary interest of the research is in morale. Material that is only of background nature for morale studies should be indexed only rather than copied out in full. For example, in Homefront material, if a five-page description of reorganization of the administrative set-up in a prefecture is encountered, the processor should merely note this fact with perhaps a few brief sentences about particularly interesting or striking features of the content. On the other hand, material on any topic that has obvious and direct implications for morale is to be extracted.

Appendix D

FIGHTING FORCES OUTLINE

A. *ORGANIZATIONAL EFFICIENCY*

1. *Food* (rations, gripes about quantity and quality, shortages)
2. *Supplies* (other than food; excludes ammunition) (Concern about home front production, attitudes toward)
3. *Communication* (includes official mail and censoring of mail)
4. *Comforts* (cigarettes, comfort kits, brothels, sake, etc.)
5. *Recreation*
6. *Personal Relations* (friction between officers and men, officers and officers, men and men, regulars and reservists, military and civilians)
7. *Coordination* (cooperation of other armed services or within a service; attitudes toward other armed services; lack of air support)
8. *Weapons* (includes quantity, quality and effectiveness of ammunition; strength of installations; does not include transport, other supplies, etc.)
9. *Pay*
10. *Numbers* (of officers, men, civilians, reenforcements)
11. *Discipline* (crimes; court martial; mutinies)
12. *Living Conditions* (weather; cleanliness and sanitation; clothing; insect pests, etc.)
13. *Vital Statistics* (casualties; numbers of men captured)
14. *Health* (medical and nursing service; diseases; medicines and lack of)
15. *Minorities* (minority or nationality groups within Army — Koreans, Formosans, etc.)
16. *Training* (instruction and regulation)
17. *Transportation* (includes travel to and from the front)
18. *Background*
    N.B.: This topic later eliminated, material under it merged with *Military*, See F, 11.
19. *Desertion* (desertion, surrender, capture)
20. *Civilians* (civilians attached to military units, including laborers)
21. *Security* (precautions; espionage and counter-espionage)

B. *MORALE*

1. *Rumors* (origin, spread, and influence; whether in rear or fighting areas)
2. *Homesickness*
3. *Ideology* (Bushido, including "no surrender" policy; spiritual superiority; Emperor; Greater East Asia; purpose of war and rightness of Japan's cause)
4. *Enemy* (attitudes toward enemy armed forces under battle conditions, fear, hate, revenge, praise, etc.; complaints about Allied use of gas, bacterial warfare, etc.; any mention of enemy in emotional context, other mention of enemy goes under *Other Peoples*, See F, 6.)
5. *Suicide* (includes attempts at suicide and self-mutilation)
6. *Measures* (taken by Japanese for improving or maintaining morale of own troops)
7. *Bombings* (strafing, reactions to own experiences in being bombed and to other bombings of military groups or installations)
8. *Defeat* (reactions to Allied successes, local and general, explanations of, etc.; reactions to Allied air superiority)
9. *Victory* (beliefs about; negotiated peace; defeatism, etc.)
10. *Post-war* (expectations, anticipations, plans)
11. *Morale* (general statements about high or low morale; overall references to morale; material on morale not covered by any of the foregoing specific headings)
12. *Leadership* (morale reactions to high command, political leadership, etc.)
13. *Emotionality* (other than as covered above; reactions to death or wounding of friends; concern about people at home; fear, hope, anxiety, satisfaction and other emotions regardless of content)
14. *Subversive Activities* (includes malingering through faked illness, etc.)
15. *Specific Military Units* (material on, sentiments about, etc.)

C. *PROPAGANDA*

1. *Allied Propaganda*
1A. *Suggestions for Allied Propaganda*
2. *Japanese Propaganda*
3. *Counter-Propaganda* (Allied and Japanese)

Appendix D

D. *INTERROGATIONS AND POWs*

1. *Japanese Methods of Interrogation*
2. *Allied Methods*
3. *Allied POWs* (held by Japanese)
4. *Japanese POWs* (Japanese as POWs; their attitudes; official policy towards POWs; returned POWs, Nomonhan Incident)

E. *OCCUPIED AREAS AND NATIVES*

1. *Organized Resistance* (resistance organizations, guerrillas, spies)
2. *Administration* (general, including conscription of native labor)
3. *Propaganda* (Japanese and Allied to inhabitants of occupied areas or natives)
4. *Caucasians* (attitudes of natives and inhabitants toward)
5. *Natives* (general dealings of Japanese with natives)
6. *Background* (background data on area)
7. *Allied Military Government*

F. *MISCELLANEOUS*

1. *Religion*
2. *Superstitions*
3. *Death and the Dead* (beliefs about, reactions to corpses, etc.)
4. *Atrocities* (Japanese and Allied)
5. *Axis* (attitudes toward Germany, Italy; stereotypes about Germans, Italians, etc.)
6. *Other Peoples* (attitudes toward and stereotypes of Allied and neutral nations; attitudes toward things Western in general)
7. *Women* (attitudes toward, treatment of)
8. *News* (reactions to; belief in news put out by Japanese, Allied, or neutral agencies)
9. *Personalities*
10. *Diaries*
10A. *Letters* (all personal correspondence, references to letters but without giving contents; official correspondence goes under *Communication*, A, 3)
10B. *Essays by POWs*

331

Appendix D

11. *Military* (all material on military topics not covered by any of the foregoing categories; organization, disposition, etc. of Japanese army; awards and citations; ruses and tricks; reinforcements or lack of, when not expressed in terms of co-ordination of the armed forces)
12. *General Psychology*
13. *Sources*
14. *Holidays*

HOMEFRONT OUTLINE

A. *ECONOMICS*

1. *Food* (includes food shortages; rationing of food; data on harvests or crop failures; ersatz foods; price of food goes under *Cost of Living*, A, 5.)
2. *Housing* (shortages and construction, except those due to bombing; fuel and fuel shortages)
3. *Clothing* (shortages; rationing; quality; changes; price goes under *Cost of Living*, A, 5.)
4. *Welfare* (social insurance; relief, but *not* including the measures taken to provide for the subsistence needs of evacuated or bombed-out civilians)
5. *Cost of Living* (changes in prices of commodities; inflation; official measures for price control and inflation control; profiteers; black markets; privileged groups; taxes)
6. *Wages* (rise and fall of wages; freezing of wages; wage differentials between various groups and resentments over them)
7. *Labor* (working conditions; tenant-landlord conflicts; hours of work and changes therein; labor organizations; workers who feel uprooted; all kinds of dissatisfaction with work; strikes and labor riots; cynicism of workers in war industry; absenteeism; prejudices against other workers)
8. *Business and Industry* (includes industry and industrialization; profits)
9. *War Production* (shipbuilding; shortages of business and industrial materials; conservation of materials for war production; production increases and decreases; dispersion of industrial enterprises)

Appendix D

10. *Manpower* (military and labor conscription; occupational recruiting and deferment; manpower shortage)

B. COMMUNICATION

1. *Radio* (except propaganda uses)
2. *Press* (includes magazines, books, periodicals)
3. *Dissemination* (telephone, telegraph, cables; news-reels; postal system, including change in postal rates; information services for civilians other than the strictly propaganda ones)
4. *Distrust* (distrust of news in press, radio, movies — whether official or not, whether obviously propaganda or not)
5. *Transportation* (means used; restrictions on civilian travel; gas rationing; shortages of various types of vehicles)
6. *Rumors* (gossip and rumors — their origin, spread, and influence)

C. VITAL STATISTICS

1. *Health* (epidemics, diseases, mental disorders, nutritional deficiencies)
2. *Medicine* (medical services; public health organizations and measures; hospital facilities; shortages of physicians, nurses and medicines)
3. *Population* (migration; mortality rates; other vital statistics)

D. SOCIAL STRUCTURE

1. *Classes* (socio-economic classes; occupational classes such as business and professional men, landlords, clerks, etc.; aristocracy; feeling of persons in low economic groups that life could be no worse if Japan lost)
2. *Factions* (military and industrial clique groups; political parties and activities; political attitudes toward specific factions; self-centered groups seeking to use the emergency to force their particular loyalties upon the nation, e.g., economic, professional, or moral pressure groups)
3. *Minorities* (Eta, Koreans and Formosans; scapegoat tendencies toward these or other groups)
4. *Subversive Activities* (Communism; liberalism; Free Japan Movement)
5. *Family* (family system; everything on domestic life)

6. *Women* (position of women, especially as changed by war conditions; women in factories, etc.)
7. *Intellectuals* (attitudes toward and of students and intellectuals)
8. *Education*
9. *Leadership* (all material on military, political, economic, religious personalities)
10. *Imperial Institution* (Emperor and Imperial family, activities of, beliefs about and attitudes toward; Imperial rescripts)
11. *Associations* (organization and activities of societies like IRRA; secret societies; attitudes of others toward such societies; also non-political clubs)
12. *Rural-Urban* (all materials on rural or urban groups, their characteristics; differences in behavior and attitudes of rural-urban groups)
13. *Sectionalism* (Honshu vs. Kyushu; ken vs. ken, etc.)
14. Recreation (movies, games, and other entertainment)
15. *Armed Services* (armed forces as a social group; disruption of ordinary social and family life through absence of fighting men; attitudes toward Japanese prisoners of war; concern expressed about men on the fighting fronts)

E. GOVERNMENT

1. *Politics* (one copy of extracts on political clubs to be filed under this heading)
2. *Control* (overall Governmental control of war effort and civilian life)
3. *Organization* (bureaucracy and changes therein)
4. *Attitudes* (general reactions of individuals and groups to government and government policy in general; feelings of remoteness of government in times of crisis; distrust of war promises of government)
5. *Policy* (overall governmental policies; confusions and contradictions in)

F. RELIGION AND IDEOLOGY

1. *Shintoism* (ceremonies; beliefs; mythology)
2. *Buddhism* (watch for distrust by Buddhists of war as such; of suspicion of being "used" in S.E. Asia to further military aims)

3. *Christianity* (missionaries, missions, and attitudes toward; revisions of Christianity to include Emperor cult; persecutions of Japanese Christians)

4. *Ceremonial Calendar* (holidays, feast days, etc.)

5. *Other Religion* (ceremonies, beliefs, myths which may not definitely be ascribed to any of the three religions above; unformalized and uninstitutionalized religious beliefs and practices not known to be connected with above three religions.

6. *Ideology* (all official ideology not covered above, discussions and statements of as well as attitudes toward; Bushido; "spiritual superiority;" indoctrination in official ideology; Japanese as Savior of Asia; Greater East Asia Co-Prosperity Sphere; belief that Japan always wins, etc.)

G. BOMBINGS

1. *Armed Forces* (reactions to bombings in Japan)

2. *Civilian* (reactions: anger, fear, migration, panic, horror, succorance, etc.; behavior of individuals in other than emotional terms)

3. *Official Measures* (evacuation and ways of handling and caring for refugees; air raid precautions; measures for deflecting aggression against officials, *i.e.*, by identification of home front and army, etc.)

H. OTHER PEOPLES

1. *Allies* (stereotypes of any nation; conceptions of life in; interpretations of Japan's past relations with; criticisms of acts or beliefs of Allied—includes Russia—nations, such as American behavior toward colored peoples; lack of righteous indignation against Americans, British, etc.; discussions of Allies' plans, etc.)

2. *Allied Successes* (fear, contempt, revenge, hate, intensified efforts; reactions to Allied superiority in production, material resources, etc.)

3. *Allied Propaganda* (contact with, reactions toward)

4. *Things Western* (attitudes toward, importations, dances, music, words, sports)

5. *Neutrals* (non-Oriental only)

6. *Oriental Peoples* (materials about and attitudes toward regardless whether occupied, enemy, or technically Allies; includes India, Malaya, Dutch East Indies, Thailand, Philippines, French Indo China)

7. Axis (material about and attitudes toward Axis nations)

Appendix D

I. *JAPANESE PROPAGANDA*
   1. *Propaganda Organizations*
   2. *Domestic* (for domestic consumption in radio, press, magazines, etc.)
   3. *Occupied Areas* (and GEA Sphere)
   4. *Foreign* (for foreign consumption)
   5. *Counter Propaganda* (answers to Allied propaganda)

J. *MISCELLANEOUS*
   1. *Customs* (other than covered elsewhere; tea ceremony, flower arrangements, etiquette, geisha houses)
   2. *War Effort* (civilian efforts other than covered elsewhere, e.g., voluntary money contributions and activities such as entertaining soldiers, carrying their luggage at the train, etc.)
   3. *Aberrations* (suicide and self-mutilations; delinquency; escapism; atrocities — includes attitudes of home front toward Japanese and Allied military atrocities)
   4. *Catastrophes* (earthquakes and floods, reactions to and measures taken to prevent or mitigate effects of)
   5. *Character* (includes theories by Japanese and foreign students of Japanese personality and character structure; Japanese humor)
   6. *Peace* (faith in Japanese victory or in possibility of a negotiated peace; defeatism; statements about times when it is thought war will end and circumstances under which it will end; attitudes toward and speculations about post-war Japan)
   7. *Emotionality* (all utterances of intense emotionality regardless of content; hopes, fear, satisfaction, anxiety in different groups and individuals; disappointment in expectations; desire for business or occupation as usual; attitudes to and about death, corpses, etc.)
   8. *Morale* (overall references to Japanese morale that do not fit under more specific topics listed earlier; includes material on friction other than as covered under factions, minorities, measures for bolstering morale of home front)
   9. *Child Training* (other than formal education; socialization; discipline; indoctrination of children in patriotism and official ideology; child welfare-methods of dealing with orphans, etc.)
   10. *Public Safety* (police and fire; public order except as related to bombing and natural catastrophes or as otherwise covered in other headings; crime)
   11. *Letters* (all personal correspondence including postcards)

Appendix D

APPENDIX II. HANDBOOK FOR PROCESSING

I. TOPICAL HEADINGS

Research notes from all intelligence materials are to be taken under the topical headings of the Homefront and Fighting Forces outlines. Notes should be made in sufficient copies so that a copy (or cross-reference sheet) may be filed under each of the appropriate topical and area headings.

The main Fighting Forces and Homefront headings under which notes will be organized in the files are indicated by capital letters (e.g., SOCIAL STRUCTURE) and need not be written on the note sheets by processors. Specific sub-headings under which notes will be filed are indicated by lower case letters in italics (e.g., *Classes*). All of the topical sub-headings under which a given note is to be filed should be typed across the top of the note sheet. The processor can then underline the appropriate heading under which each copy of the note is to be filed.

II. AREA HEADINGS

The area headings will be used for filing both POW extracts and notes from non-POW intelligence materials. (See list of Area Headings at the end of Appendix II.) As with the topical headings, the main areas (e.g., CENTRAL PACIFIC ISLANDS) indicate divisions under which the notes will be organized in the area file. They are to be written on the note sheet *only* in the following cases: 1) when the sub-area is not known, 2) when the sub-area does not appear on the accompanying list, or 3) when the material in the note applies to the whole area rather than to a particular sub-area within it. The sub-area should *always* be written on the note when it is known, *plus the specific locality*. A general rule to follow is that sufficient place identification should be given so that an analyst using the note will be able to locate the place to which the material applies, or in the case of POW notes, the place of capture of the POW.

III. DATE HEADINGS

The area heading should be followed by the date to which the material in the note applies. In the case of POWs this will be the date of capture. If the date reference of the note is not clear from the context, the date of the report may be used, preceded by the word "prior."

Appendix D

IV. *NOTES ON THE USE OF TOPICAL, AREA, AND DATE HEADINGS IN FILING*

One complete set of notes on a given item (preferably the original) is allotted to the Area File if one of the areas outside Japan is involved. Within the Area File notes are filed chronologically. It will be found that some Fighting Forces material does not have any place reference, or the place reference is too general to fall under any one of the area headings (e.g., an order issued from GHQ Tokyo re Japanese attitude toward POWs that applies to all areas). To cover these cases a GENERAL or "overall" area has been set up and one copy of all Fighting Forces notes that cannot be assigned to a specific area will be filed chronologically here.

Homefront notes concerning Japan proper (four home islands) are filed chronologically under each topical sub-heading. In writing the topical sub-headings across the top of the note the most important heading should appear first and the complete original copy of the notes should be filed under it. (The "JAPAN" area is reserved for Fighting Forces material that concerns troops or military activities and installations within Japan proper; it is not to be used for Homefront material on Japan proper.)

V. *NOTES ON FORM OF RESEARCH NOTES AND INDEX CARDS*

The bibliographical heading of research notes should contain on the first line (below the topical and area headings) the MIS Library number (or place where the document may be found), the source (see list of source abbreviations for intelligence reports that we handle frequently), the report number if in a numbered series, the date of report. The second line of the heading should give more specific identification and description of the item, including number of pages. In the case of captured documents this would include document number, title, place and date of capture, etc.

For each document on which notes are taken an index card is made with this same bibliographical heading, titles of articles on which notes have been taken, and notation of where one complete copy of the notes has been filed. This notation should refer to the area and date in all cases except Homefront notes concerning Japan proper, where the most important topical sub-heading and date should be used.

The color of note paper to be used for different sources is as follows: white for information from POWs; blue for captured military documents; green for Japanese civilian sources (e.g., Japanese newspapers, periodicals, radio, etc.); yellow for secondary reports by Allied sources (e.g., Allied estimates of Japanese military or civilian situation, etc.)

AREA HEADINGS

A. NEW GUINEA

1. Buna, Gona
2. Lae, Salamaua
3. Huon Peninsula
4. Wewak, Hollandia, Aitape
5. Biak, Maffin Bay, Noemfoor, Manokwari, Sansapor, Wageo, Schouten Is., Vogelkop
6. Moluccas (add specific island)

B. SOLOMONS – BISMARCKS

1. Guadalcanal
2. New Georgia
3. Bougainville
4. Tulagi
5. New Britain
6. New Ireland
7. Admiralties (add specific island)

C. CENTRAL PACIFIC ISLANDS

1. Saipan
2. Tinian
3. Guam
4. Carolines (add specific island)
5. Marshalls (add specific island)
6. Gilberts (add specific island)

D. INDIA – BURMA

1. Arakan
2. Imphal-Manipur
3. Myitkyina

E. PHILIPPINES

1. Leyte
2. Luzon
3. Mindanao

F. NEI (Netherlands East Indies)

1. Borneo

G. CHINA

H. OUTLYING ISLANDS – JAPANESE

1. Iwo Jima
2. Okinawa

I. SEA (Southeast Asia)

J. FORMOSA

K. KOREA

L. MANCHURIA

M. JAPAN (for Fighting Forces material only)

N. GENERAL (for Fighting Forces material only)

APPENDIX III. IR CARD AND HANDBOOK-KEY *

Background Items

A. Identification of POW and Report
B. Date of Interview or Report
C. Rank
D. Place of Capture
E. Date of Capture
F. Age at Time of Capture
G. Home Province
H. Racial Group
I. Marital Status
J. Military Unit
K. Education
L. Occupation
M. Interviewer's Estimate of Intelligence
N. Interviewer's Estimate of Cooperativeness
O. Service Status
P. Years of Service
Q. Areas of Activity

Attitude and Situational Factors

R. Circumstances of Capture
S. Attitude toward Being POW
T. Influence of Allied Propaganda
U. Faith in Common Purpose
  A. Positive
  B. Negative
V. Faith in Leadership
  A. Positive
  B. Negative
W. Faith in Other Members of Group
  A. Positive
  B. Negative
X. Organizational Efficiency of Group
  A. Positive
  B. Negative
Y. Health and Emotional Balance
  A. Positive
  B. Negative

* The Handbook-Key has been abbreviated here. Only the main topics are listed. Under each of these main topics is a series of numbered sub-categories. Illustrations of the sub-categories under R. *Circumstances of Capture* and V. *Faith in Leadership* are given in the text (p. 316).

A.		B.		C.
D.		E.	F.	G.

```
H.  1 2 3 4 X
I.  1 2 3 X
J.  2 20 38 50 51 X
K.  1 2 3 4 5 6 7 X
L.  1 2 3 4 5 6 7 8 9 X
M.  1 2 3
N.  1 2 3
O.  1 2 X
P.  0 1 2 3 4 5 6 7 8 9 10 X
Q.  1 2 3 4 5 6 7 8 9 10 11 12 13 14 15
    16 17 18 19 20 21 X
R.  1 2 3 4 X
S.  1 2 3 4 5 6 7 X
T.  1 2 3 4 5 6 X
UA. 1 2 3 4 5 6 X
UB. 1 2 3 4 5 6 X
VA. 1 2 3 4 5 X
VB. 1 2 3 4 5 X
WA. 1 2 3 4 5 6 7 8 9 10 X
WB. 1 2 3 4 5 6 7 8 9 10 X
XA. 1 2 3 4 5 6 7 8 X
XB. 1 2 3 4 5 6 7 8 X
YA. 1 2 3 4 5 6 7 8 9 10 11 X
YB. 1 2 3 4 5 6 7 8 9 10 11 X
```

APPENDIX IV. COLUMN HEADINGS OF POW CODE *

Background Columns

1-4 Identification (FMAD ser. no.)
5 Source
6-7 Date of Report of Interrogation
8 Rating
9 Classification of Service
10-11 Place of Capture
12-13 Date of Capture
14-15 Age at Time of Capture
16-17 Place of Registration, Induction, Residence or Birth
18 Urban or Rural
19 National-Cultural Group or Sub-Group
20 Marital Status
21 Education
22 Occupation (by major industry)
23 Occupation (by status)
24 Secondary Occupation
25 Interrogator's Estimate of Intelligence
26 Attitude as POW
27 Interrogator's Estimate of Reliability
28-29 Branch of Service
30 Type of Military Duties
31 Length of Service in Area
32 Length of Time Away from Japan
33 Total Length of Military Service
34 Service Prior to Last Induction
35 Combat Experience

Attitude and Situational Columns

36 Circumstances of Capture
37 Physical Condition at Capture
38 Desertion
39-40 Attitude toward Being POW
41 Future Plans
42 Suicide
43 Contact with Propaganda
44 Overall Reaction to Propaganda
45 Leaflets
46 Public Address System
47 Radio
48 Allied News Releases
49 Leaflets, Postcapture Reaction
50 Official Policy re Allied Propaganda
51 Faith in Purpose of War
52 Faith in Victory
53 Faith in Japan as Savior of Asia
54 Faith in Military Ideology
55 Emperor
56 Faith in Government Leaders
57 Faith in High Command

58 Faith in Business and Industrial Leaders
59 Faith in Reliability of Official News
60-61 Faith in Immediate Associates
62 Faith in Armed Services
63 Faith in Homefront
64 Faith in Germans
65-66 Attitudes toward the Enemy, Captured Peoples and Natives
67 Morale of POW's unit
68 Supplies, Ammunition, and Pay
69 Rumors
70 Organizational Efficiency
71 Numbers of Officers and Men
72 Training, Efficiency and Discipline
73 Quantity and Quality of Japanese Equipment
74 Food and Medicine
75 Psychobiological Status of Individual POW
76 "Gang Punches"

* Only column headings are given here, and the wording has been simplified in some cases. Under each heading is a series of sub-categories or code "punches." For examples of punches see pp. 319-320 of the text where the punches under columns 36, 37, and 63 are listed.

INDEX

NOTE: The letter *n* following page number indicates
that the reference is to be found in footnote.

Index

Index

Index

Emperor, Japanese, 24, 46, 50, 51, 54, 55-56, 66, 72, 73, 87, 89-94, 103, 109, 115, 120, 121, 151, 166, 167, 229, 230, 231, 252, 253, 255, 258, 263, 268, 282, 312, 316, 330, 334, 335; as symbol, 92-94, 230, 252, 253

Empiricism, 155, 173, 200, 307

Encyclopedia of Social Sciences, 157n

Energy, definition of, 162

Entomology, 157, 158

Eskimos, 113

Espionage, 329, 331

Eta (Japanese low caste), 246, 333

European Recovery Plan, 107

Evacuations of population, 59, 61, 66-67, 234, 251, 253, 274, 282, 283, 288-289

Evaluating morale, 79, 81

Evaluation of social-science research, 160

Evolution, 130, 189

Extinction of human race, 36

"Face," 261

Factory workers in war effort (Japan), 59, 233, 234, 242, 279

Failure, attitude of policy maker toward, 174-175; attitude of social scientist toward, 174-175

Fair employment practices, 191

Faith in common purpose, 78, 311, 312, 316; in leaders, 78, 86, 248, 311, 312, 316, 330, 334; in other members of group, 78, 86, 89, 229, 253, 311, 312, 316; *see also* Criticism of war leaders.

Faith in justice of war, Japanese, 50, 62, 93, 225, 252, 253, 254, 266

Faith in war, foundations of (Japanese), 50, 51

Family life, disruption of, 61, 67, 113, 189, 190, 206, 235, 253, 259, 334

Family life, structure of (Japan), 91-92, 247

Far East, 44, 149, 166, 223, 225

Far East, Deputy Director for the, 60, 225

Far Eastern experts, 44, 117, 166, 305, 306-307

Farmers, Japanese, 268, 269, 272, 274, 275, 306

Fear of consequences of defeat, 63, 81, 231, 235, 247, 258

Fear of invasion, 59, 62, 72, 235, 243, 257, 266

Federal Communication Commission, 177, 310

Federal Personnel Council, 198

"Fellow travelers," 192

Fertilizers, 109, 275

Field of activity in social-science research, 176, 180-181, 182

Fighting Forces outline (FMAD), 308, 309, 328-332; *see also* Morale, military (Japanese)

Five factors in Japanese morale, 50-51, 252-255, 311-312

FMAD, *see* Foreign Morale Analysis Division

Followership, 199

Food and Agriculture Organization of U. N., 109, 189

Food, relation of, to morale, 60, 67, 68, 69, 71, 73, 109, 166, 167, 232, 233, 245, 249, 265, 267, 275, 283, 284, 329, 332; *see also* Malnutrition; Starvation

Forced savings, 233

Foreign Morale Analysis Division (FM AD), 43 *et seq.*, 58-75, 76, 115, 117-125, 291; achievements of, 117-119; analysis of reports, 79, 83-84, 85 *et seq.*, 118, 265; area headings, 309, 337-339; attitudes of POW, 313, 316, 322, 325; conflict with policy makers, 138-140, 148, 170-173, 175-179, 230n; failures of, 117, 120-126; findings (1944), 52; findings inadequately considered, 120-122, 126-127, 170; future possibilities, 327-328; government attitude toward, 117-118, 120-128, 129, 133-140, 148, 170-173, 175-179; I R card, 314 *et seq.*, Appendix III; methods and procedures, 45, 76-84, 296, 307-326; organization, 298-301; outline of topics studied, 329-336; personnel, 45, 52, 223-225,

Index

Index

Ideologies, conflicting, 94, 115-116, 190, 261, 262, 296, 334-335; see also Cultural patterns
Idleness, enforced, 77, 108, 112, 232
Imperial Institution, see Emperor, Japanese
"Impregnable morale," no, 85
Indians, American, 113, 164-165, 190
Industrial revolution, 114
Industrialization in Japan, 22, 61
Industry in Japan, decentralization of, 61, 233, 245, 332
Inflation, 61, 69, 257, 271, 332
Innovation, resistance to, 129-132, 203; instances of, 130
Intellectuals in Japan, 246, 263, 269, 306, 334
Intelligence Agency (U.S.), 128
Interdependence of nations, 111, 207
Interdependence of plants and animals, 157-158, 217
International Labor Organization, 189
International Relations, 101, 102, 111, 180, 184, 189, 191-193, 195-197, 201, 217
Interpretation of information, importance of, 113, 143, 163, 176, 178-179, 181
Interrogation reports, how handled, 83, 123, 264; see also Prisoner-of-war interrogation
Interviews as source of social-science information, 180
Invasion, 62, 75, 249, 250; fear of, 59, 62, 72, 235, 243, 257, 266; see also Fear of invasion
I R A A (Japanese political party), 68, 279
I R A P S (Japanese political party), 68, 279
"Iron Curtain," 180
I R R A, 334
Isolation, 77, 91, 232
Isolationism, 205
Italy, 259, 331
Iwo Jima, 90, 283, 286

Japan, research on, by University of Michigan, 187

Japanese Americans in U. S., 193, 299
Japanese Behavior Patterns, 307n; see also Chrysanthemum and the Sword, The
Japanese culture, experts on, 44, 224-225; see also Far Eastern experts
Japanese fleet, 286
Japanese language: broadcasts by U. S., 285; experts in, 44, 224-225
Japanese prisoners in the U. S., 123-124
Japanese Relocation Camp, 44, 124, 133, 138, 165, 299
Jobs, wartime placement in, 43
Johns Hopkins, 214, 215
Joint Morale Survey, 225, 300, 327; see also Foreign Morale Analysis Division
Journal of Social Issues, 127n
Justice of war, Japanese faith in, 50, 62, 93, 225, 252, 253, 254, 266, 315, 330
Justification for Hiroshima bombing, 34

Kamikaze pilots, 188
Kamikaze spirit, 277
Kaya (Finance Minister), 270
Knowledge of nations necessary, 101-106, 191, 193; see also International relations
Koiso Cabinet, 285
Korea (or Koreans), 22, 67, 242, 246, 266, 329, 333; Russians in, 167
Kyoto, 21, 66
Kyushu, 268, 282, 289, 290, 334

Labor-management relations, 70, 113, 114, 189, 190, 191, 192, 217, 332; see also Unions
Lack of time in present dilemma, 38-39
Leadership, dynamic principle of, 163
Leadership, preparation for, 199, 200-201
Leaflets used in psychological warfare, 49, 52, 53, 95, 118, 287
Lessons from Hiroshima bombing, 35-40
Letters, captured, 44, 82, 83, 270, 271, 272, 331, 336

Index

349

Index

Index

351

Index

Religion, relation of social science to, 205, 208, 218

Relocation Camp, Japanese, 44, 124, 133, 138, 165, 299

Report of Foreign Morale Analysis Division, 58-75, 227-289, 307n; analysis of, 79, 83-84, 85 *et seq.*, 118, 265

Report on Japanese home front (Bombing Survey), 60-75

Research and Development Board of Nat'l Military Establishment, 198

Resistance to innovation, 129-132, 203; instances of, 130

Responses, positive and negative, 79, 81, 86, 316, 319, 320

Restriction of movement, 77, 232

Retaliation unsatisfactory, 104

Ridicule, effect of, 77, 108, 112, 233

Righteousness of war, Japanese faith in, 50, 62, 93, 225, 252, 253, 254, 266

Risus sardonicus, 219-220

Romulo, General, 46

Ruling class in Japan, 72

Rumor, effect of, 67, 69, 193-194, 202, 203, 250, 257, 274, 284, 287, 330, 333

Rural population (U. S.), needs of, 190

Rural soldiers (Japan), morale of, 49, 51

Rural *vs.* urban population (Japan), 245, 269, 334

Russia, 75, 167-168, 187, 188, 191-192, 193, 195-196, 235, 335

Russians, three kinds of, 167

Saipan, 47, 62, 73, 266, 267, 285

Sakomizu, Hisatsune, 69, 70

Sakurai, Maj.-Gen., 283

Salpêtriére, 216

Scurvy, earlier attitude toward cure for, 130

Secret societies (Japan), 68, 249, 334

Sermon on the Mount, 206

Sexual satisfaction, deprivation of, 77, 232

Shikoku District, 282

Shimada (Agriculture Minister), 283

Shimane, 30

Shimonoseki, 21

Shintoism, 46, 92, 118, 334

Shipping (from Hiroshima), 22

Slums, 113, 214-215

Social behavior, 43, 44, 66-67, 69-71, 72, 144, 148, 149-150; *see also* Behavior patterns

Social conflicts, 61, 67-68, 70-71; *see also* Stress

Social morphology, 156

Social pathology, 193

Social physiology, 156

"Social Research in Political Decision," 127n

Social science, 43 *et seq.*, 120 *et seq.*, 297-298; aims of, 144, 180; applied to peace, 180 *et seq.*; applied to world events, 201-202; causes of difficulty with government, 129, 133-140; conflict with policy makers 136-140, 148, 170-173, 175-179; differences between social scientists, 144-145; difficulties of getting government cooperation, 117-118, 120-128; government use of, 180-184, 190-191; public understanding necessary, 181, 199-204, 209; relation to religion, 205, 208, 218; remedy through, 39-40; sources of information for research, 181; subjects for research, 180; training for, 183-184, 191, 198, 200-201, 225; training of government personnel in, 43

Sociological Branch of M I S, 300

Sociology, experts on, 224-225

Solutions to present dilemma, 39; *see also* Present problems

Sources of information, 301-307; multiple sources of, 79, 82, 86, 264-265; nature and value of, 79, 82-83, 265; *see also* Diaries; Documents; Letters; Prisoner-of-war interrogation

Southeast Asia, research on, 187

Spanish Americans (in U. S.), 113

Special Attack Corps (Japan), 243, 276, 282, 283

Speeding up procedure in social-science research, 134

Index

Index

Date Due